Marketing
in the
Tourism Industry
THE PROMOTION OF DESTINATION REGIONS

Edited by Brian Goodall and Gregory Ashworth

ROUTLEDGE

First published 1988 by
Croom Helm Ltd

Reprinted 1991, 1992, 1993, 1994 and 1995
by Routledge
11 New Fetter Lane, London EC4P 4EE

Simultaneously published in the USA and Canada
by Routledge
29 West 35th Street, New York, NY 10001

© 1988 Brian Goodall and Gregory Ashworth

Printed and bound in Great Britain by
Antony Rowe Ltd, Chippenham, Wiltshire

British Library Cataloguing in Publication Data
A catalogue record for this book is available from the British Library

Library of Congress Cataloguing in Publication Data
A catalogue record for this book is available from the Library of Congress

ISBN 0-415-04545-2

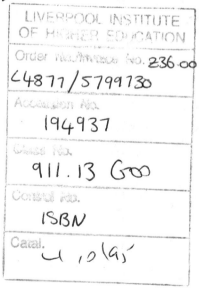

CONTENTS

List of Tables
List of Figures
Contributors
Preface

TABLES

FIGURES

CONTRIBUTORS

Dr Gregory ASHWORTH	Reader, Dept of Urban and Regional Planning, Geografisch Instituut, Rijksuniversiteit, Groningen.
Jan BERGSMA	Lecturer, Dept of Geography, Geografisch Instituut, Rijksuniversiteit, Groningen
Stan BOWES	Head of Marketing and Membership, Thames & Chilterns Tourist Board, Abingdon
Dr Bryan BROWN	Reader and Deputy Head of Department, Department of Tourism, Dorset Institute of Higher Education, Poole
Maurice BUCK	Director, Meadway Travel Ltd, Reading
Dr Erlet CATER	Lecturer, Dept of Geography, University of Reading
Brian GOODALL	Head of Department and Consultant Director of NUTIS, Dept of Geography, University of Reading
Martinus KOSTERS	Deputy Director, Nederlands Wetenschappelijk Instituut voor Toerisme en Rekreatie, Breda
Dr Thea SINCLAIR	Lecturer, Keynes College, University of Kent at Canterbury
Michael STABLER	Lecturer, Dept of Economics, University or Reading
Charles SUTCLIFFE	Northern Society Professor of Accounting and Finance, Dept of Economics, University of Newcastle upon Tyne
Dr Henk VOOGD	Professor of Planning, Dept of Urban and Regional Planning, Geografisch Instituut, Rijksuniversiteit, Groningen

PREFACE

The emergence of tourism as a global and, in many cases, a national and regional growth industry has been matched by both an increasing realisation on the part of governments of the contribution tourism can make to economic and social progress and an increasing attention from academic researchers. But tourism is not necessarily a key to a golden future for the destinations visited by the holiday hordes. Destination regions have to work increasingly hard to create or maintain a share of the tourism market. Not all can be, indeed will not be, successful. Much depends on how destination regions market their 'images', i.e. whether they are successful in persuading potential tourists that they will enjoy 'the holiday of a life-time' if they choose a particular destination. It is this problem of marketing destination regions that provides an underlying theme for this book.

The contributions originated in the second international workshop organised by the Geographical Institutes of the Universities of Groningen (The Netherlands) and Reading (United Kingdom), which was held at Reading from 21 to 24 September 1986 to consider the role of the tourism industry in promoting destination regions. The articles presented here were produced after the workshop had taken place and thus incorporate the authors' responses to the discussion prompted by the original paper. The emphasis is on an interdisciplinary and applied approach, involving not only economists, geographers and planners but also practising tourism managers. It is therefore the editors' expectation that this collection will appeal to a wide readership of researchers, planners, managers and students concerned with tourism.

As in any such collection, the contributions may be treated as self-contained studies in the theory and practice of an aspect of leisure sciences, but this was not the primary intention of the organisers of the workshop nor of the editors of this volume. The workshop focused on a clearly formulated and rigorously applied theme which governed the choice of subject matter and the nature of this theme provides both the framework outlined in the introductory chapter and the basis for the concluding discussion.

The editors wish to thank not only their academic and professional colleagues who have contributed to this volume but also those participants in the workshop from the tourism industry in the mid-Thames Valley who outlined current policies of their organisations and demonstrated practical achievements: namely Dr B. Hughes (Thames Water Authority), Mr B. Berenjyskyj (British Waterways Board), Mr Fisher (Greenham Lock Marina), Mr K. McGarry (Leisure & Arts Office, Royal Borough of Windsor and Maidenhead) and Mr K. Messenger (Madame Tussauds, Windsor). In addition the editors must acknowledge the financial support of the Departments of Economics and Geography at the University of Reading which made the workshop possible and the British Council (Amsterdam Office) towards the costs of the Dutch participants. In particular we recognise our debt to, and thank most sincerely, Rosa Husain for preparation of the camera-ready typescript and Sheila Dance for preparing the diagrams.

B.G. and G.A.

HOW TOURISTS CHOOSE THEIR HOLIDAYS: AN ANALYTICAL FRAMEWORK

Brian Goodall

THE HOLIDAY HABIT

Taking holidays is major international business. The market is world-wide and tourism is an international growth industry. Increased real disposable income, longer holidays with pay, improved opportunities for mobility, better education and wider dissemination of information have all contributed towards changing people's attitudes about taking their holidays away from home. First robotization in the factory and now computerization in the office have so standardized work that, for those in employment, there is an increased need for periods away from humdrum everyday routine.

Since the beginning of the 1960s world tourism, as measured by international tourist arrivals, has grown at a rate of over 6 per cent each year and the underlying trend, despite some instability in the mid-1980s, allows continued growth in demand for holidays to be forecast.

A holiday is seen by the individual and the family as a most desirable product. Once indulged in the holiday habit enjoys a high ranking in people's future budgets: even an increasing consumer priority. Holidays are a mainstay of behaviour patterns in advanced western societies and any survey of holiday intentions will lend support to the importance attached to holiday-making.

Sustained growth in aggregate tourist flows masks variation in the types of holidays taken and destinations visited, the latter responding particularly to floating exchange rates and oscillating fuel prices. Tourism is a highly competitive industry and the message conveyed to the potential holiday-maker is one of increased choice. More destinations, in more countries, are available; a wider variety of holiday types,

1

especially activity ones, are on offer; whilst
travel, accommodation and timing arrangements are
now sufficiently flexible for individual tailor-
made holidays. The potential tourist appears spoilt
for choice!

Tourists have high expectations of their
forthcoming holiday and also demand value for
money. Given such choice between numerous
competing destinations they will favour those
holidays which offer the fullest realisation of
their expectations. But how do tourists choose
their holiday?

THE HOLIDAY SELECTION PROCESS

A holiday is a high-risk purchase because,
unlike most other retail purchases, the tourist can
neither directly observe what is being bought, nor
try it out inexpensively. Previous experience of
the holiday-maker or his acquaintances is similarly
a poor predictor of future satisfaction as the
conditions determining success are specific in time
and space. Holiday planning (whether and where to
go) takes place over a long time, although the
planning horizon differs between types of tourist.
This planning and anticipation, which in Western
Europe is in full swing by January for holidays to
be taken in the summer, is an important aspect of
the experience itself and a potent source of
satisfaction. This implies, as conceptualised in
Fig. 1.1, a process which is systematic and
sequential. Such conceptualisation, however,
acknowledges the importance of a behavioural
perspective in understanding how people make
holiday decisions. At best the tourist is a
satisficer acting within implicit and explicit
constraints of an uncertain environment.

Motivations

For any individual the decision to take a
holiday stems from both needs and desires. On the
one hand needs are intrinsic, an innate condition
arising from a lack of something necessary to the
individual's well-being, and reflect emotional,
spiritual and physical drives. On the other hand
desires are extrinsic, a feeling that the
individual would get pleasure or satisfaction from
doing something, and are acquired through and

2

dependent on the value system prevalent in society. Together, needs and desires determine motivations, i.e. definite and positive inclinations to do something. Motivations for pleasure travel contain push factors related to the home environment, such as break from work, escape from routine, or respite from everyday worries, and pull factors related to the stimulus of new places and the attractions of destinations. Motivations have been classified (see, for example, Mathieson & Wall, 1982; Murphy, 1985) as (i) physical (or physiological), e.g. search for relaxation, health, sport, or challenge; (ii) cultural, i.e. the wish to learn about foreign places; (iii) social, e.g. the visits made to friends and relatives, or for prestige or status reasons; and (iv) fantasy (or personal), i.e. escape from present reality. Such motivations, weighed against other circumstances affecting the individual, influence the propensity to take a holiday but not the decision to go to a particular holiday destination.

Images

Having decided to take a holiday what influences the individual's choice of destination? To convert motivations into a holiday trip requires the identification of the tourist's preferences and a knowledge of holiday opportunities. Mental images are the basis of the evaluation or selection process (see dashed ellipse in Fig. 1.1). All activities and experiences are given mental ratings, good or bad, and each individual, given their personal likes and dislikes, has a preferential image of their ideal holiday. This conditions their expectations, setting an aspiration level or evaluative image, against which actual holiday opportunities are compared.

An individual's perception of holiday destinations, i.e. their travel awareness, is conditioned by the information available. At any given time each individual, as shown in Fig. 1.1, is aware of only part of the total holiday opportunity set. From information available regarding this perceived opportunity set the potential holiday-maker constructs a naive (or factual) image of each destination. That information may be derived from formal sources, e.g. travel agents, holiday brochures, or informal sources, e.g. friends. Amongst the perceived

3

Figure 1.1: The tourist's holiday decision

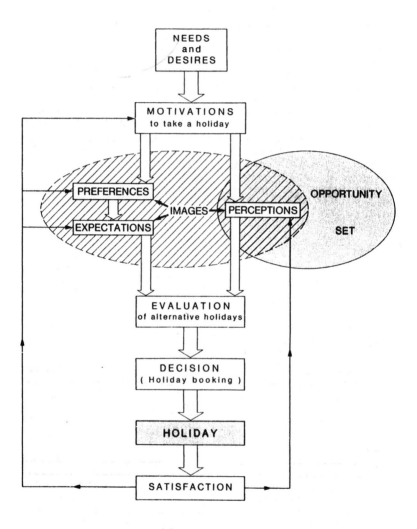

opportunity set will be several destinations which appear to meet the individual's holiday expectations and these must be evaluated further, according to criteria such as family, home and work circumstances; value for money; and destination attractions. This combination of holiday trip features and destination resources constitute the basis for holiday selection within the constraints imposed by generation point characteristics. Having identified the holiday in a particular destination which appears to exceed the aspiration level by the greatest amount the tourist makes a booking. Between booking and departure there is an anticipatory phase during which an individual's expectations and perceptions may be refined as more information is obtained. Then comes the holiday, which may or may not come up to expectation. The tourist enjoys a certain level of satisfaction from the holiday and this induces feedback effects (see Fig. 1.1) on motivations, preferences, expectations and perceptions of a reinforcing nature, where a highly satisfactory holiday experience, or of an adaptive or modifying nature, where the experience, in part or overall, was not up to expectation. Thus, at any point in time, each tourist has a certain accumulation of mental images about a variety of holiday experiences in a number of destinations.

CHOICE OF RESORT

Tourists vary not only in respect to their accumulated knowledge of holiday experiences and opportunities but also in terms of the extent to which their choice of holiday destination is a systematised process. A behavioural, rather than a normative economic perspective is therefore required to understand how people reach decisions and act upon their experiences (see also Mathieson & Wall, 1982). Thus the tourist's annual holiday choice may be conceptualised in more detail as a search process (see Fig. 1.2) which acknowledges tourists differ in their abilities to obtain and use information about holiday opportunities.

The potential tourist interacts with an environment (comprising nested behavioural, perceptual, operational and phenomenal elements) which determines not only the holiday opportunities available but also the tourist's motivations and preferences regarding holiday-making. Once the

Figure 1.2: The tourist's annual holiday search process

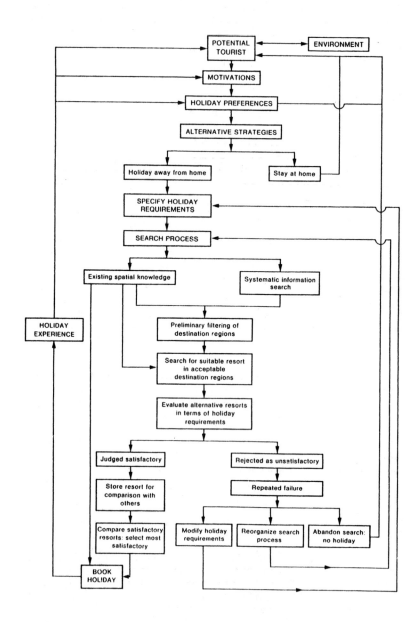

decision to go away on holiday, rather than stay at
home, has been made the requirements of the holiday
must be specified: these will depend on factors
such as whether the tourist will be accompanied by
family or friends, the type of holiday sought is
activity- or touring-based or is a traditional
seaside one.

The search process

The tourists then begin a search process to
find the holiday which best matches their
requirements within the limits imposed by what they
can afford and the timing of their other
commitments. Considerable variety exists in the
search behaviour of potential tourists with
planning horizons and preparations differing
markedly between types of tourist. At one extreme
is the 'impulse buyer' who, walking along the high
street, is attracted by a 'cut-price immediate
departure package' advertised in the travel agent's
window. This tourist makes up his mind on the
spot, enters the travel agency, books up, and is
away on holiday in a matter of days. Here the
planning horizon is at its shortest and the
decision is obviously made on the basis of existing
spatial knowledge. At the other extreme is the
'meticulous planner' - the tourist who obtains up-
to-date information from travel agents, tour
operators' brochures, tourist boards and similar
organisations and compares prices in detail before
putting together a tailor-made package. Here the
planning horizon approaches a full year with
advance preparations for next year's holiday
beginning as soon as the previous year's is
completed. In this case once a firm booking is
made preparations continue in respect of obtaining
additional information on the attraction of the
selected resort, e.g. opening times of historic
houses or safari parks, routes for scenic drives or
excursions. In between these two extremes holiday
search behaviour involves an enormous variety of
combinations of existing spatial knowledge and
specific information gathering.
    Novelty is an important requirement of a
holiday destination but for many would-be tourists
this may be offset by the worry and uncertainty of
coping with the unfamiliar. This balance of
opposing requirements of novelty and security is
seen as especially relevant to determining where

people are prepared to go abroad (Social & Community Planning Research, 1972). Thus a preliminary filtering of destination regions/countries is made by many tourists in which their existing spatial knowledge is important in ruling out some destination areas because 'people there are reputed to be unfriendly', 'the food is disliked', 'there are bound to be language difficulties', etc. Where existing knowledge comprises good previous holiday experiences the potential tourist may by-pass this first stage and proceed directly to the search for a suitable resort in an acceptable destination area. Whilst there is a degree of repeat visiting to countries, there is evidence that tourists display greater originality when it comes to choosing resorts within these countries (Carrick, 1985). For some tourists an earlier holiday decision, such as the purchase of a second home or time-share interest, may condition subsequent holidays to the extent that they appear habitual (unless, for example, second-home owners and time-sharers participate in exchange schemes).

Evaluation of alternatives

Returning to Fig. 1.2 and the search for a suitable resort: each resort considered by potential tourists must be evaluated against their detailed holiday requirements. Where the first resort which meets these requirements is selected the tourist is acting very much as a satisficer (although this should also be viewed in terms of the propensity of the tourist to visit new resorts on each vacation). Where several resorts which fulfil the requirements' test are stored for comparison the tourist is practicing a form of optimizing behaviour within a context of bounded rationality, the assumption being that the resort selected is the one which it is anticipated will best satisfy the tourist's requirements. If the potential tourists are unable to find an acceptable resort then they must consider modifying their holiday requirements and/or reorganising their search process: failing that they abandon the search and do not go away on holiday.

It must be emphasized that the search process undertaken by a potential tourist seeking a new destination to visit is restricted to obtaining information in a secondary form: namely, tour

8

operators' brochures, official guide books, tourist
board promotional literature, advice from travel
agents, friends' comments about their holidays.
Site visits, which are an integral part of search
processes in the case of house purchase or factory
location, are not made by the potential tourist: at
least, that is, not until he/she actually goes on
holiday - by then the commitment has already been
made. If the holiday turns out to be less than
satisfactory it becomes part of the tourist's
accumulated experience which will influence
motivations, preferences and requirements for
subsequent holidays. However, it has been argued
(Gitelson & Crompton, 1983) that systematic
information search of external sources is used much
more frequently in making holiday and travel-
related decisions than in consumer decisions to
purchase most other types of product. This
reflects, of course, the tourist's propensity to
visit new destinations on each holiday. Main
holidays taken by tourists tend to be better
planned than second or subsidiary ones (Marketing
Sciences, 1982).
     Choice of holiday resorts and the extent of
holiday travel depend, for most tourists, as much
on the amount of free time people have and when it
occurs and what they can afford to spend as it does
on the intrinsic attractiveness of the special
facilities and natural resources of the resorts.
The point of decision may not always be as precise
as conceptualised and is made in terms of an image
efficiency or anticipated experience criterion
(kept within the tourist's time, money and other
limits)(Gunn, 1972). Where prices are comparable
image is the decisive factor in holiday choice.
     So far the analysis has assumed that choice of
holiday resort was a package involving travel,
accommodation and, probably, excursions. This
certainly holds true for inclusive tours abroad but
there is a clear difference in the way people
regard accommodation as a component of a holiday
abroad compared to a home country one (Marketing
Sciences, 1982). For holidays abroad accommodation
is seen as part of the total package but for a home
country holiday the choice of accommodation will
be a separate consideration in which economic
factors, rather than preference, govern that
choice. There is also a preference, especially in
the case of home country holidays, for destinations
that can be reached inside a day's travel (Social &
Community Planning Research, 1972).

HOLIDAY SELECTION AS AN ANALYTICAL FRAMEWORK

Participation in tourism is voluntary and personal. Destination areas are competing to attract holiday-makers and the discussion above highlights the importance of the would-be tourists' mental images of possible holiday destinations, i.e. tourism products. Likewise, marketing and consumer researchers frequently stress the role of image in consumer product preference (Hunt, 1975). Although such images represent, in the case of holiday-making a very personal, composite view of a destination's tourism potential the images held by any person are not static, unchanging. At any given time a person possesses a certain accumulation of images about a great number of holiday experiences, some personal but many second-hand. These images, for each person, will be modified and added to with each additional experience and by further exposure to a variety of information sources.

The implications for tourist destinaton areas are clear. First, unless a given destination figures amongst a would-be tourist's current set of mental images it has no chance of being selected as the holiday base. Second, where it does figure in the tourist's image set a very positive image of that destination must be projected in the tourist's mind for it to be selected in preference to an alternative. Third, where the tourist is successfully enticed to a destination it is equally important that the satisfaction derived from the holiday at least matches the expectations created by the image - otherwise the tourist will not wish to return and will not recommend that destination to friends (indeed, the dissatisfied tourist may be instrumental in implanting a negative image in the minds of friends).

Personal images can therefore not only be influenced by, but can be manipulated, even created by forces external to the individual. Here is an opportunity for the tourism industry. In practice, however, it must be admitted that these personal images are more often created as a result of the tourists' general media exposure (an area over which the tourism industry has no control) than the promotional activities of tourism organisations. But it is during the formulation and reformulation of mental images held by holiday-makers that the demand and supply sides of the tourism industry are first drawn into explicit contact. Hence the importance of promotion, or advertising, to a destination area: the need to project and make widely known an image that will attract tourists. The effective transmission of the 'official' image of a destination area via promotional activities of the tourism industry is another matter!

How do tourism organisations seeking to promote potential destination areas establish what holiday-makers want and whether an area can satisfy those wants? Tourist boards, tour operators and other firms and organisations within the industry need to obtain systematic information on potential markets for their products. To market a tourism product successfully requires that product to be tailored accurately to identified patterns of consumer demand. Market researchers use a specialised form of in-depth interviewing of consumers - protocal research - which focuses on the decision-making process underlying market behaviour. In the case of tourism its use has been primarily to identify holiday intentions (Marketing Sciences, 1982) but there may be a gap between intent and actual behaviour. An alternative, commonly used approach is to study overt behaviour, i.e. where tourists actually go, and to use these 'visitation rates' as a surrogate for tourist preferences.

With European countries now recording well over 200 million tourist arrivals every year, three-quarters of whom come from another European country, and with the pronounced flows to particular destination countries, such as Spain, it is understandable why current behaviour is taken as a measure of tourist preferences. In Chapter 2 Brian Goodall reviews patterns of tourist flows between European countries but notes that those patterns, and changes in them, reflect not only tourist preferences but also the opportunities the tourism industry makes available in the market in the tourist's home country. Supply can generate its own demand (especially where much of the demand is 'latent'), as well as vice versa, and increasingly for the mass tourism market it is the activities of the industry, especially the tour operators, that largely determine the volume flows. However, not all tourists wish to be packaged on an inclusive tour along with the hordes going to the most popular destinations. Some - the more adventurous, independent, explorer types - seek something different. In that context Erlet Cater, in Chapter 3, discusses the tourism potential of the least developed of the Third World countries: countries which have yet to break into the international tourist circuit. She also argues that the development of tourism in such countries will not be unequivocally beneficial.

Before choosing a holiday the would-be tourist needs a certain amount of information. Without such information the tourist would be unable to form naive images of potential destinations. Unless tourists are planning holidays, using their own cars in their home country, visiting friends and relatives, information will need to be collected and reservations will most likely need to be made. How do would-be tourists obtain the necessary information and develop an awareness of the range of holidays and destinations (the opportunity set) available? Information is drawn from sources both internal and external to the tourist (Gitelson & Crompton, 1983). Internal sources represent a person's past experiences: whilst these may impart knowledge of places previously visited further information is required on new destinations, as well as on current travel arrangements, accommodation, and price levels. External sources providing this additional information may be either formal, e.g. travel agencies, tourist information offices which have to be actively sought out, or informal, such as friends and relatives. Destination-specific literature and the media, which are non-personal and formal sources, generally perform an informing function, i.e. helping a tourist to generate naive images, whereas friends and relatives, as well as travel agents, assume an evaluating or legitimizing function, i.e. influence a would-be tourist's preferential and evaluative images.

Much activity in the tourism industry is aimed not only at informing the would-be tourists of the opportunities but also at being persuasive, creating a favourable image of a particular destination or tourism product, such as a cruise. Tour operators use television and other media advertisements to proclaim the availability of their holiday brochures, which are designed to persuade the holiday-maker to purchase from tour operator 'A' rather than tour operator 'B'. Most tour operators' brochures are distributed via travel agents who act as impartial advisers on the opportunities for and detailed availability of holidays. Tourist boards, national and regional, seek to promote a favourable image of their

particular destination area by various means, e.g.
the distribution of literature, 'trial visits' for
representatives of tour operators and travel
agencies. On arrival in the holiday locality
tourist information offices provide a range of
information and services, especially relating to
current events, for the tourists. Focus is here
placed on two aspects of information provision in
the tourism industry. First, in Chapter 4, Maurice
Buck expands on the role of the travel agency in
informing and advising holiday-makers of the
opportunities available, and draws a distinction
between the independent and multiple travel agency
in respect of the nature and quality of the service
offered to the public. In addition he discusses
the pressures travel agencies face from tour
operators (whose products the agencies are
retailing). Second, the view of the destination
area seeking to establish or improve its image is
outlined by Stan Bowes in Chapter 5. He provides a
review of the structure, functions and policies of
tourist boards, using the Thames and Chilterns
Tourist Board as a case study. Innovative
promotion of the area's tourism products is
highlighted which requires acknowledgement of the
extent to which the holiday market is a highly
segmented one.

Destinations compete, even in a growing
market, for tourists since their products are often
close substitutes. Thus the European 'sunlust'
tourist wanting sun, sand and sea in a fully
serviced package will find very similar holidays
available in Spain, France, Italy, Yugoslavia,
Greece, Tunisia, as well as outside the
Mediterranean. The image projected of a
destination area by its tourism agencies and by
tour operators offering holidays there is critical.
A positive image, a high profile is essential to
keep the tourists coming. That image can be
damaged by circumstances beyond the control of the
tourism industry as witnessed by the publicity in
1985,6 given to both the bomb threats by ETA (the
Basque separatist movement) and the muggings in the
case of Spanish coastal resorts. Established
destinations cannot rest on their laurels but need
to reappraise their attractions and supporting
facilities in order to compete with new
destinations equipped with the most modern hotels
and facilities. Much effort in the tourism
industry is therefore directed at formulating and
marketing destination images and the range of

destinations getting in on the act is forever widening as new market segments are tapped. How can tourists be seduced? Do the images conveyed by the destination agencies and the tour operators measure up to the preferential images of the would-be tourist and do they succeed in attracting tourists? Chapters 6 to 12 are all concerned with aspects of these questions.

Attention rightly focuses on the attractions and facilities of the holiday destination but the holiday experience, like the outdoor recreation experience (Clawson & Knetsch, 1966), can also be viewed as a five-phase experience with anticipatory, outward travel, holiday resort experience, return travel and recollection phases. Minimal attention has been given to the travel phases of the overall experience. Such neglect may be acceptable in the case of the British tourist off on an inclusive tour to the Spanish sun where outward and return travel by charter flights at unsocial times adds little or nothing to the satisfaction derived from the holiday. But the travel element could be important in raising the level of satisfaction enjoyed: for example, on the continent of Europe where surface travel to holiday destinations is quite common. Such traffic, based on the use of the private car, normally uses the quickest route but if travel adds positively to the holiday experience some detour(s) may be acceptable. Special tourist routes can be planned, i.e. long-distance routes connecting the tourists' home area(s) with their holiday area(s). In Chapter 6 Jan Bergsma discusses the planning of one such route in the northern Netherlands - the Green Coast Road which offers Danes, Germans and Swedes heading for the Dutch, Belgian and French coasts supplementary opportunities. Where tourists are persuaded to make a detour, even an overnight stop, en route to or from their holiday destination the economic benefits from tourism are spread more widely and intermediate regions can participate in tourism.

Destination images reflect not only the natural attractions of an area, which are usually the basis of initial tourism development, but also facilities which have been created, from recreational, e.g. golf courses, to supporting ones, such as hotels. At the extreme the tourism rationale may be wholly created, as in the case of Disneyland or Legoland. In Chapter 7, Henk Voogd outlines efforts in central Limburg to realise the potential of the worked-out gravel pits along the river Maas for water-based recreation: creating facilities attractive to German tourists. The necessary investment funds for tourism development are often drawn from outside the destination region and subsequent operation may also use external production factors and supplies. The economic benefits of tourism development may then be reduced for the destination region - a line of argument Thea Sinclair and Charles Sutcliffe take up, in Chapter 8, in their case study of the hotel sector in Malaga.

Once tourists have arrived at a destination they may be persuaded to undertake extra or different activities to those anticipated in their preferential holiday image. Thus in Chapter 9, following a theoretical discussion of image in economic demand theory, Mike Stabler reports on a study which relates availability and use of publicity material available in the coastal resorts of Languedoc-Roussillon to the evaluative images the holiday-makers hold of those resorts. His conclusion points to a marked difference between the promotional images of the 'suppliers' of tourism products and the naive and evaluative images held by tourists. Identification of a particular tourism product is the theme of Chapter 10 in which Greg Ashworth examines the potential for heritage tourism and considers the problems of effective marketing of the historic city as a tourism product. Destination areas, amongst the first into the business of attracting tourists, which have lost their competitive edge are forced into a reassessment of the image they seek to project. This is especially true of traditional seaside resorts in northern Europe. Bryan Brown, in Chapter 11, emphasizes that promotion has always been a prominent feature of major British seaside resorts but he concentrates on their current problems, illustrating the varied approaches these resorts are now adopting to promote their future in tourism. Stabler, Ashworth and Brown all agree on the requirement for destination areas to market their tourism product(s) effectively, i.e. promotion which creates in the tourists' minds a naive image which matches their preferential image.

Tourism, especially in Europe, remains largely a private sector industry but one in which government, from local to national levels, takes an increasing interest. Governments can be involved directly in the entrepreneurial process of tourism development but more frequently they perform a supporting or co-ordinating role in marketing. In Chapter 12 Greg Ashworth and Mike Stabler combine to evaluate the relative success of a government tourism development planning agency, Le Mission, in Languedoc-Roussillon. Even where government does not involve itself as entrepreneur in the tourism development process it must consider its role in supporting the promotion and marketing of tourism. Here there is scope for improvement and, in Chapter 13, Martinus Kosters calls on governments, at national, regional and local levels, to adopt a professional management approach to their involvement in tourism promotion which acknowledges the various changes tourism demand and supply are currently undergoing.

In conclusion (Chapter 14) Brian Goodall and Greg Ashworth consider the problems faced in matching the demand and supply images of tourism. Tourist images certainly influence holiday-makers' choice of destinations: therefore the perceptions held by potential tourists about a destination will be a significant influence on that destination's viability as a holiday centre. There is a difference between exposure to information and effectiveness of information. Tourism promotion must convey an appropriate image of a destination area's attractions: the lessons for tourism management are clearly indicated.

REFERENCES

Carrick, R. (1985) Typing Tourists, Dept of Geographical Sciences, Huddersfield Polytechnic, Huddersfield

Clawson, M. & Knetsch, J.L. (1966) Economics of Outdoor Recreation, Johns Hopkins Press for Resources for the Future, Baltimore

Gitelson, R.J. & Crompton, J.L. (1983) The planning horizons and sources of information used by pleasure vacationers, J. of Travel Research, 23 (3), 2-7

Gunn, C.A. (1972) Vacationscape: Designing Tourist Regions, Bureau of Business Research, University of Texas, Austin

Hunt, J.D. (1975) Image as a factor in tourist development, J. of Travel Research, 13 (3), 1-7

Marketing Sciences (1982) The British Domestic
    Holiday Market - Prospects for the Future,
    Report prepared for the Scottish, Wales and
    Northern Ireland Tourist Boards and the
    British Tourist Authority, London
Mathieson, A. & Wall, G. (1982) Tourism: Economic,
    Physical and Social Impacts, Longman, London
Murphy, P.E. (1985) Tourism: A Community Approach,
    Methuen, London
Social & Community Planning Research (1972)
    Attitudes to Holidays in Scotland and Wales,
    Social & Community Planning Research, London

Chapter 2

CHANGING PATTERNS AND STRUCTURE OF EUROPEAN TOURISM

Brian Goodall

The 1960s was a period of 'explosive' growth for tourism and a volume growth of 6-7 per cent a year was resumed after the energy crisis of the early 1970s (Shackleford, 1979). Tourist demand has been less stable in the 1980s with a flattening of demand in the period 1980-3 (OECD Tourism Committee, 1984), a revival signalled in 1983 and consolidated in 1984 (OECD Tourism Committee, 1985) and 1985 but falling back in 1986 if media reports to date are correct. Holidays abroad are therefore an established fact of life for millions of people resident in the developed countries.

International tourism is, for the most part, freely traded and there is increasing import and export penetration of all the major tourist markets. Europe dominates both tourist destinations and origins, a situation which has changed little over the past two decades. Between 1967 and 1981 international tourist arrivals (excluding day-trippers or excursionists) in Europe from other continents almost doubled (+94 per cent), as did tourist movements between European countries (+93.5 per cent) (Commission of the European Communities, 1985). European countries account for some 70 per cent of all international tourist arrivals and generate about two-thirds of all international tourists. Well over 200 million tourists visit European countries each year: of this number 84 per cent originate in another European country. Even so it should be remembered that international tourism accounts for only 15 per cent of all tourists since it is estimated that the ratio of international to domestic tourism is of the order of 1:8 (Commission of the European Communities, 1985). Europe's importance in tourism statistics is, in part, due to the large number of contiguous countries within the continent, as compared for example with North America.

The growth of European holiday tourism reflects higher standards of living, broader social and cultural horizons, greater mobility at declining cost, and increased leisure time. However, tourist flows change their volume and direction over time: shift from one country to another, from one type of destination to another, from one form of accommodation to another. In the past seaside (especially), lakeside and mountain destinations have been favoured but now holidays have expanded to include 'capitals' tourism, cultural tourism, historic itineraries, and the search for adventure and activity. Where destinations abroad are involved tourists express a marked preference for inclusive tours. It will be argued that the main patterns of European tourist movement can be explained in terms of the structure of the tourism industry and changing economic, social and political factors. In conclusion the future directions for European tourism and the organisation of Europe's tourism industry are commented upon.

PATTERNS OF EUROPEAN TOURISM

The volume of international tourist travel has more than doubled over the last 20 years, with an even greater boom in domestic tourism. Comparative analysis is complicated because international tourist statistics are not available on a common basis for all European countries. They use different bases for recording visitors, e.g. Eire excludes excursionists but Greece includes them; Austria records visitors in the hospitality sector whilst Sweden returns numbers of nights spent by foreign tourists. Definition of the hospitality sector varies, being confined to hotels in some countries, e.g. Finland, but covering all registered tourist accommodation, including camp-sites, in others, e.g. Denmark. Some countries keep records under all headings, e.g. Yugoslavia, others have statistics available only under a single heading, e.g. Finland. No country has accurate records of those staying with friends and relatives which is generally between 10 and 30 per cent of the total. Caution therefore has to be exercised when interpreting gross national figures of international tourists since a country making returns on the basis of foreign tourist arrivals in hotels will underestimate numbers compared to a

country recording all foreign visitors at its
frontiers. In addition there is no agreement on who
constitutes a tourist. Available statistics are
taken at their face value and it is assumed that
the proportions of international tourists visiting
a country from other countries are representative
irrespective of the recording basis.

Origins and destinations

Spain dominates tourist destinations, and has
done so for the past 20 years. In 1984 Spain
hosted some 43 million visitors, i.e. nearly 1 in 4
of the tourists visiting Europe. France was second
with 33 million visitors, and only Italy (19
million), Austria and the United Kingdom (both 14
million), of the other European countries, topped
10 million visitors. Such figures based on
arrivals exaggerate the importance of transit
countries, such as France and Austria, and
conversely underestimate the importance of 'long-
stay' destinations, especially the United Kingdom
which has the longest-staying tourists in Europe.
Figure 2.1 illustrates the relative importance
of the countries of origin of tourists visiting
Western Europe. Circles are shown the same size for
each country because of the varying basis of the
statistics mentioned above. For each destination
country countries of origin are named where they
account for more than 10 per cent of visitors,
otherwise the groupings 'Rest of Europe' and 'Rest
of World' are used. What stands out is the
importance of West Germany as a source of tourists,
since Germans account for over 10 per cent of
visitors to every Western European country except
Eire. The United Kingdom and the USA are also
important sources for nearly half of the countries
studied. A distance-decay factor operates
demonstrating the importance of nearest neighbours
as sources of a country's visitors, e.g. Italians
going to Yugoslavia, Swedes visiting Finland,
Germans in The Netherlands: this dependency is most
marked in the case of Eire on the UK.
Whilst the propensity to holiday abroad is
highest amongst the Danes, Dutch and Germans, in
terms of the number of international tourists
generated France, the United Kingdom and West
Germany all 'export' well over 20 million tourists
each year (with Germany approaching 40 million).
Only The Netherlands (c. 14 million) of the other

Figure 2.1: Origins of tourists visiting Western European countries

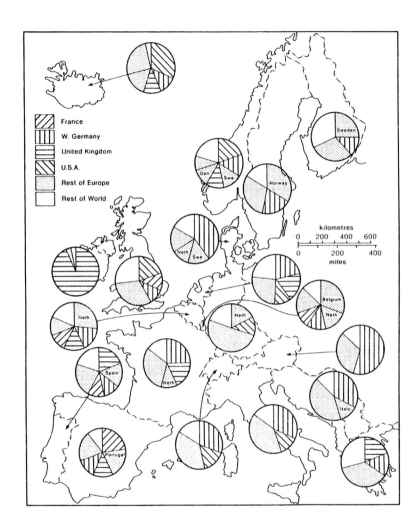

European countries exceeds 10 million.

Statistics of tourist arrivals may be reorganised to show (see Fig.2.2) the destinations favoured by tourists from each Western European country, although a 'Rest of World' category is not possible. Again circles are the same size for each country because of the variable statistical base

Figure 2.2: European destinations favoured by tourists from Western European countries

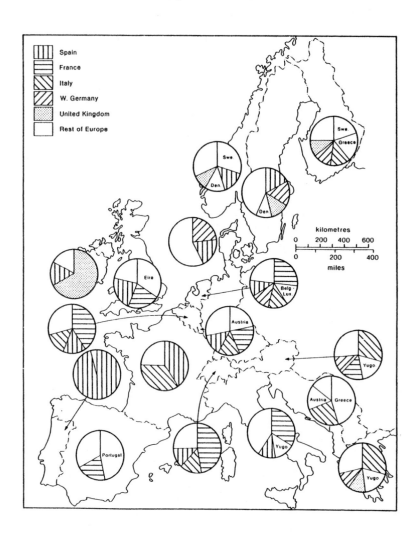

and countries are named only where they account for at least 10 per cent of tourists from the country. Clearly, Spain is the favoured destination for tourists from most Western European countries, with France and Italy very much second best. The flow of tourists generated by European countries as a whole continues to favour European destinations, with the overwhelming majority being within two hours' flight time of the origin country.

The relationship between origins and destinations may be generalised as a core-periphery model of tourism movement since those European countries which generate tourist flows are not the ones which usually receive them: there is little reciprocity. The flow is basically from the industrialised and urbanised countries of northern Europe, with their cool and often rainy summers, to the southern countries, where sunshine and warmth are guaranteed, but with their generally less well-developed economies or to the Alpine countries for winter sports. Such tourist flows are of marked significance for the balance of payments of individual countries, with those of southern Europe (especially Spain, Greece and Italy) enjoying a sizeable surplus on their 'travel account' whilst those of northern Europe (most marked in the case of The Netherlands and West Germany) are in deficit.

Holiday tourism

It is argued here that holiday tourism is the most significant element in these flows. The statistics used, however, cover more than holiday-making, but information on purpose of visit is not generally available. The proportion of tourists on holiday will vary between countries, with business tourism generally being more important the higher a country's level of economic development. The nature of the variation can be illustrated for selected countries: holiday-makers account for 85-90 per cent of all tourist arrivals in countries such as Greece, Portugal and Spain but only 50 per cent of visitors to the United Kingdom. Where visit purpose is distinguished private (as opposed to business) journeys are subdivided into holidays, visits to friends and relatives (VFR), and other (e.g. educational visits). The VFR category is significant for certain countries, e.g. 40 per cent of all tourists visiting Eire.

The volume product of the European holiday market is the inclusive or 'package' tour: a user-oriented 'sun and fun' holiday (alternatively the 4 S's - sun, sand, sea and just a slight suggestion of sex) to the Mediterranean, taken in summer, travelling by air, and hotel based. This style of

23

Figure 2.3: Average monthly hotel occupancy rates for selected countries

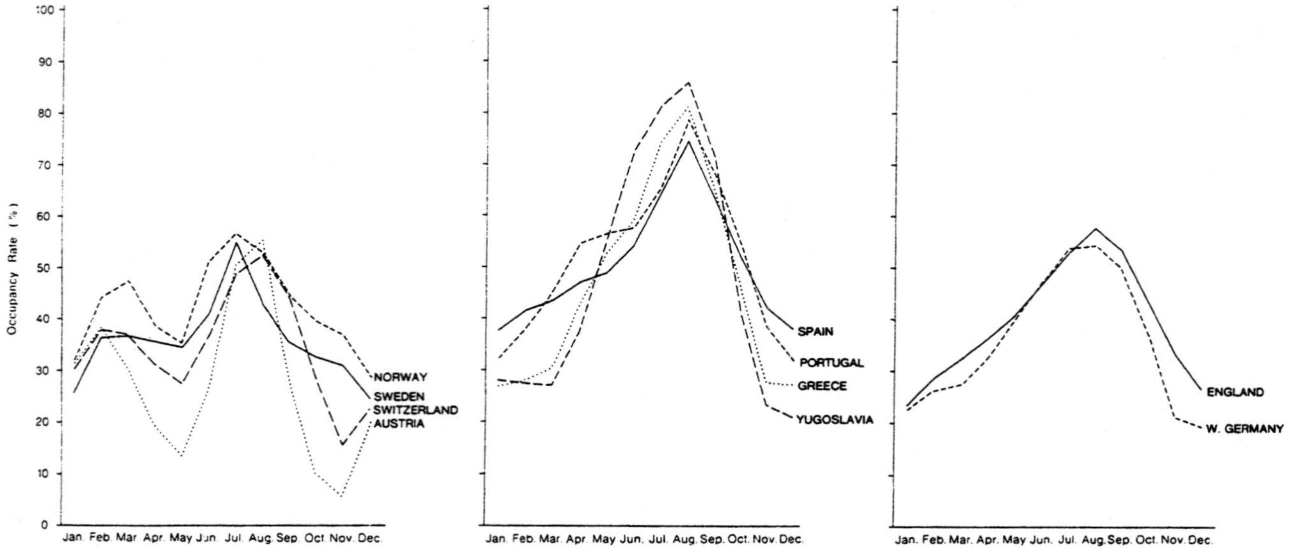

(i) Winter Sports

(ii) 'Medsun'

(iii) Industrial

holiday has accounted for much of the growth of holiday tourism since 1960. Such tourism is also markedly seasonal, as illustrated by hotel occupancy rates for the 'Medsun' and other countries in Fig. 2.3. Within destination countries there is intense spatial concentration of holiday-makers, e.g. five provinces (Balearic Islands, Gerona, Barcelona, Malaga and Alicante) account for one-half of Spain's recorded bedspace (Pearce & Grimmeau, 1985). The tourists are catered for in purpose-built 'identikit' resorts isolating them from the surrounding region and host population, creating what Simpson (1968) called the 'ocean liner' atmosphere. New resorts were developed between 1955 and 1965 along the Costas del Sol and Blanca in Spain, the Italian Riviera di Ponente and di Levante, on the Adriatic coast north of Rimini, and along Yugoslavia's Dalmatian coast. Since 1965 the Costa Dorada in Spain, the Balearic Islands (especially Majorca), the Algarve coast of Portugal and the Greek Islands of Corfu and Rhodes have been developed whilst, most recently, Morocco, Tunisia and Turkey have been investing in similar developments, as have Bulgaria and Romania.

The rise in the number of persons holidaying abroad from northern European countries has largely been at the expense of domestic tourism in those countries (although second and short-break holidays, which are overwhelmingly domestic, are not insignificant in these countries). For example, in the United Kingdom the proportion of adults (60 per cent) taking a holiday away from home has remained constant over the last 15 years whereas the proportion holidaying abroad has more than doubled (from 10 to 24 per cent) (British Tourist Authority, 1985). Economic recession in the 1980s has not had a major effect on holidays abroad, the Trade and Industry Committee (1985) arguing that unemployment affects domestic tourism hardest. The relationship between declining disposable income and holiday-making has also been investigated by Ashworth and Bergsma (1987) who concluded from Dutch evidence that the amount, as opposed to the type, of foreign tourism has been largely unaffected by stable or declining incomes.

But mass tourism is changing: witness the growth of extra-hotel holidays, the increasing importance of winter sports tourism, of second holidays, and of other activity and special interest holidays. The growth in popularity of winter sports is an especially noteworthy development of the last decade. Skiing has a mass support based on the Alpine model (with which other places have difficulty in competing, e.g. the attraction of Norway's ski resorts is reduced by the short length of day, Scotland's because of uncertainty of snow, and the Pyrenees lack access). In addition there are signs that European tourists are looking to the extra-European holiday market.

The evolution of the European tourism industry has paralleled the growth of mass tourism and the structure of the industry helps explain the patterns described above. Moreover, changes currently taking place in the structure of the industry may well be instrumental in promoting new directions in mass tourism.

STRUCTURE OF THE EUROPEAN TOURISM INDUSTRY

The tourism industry is primarily a private sector industry, one which is characterised by strong concentration in small enterprises, especially in destination areas (Commission of the European Communities, 1985). Its functional rationale involves the process of concentration and dispersal whereby individual tourists are sorted, grouped and packaged at origins to be shipped, usually in bulk, to the destination region where they are dispersed to hotels/resorts. The tourist taking an inclusive tour is purchasing transport, accommodation and transfers as a 'package', and probably also additional services such as car hire, excursions or theatre entertainment at the destination. These elements are 'packaged' by a tour operator and Fig. 2.4 illustrates the four directions the system of distribution in the tourism industry takes in Europe. Most common (i) is where the tour operator is an independent enterprise, responsible for packaging a holiday by reserving the necessary accommodation, transport, etc., and retailing the holiday to tourists through a network of travel agents. A second version (ii) cuts out the travel agent with the tour operator selling direct to the tourist: this accounts for 10-20 per cent of inclusive tour sales in many northern European countries. Much less common (iii) is where the travel agent assumes responsibility for the packaging, a system largely confined to Italy (Commission of the European Communities, 1985). In (iv) the producer of a basic service, e.g. an airline or hotel chain, assumes the role of the tour operator and sells direct to tourists. Emphasis is therefore on the role of the tour operator in the changing structure of the tourism industry.

Figure 2.4: Alternative chains of distribution in the tourism industry

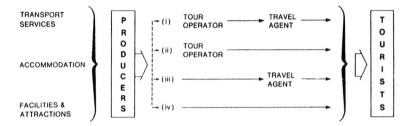

The tour operator

Tour operators came to the fore as producers of standard holidays in the 1960s. The key to their success is that their holiday prices are lower than the sum total of the services contained in the package if purchased individually because they achieve economies in transport, particularly via group charter flights, and season length. In the 1960s tour operators pioneered destinations, generating purpose-built resorts. For many tourists the country visited matters little: what matters most is the promise of reliable sunshine, warm temperatures, a beach to lie on, warm water to swim in, and clean and cheap hotels and restaurants (Matley, 1976). Thus in the first wave of foreign travel in the 1960s the standard 'package holiday' was created by tour operators to connect Spanish hoteliers and property developers with British and German demand for guaranteed sun, cheap booze, and a noisy night life. These developments were for the mass tourist market and the larger the market the less distinctive the destinations. Such 'identikit' destinations are the result of comprehensive market research, providing a degree of uniformity the tourist finds comforting (Holloway, 1985).

The 1960s boom in air travel was short lived for the 1970s energy crisis altered the economics of operating aircraft. The price factor is now more important in determining tour operators' strategies and is the single most important element in their choice of destinations. This central role of price in organised tourism helps explain the strong similarity of products offered by tour operators in a highy competitive market. In an effort to reduce transport costs by maximising occupancy of aircraft seats and to limit risks by operating in proven markets and areas tour operators are now less pioneering and are not prepared to wait too long for the success of a destination.

The tour business is more concentrated than travel retailing but there are still very many operators. Almost all tour operators limit their main selling operations to their home countries and very few control a large proportion of their home market. In the United Kingdom, for example, there were, in 1984, some 625 tour operator members of ABTA (Association of British Travel Agents) and some 700 air tour operators licensed by the Civil Aviation Authority: if coach operators and cruise companies are included it is estimated that there are currently some 800 tour operators of all sizes and types, with the 30 largest operators commanding three-quarters of the overseas market (Keynote Report, 1985).

The largest or mass-market tour operators concentrate on general air tours of the standard 'summer sun' format: they are based in the tourist-generating country and seek to promote outward travel. Notable, in recent years, has been the progress of integration within and between sectors of the tourism industry. Consequent upon the major growth of inclusive tours and the ruthless competition of the 1970s there has been horizontal integration amongst tour operators and vertical linkage of operators, especially with airlines. Such integration is most advanced in West Germany where nearly 66 per cent of all tours are sold by two operators - Turistik Union International (TUI, formed in 1968 by the merger of Touropa, Scharnow, Hummel and Tigges) and Neckermann and Reisen (established in 1963 by a mail order/department store and comprising GuT Reisen, Club Reisen, Terramar and Club Aldiana): mergers have similarly created SUNAIR (Belgium) and Holland International (Netherlands). The link between tour operators and

airlines is greatest in the case of the United
Kingdom where a greater proportion of inclusive
tours going abroad use air travel. Either,
airlines own tour operators, e.g. KLM (Holland
International), Air France (Sotair), British
Airways (British Airtours, comprising Sovereign,
Enterprise, Flair, Martin Rooks), British
Caledonian (Blue Sky); or tour operators own an
airline, e.g. Thomson Holidays (Britannia Airways),
Intasun (Air Europe), Horizon (Orion Airways),
Tjaereborg (Sterling). Firms from outside the
tourism industry have also shown an interest, as
the ownership of other tour operators indicates,
e.g. banks (Thomas Cook is owned by the Midland
Bank, Voyages Conseil by Credit Agricol),
(Commission of the European Communities, 1985).
What is perhaps surprising is the limited forward
integration to date of tour operators into travel
retailing.

Most common are **specialist tour operators**,
small- to medium-sized firms which are independent
companies or subsidiaries of transport carriers,
accommodation organisations (or even mass-market
operators). Specialisation may be based on
inclusive tours offered (i) to particular
destinations, e.g. 'national' operators such as
Yugotours or Olympic (Greece); (ii) using
particular, often self-catering, accommodation,
e.g. Canvas Holidays (camping), OSL (villas); (iii)
using specific transport, e.g. cruises (P & O,
Royal Viking), coach tours (Wallace Arnold) or
long-haul air (Kuoni); (iv) to particular age
groups, e.g. over 50s (Saga), youth (Club 18-30,
part of Intasun), and (v) to specialist interests
such as safaris and art, e.g. Prospect Art Tours.
Tour operators using direct-sell methods, e.g.
Portland (Thomson Holidays), Tjaereborg, Martin
Rooks (British Airways) have also been singled out
but these firms are competing for the mass-market
trade. Mention should also be made of **domestic
tour operators**, providing inclusive tours to
destinations within the country in which the
tourist resides, and **incoming tour operators**, based
in the destination country and selling to foreign
visitors tours only to that destination.

The travel agent

Inclusive tours are sold by unique means,
revolving around the tour operators' brochures

which holiday-makers usually obtain from their local travel agent, although in most European countries operators send brochures to old clients. Even with telephone ordering of brochures the majority still make their booking via the travel agent. The tour operator therefore shoulders the risks in setting up inclusive tours since the travel agent does not buy the package from the operator for resale to the consumer but reserves the package only after the holiday-maker has decided to buy. It is the tour operators' strategies which dictate the market opportunity available to travel agents in the various European countries, i.e. the extent to which the tour operator uses the travel agent as retailer and it is only in Italy (where the tour operator sector is weak) that travel agents create tour programmes. In general, tour operators are heavily dependent upon travel agents who sell about 90 per cent of their foreign inclusive tours. For the agents straightforward foreign holiday packages comprise 75 per cent of their business (Keynote Report, 1985) with, in the United Kingdom, 80 per cent being sold via 20 per cent of the travel agencies (Holloway, 1985).

The number of travel agencies has increased rapidly over the past 20 years, reaching over 7,000 in the United Kingdom and nearly 8,000 in West Germany. With the more difficult economic conditions since the mid-1970s tour operators have become more selective in appointing travel agents to represent them (as well as opening their own agencies, e.g. Thomson Holidays owns the Lunn Poly chain), and experimenting in some cases with direct sell. In addition horizontal integration is discernable with the retail travel business becoming increasingly concentrated in multi-branch agencies, e.g. Hogg Robinson in the United Kingdom have absorbed Wakefield Fortune, Renwicks and Ellermans; Pickfords have embarked on an agency expansion programme. This is a trend favoured by the rapid increase in computerization of booking systems by tour operators: Thomson and Horizon Holidays both take over 80 per cent of their bookings through viewdata systems (Cowie, 1986).

Tour operators' profit margins have been squeezed not only as a result of increased competition but also as a result of the trend to late booking witnessed in recent years. This means a later inflow of money and worsens the operator's liquidity position. The competitive situation also prompted the recent procedure of 'reissuing' brochures (when the first operator to publish a brochure brings out a new one with lower prices in order to compete with other operators who have undercut him). The retail market, as a consequence, is moving away from the independent travel agency. Even so, in the United Kingdom, the top 20 travel agency groups account for only 30 per cent of all outlets. In West Germany tour operators have succeeded in stratifying travel agents with some 2,000 selling TUI products and not Neckermann ones and vice-versa (Commission of the European Communities, 1985). Independent travel agencies have begun to band together to form consortia and in addition to the 'selective' specialisation mentioned above agencies have become more specialised in other respects, e.g. the Business Travel Centre founded in 1982.

The accommodation sector

The major increase in European tourism since 1960 has not guaranteed success for all sectors of the industry, notably the hotel trade, where the numbers of hotels and beds have decreased in some countries. The once-popular, fully-inclusive holiday in serviced accommodation is no longer wanted by the modern tourist seeking flexibility and there has been a significant switch to extra-hotel tourism, in all its forms - tourist villages, caravan and camping sites, second homes, time-share, home exchange, agrotourism, social tourism. The concept of the club, epitomised by the Club Mediterranee, which acts as both tour operator and accommodation chain, is an especially noteworthy development, adding sports to the usual tourist menu of sun, sand and sea.

As a consequence there has been restructuring in the hotel sector, bringing greater concentration and greater standardization (the International Standard Hospitality or ISH). This has been achieved not only through ownership but also by franchising, e.g. Holiday Inns. The hotel sector has also responded by upgrading serviced accommodation, e.g. each hotel room with private bath, and by competitive pricing. Certain summer resorts keep hotels and facilities open for tourists seeking relief from northern winters and attract them with cheap off-season rates: this applies particularly to the more southerly resorts, e.g. the Canary Islands, Madeira. The policy of marginal cost off-season pricing produced rock-bottom prices in the 1970s for 'mini-packages' or 'bargain breaks' of 3-4 days' duration, which introduced a new clientele to the idea of holidays abroad, as well as attracting pensioners for 3-4 months. Now, hotels are seeking to maintain, even increase, their share of traditional family summer holidays, e.g. Ryans Hotels in Eire make no accommodation charge for children sharing a room with parents and arrange special activities for children, including 'play-school' and creche facilities at their Killarney and Sligo hotels.

Structure and patterns

Three factors have been critical to the increase in European tourism over the last 15 years - rising living standards, rates of exchange, and air routes' over-capacity. The first fuelled the demand; the latter two conditioned the industry's response. The development of air transport, in particular the growth of group charter flights, solved the problem of access to destinations within easy transfer of at least a seasonal international charter airport: (transport costs depending on charter rights into a country, distance flown and ground handling charges). Accommodation and other costs to be met abroad are the outcome of exchange rates, inflation and the competitive environment. Tour operators exercise choice here in putting together their holiday programmes. For example, whilst the Greek, Italian and Spanish currencies have been relatively weak against the northern European ones over the last decade, the rate of inflation in Italy has been higher than in Greece or Spain and Italy has been most heavily penalized by tour operators as a result of the strong Mediterranean competition. It should, however, also be remembered that the tourist boom in Greece and Spain was, in part, politically inspired (Commission of the European Communities, 1985).

The dependence on air charter is, of course, much less important in continental Europe where the majority of holidays, even to the Spanish, Italian and French Mediterranean coasts are taken by motor car. The car has proved to be not merely a transport mode but has shaped the rise in self-catering, almost impossible without a car, and the choice of destinations within holiday regions.

Now that two holidays abroad per year are within reach of many people, a 'relaxing' summer holiday is often complemented with an activity holiday (skiing, camping, leisure learning, etc.). The increasing sophistication of the tourist has given rise to a more segmented market, with opportunities for specialist tour operators: the latter can set up a tour programme at short notice (and withdraw equally quickly from current commitments) and they therefore respond more quickly to market changes than the mass-tourism operator. The importance of satisfied customers to both tour operators and destinations cannot be underplayed, for over half the bookings are for 'repeats' (Trade and Industry Committee, 1985).

PROSPECT

Future holiday-makers

European tourist demand has considerable potential for volume and value growth since the proportion of persons holidaying abroad remains small. For example, only 24 per cent of British adults took an overseas holiday in 1984 (Keynote Report, 1985) and a 1 per cent increase in their numbers would generate 400,000 new consumers each year. Which age groups have the highest propensity to travel? The family holiday has been regarded as the corner-stone of tour operators' business but higher than average propensities to travel are to be expected amongst the young unmarried and the retired. Demographic trends are important and by the year 2000, every fourth person in Europe will be at least 65 which suggests the 'Golden Oldies' market will live up to its name, especially since retired people have the freedom to take their holidays at any time of year, and the next generation of 'seniors', unlike the last, is accustomed to foreign travel.

People expect more leisure time. The balance of both employee and employer preferences is for greater holiday entitlement rather than for a shorter working week (Shackleford, 1979). In 1970 four weeks' paid holiday was the norm for only 20 per cent of British workers, by 1980 it was the right of 90 per cent and can be expected to increase by up to a further week by 1990. French workers already have an entitlement to five weeks' paid holiday.

Tourists are now more experienced and demanding. The desire for greater flexibility, allied to the availability of 'convenience' foods and more adventurous eating habits, suggests that the swing to self-catering will continue. In this context the substantial and growing VFR market should also be acknowledged. A growing minority is looking for a more adventurous holiday. Perhaps the days of the 4 S's holiday are numbered! A recent report (Webster, 1986) suggests a revolution of the French annual grande vacances with the average French holiday-maker prefering countryside and activity holidays (reflected in the 50 per cent drop in Riviera bookings for 1986). Short and additional holidays will be of increasing importance and more tourists will be demanding made-to-measure holidays. Even in the face of further falls in the value of sterling British tourists will trade down rather than forgo foreign holidays altogether.

The tourism industry

Future transport possibilities have a major bearing on tourism. Aviation experts agree that the development of the jet aircraft has reached a point where productivity and efficiency have peaked - real travel costs are therefore unlikely to decline (Holloway, 1985). Energy prices will therefore largely determine transport costs over the next two decades: the higher they are the more 'organised', rather than individual, tourism will be favoured. Private car holiday-making will suffer most. However, policy over the regulation of competition in the air transport market is also a key factor in shaping future trends in Europe, where scheduled fares are governed by 'system number two' in which fares are fixed in collusion by the two airlines (usually state owned) that have been 'given' the route by the governments involved. (It therefore costs, for example, at 1985/6 winter economy-class rates eight times as much per kilometre to fly from London to Paris as from London to Los Angeles.) A shift to an 'open-sky' policy in Europe could defer any redistribution of tourist flows from traditional European destinations to less developed countries.

The inclusive tour will survive as the standard format for foreign holidays but there will be greater variety of packages and more 'up-market'

offerings to meet the demand for made-to-measure
holidays. Activity and special interest holidays
organised by specialist operators will proliferate
to cater for the more educated and adventurous
tourist market. There will be a move towards tours
which provide a mixture of relaxation and activity,
involving two centres, one of which has a cultural
base for tourism. Breaking the monopoly of the
beach/sun image will help overcome seasonality and
will be critical to efforts, in Spain for example,
to exploit other aspects of the country's tourism
potential.

The flexibility demanded by more and more
tourists can be met by developing one of the two
main forms of inclusive tour - the ITX or inclusive
tour by excursion ticket on scheduled air services
(the other, the ITC or inclusive tour by charter
caters to mass-market travel in the cheaper price
ranges to give high load factors on aircraft).
There are two versions of ITX: (i) IIT =
independent inclusive tour, in which the tourist
travels to his destination separately, and (ii) BIT
or GIT = bulk or group inclusive tour, where travel
is along with other tourists. ITXs, coupled with
accommodation vouchers, car hire or special rail
passes, etc., provide the tourist with a truly
flexible product.

The industry will remain highly competitive,
necessitating further structural adjustments. In
the United Kingdom, for example, there has been a
'price war' for 1986 summer sun holidays between
the leading mass-market tour operators: it was
started by Intasun, the second largest operator,
reducing prices by an average 12.5 per cent;
Thomsons, the largest operator, retaliated with an
average 17 per cent cut. Despite the significant
increase in bookings which resulted, profit margins
are being squeezed with Horizon, the third largest
operator, announcing (20 August 1986) first-half
year trading losses of £5.4m (cf. profits of £10.7m
for the comparable period in 1985). Some tour
operators will be forced out of business (e.g.
Sierra Holidays ceased trading, 2 August 1986).
Further mergers are likely, e.g. Horizon are
currently negotiating to take over Blue Sky and
Arrowsmith. The stock market is cautious regarding
the short-term prospects of the industry as
evidenced by the difficulties experienced in
placing shares amounting to 7.5 per cent of the
equity of the International Leisure Group (owners
of Intasun) in August 1986 - it took two attempts

and institutional investors forced a substantial discount. Questions arise about the future of travel retailing. On the one hand, the demand for made-to-measure holidays is seen as preserving a role for the travel agent (Commission of the European Communities, 1985), even though the image may become more of a 'supermarket' one with the entrance of non-travel agents, such as W.H. Smith in the United Kingdom, into the travel scene. On the other hand, Holloway (1985) acknowledges that advances in computerised reservation systems are likely to permit the tourist to select his holiday, book it and pay for it by direct debit to his account from his armchair and suggests this will encourage impulse buying, resulting in a further decline in traditional patterns of advanced booking. Indeed he goes on to suggest that if the tourist can 'package' his own arrangements at home at the touch of a button and call up on his own TV screen images of the destinations he wishes to choose from, not only travel agents but also tour operators could become obsolete.

PERSPECTIVE

A further increase in mass tourism on the scale witnessed between 1960 and 1980 is unlikely since the slow-down in the growth of economic wealth in the developed countries is not expected to be reversed dramatically in the next decade or so. Moving from an industrial to a post-industrial society has consequences for life-styles, especially leisure, and whilst in the 1980s people will not forgo holidays they exercise greater caution in their expenditure patterns, e.g. reduction in length of stay, greater use of supplementary accommodation, and switching of destinations to nearby countries or other places which appear more attractive because of favourable exchange rates or where competition has improved the price/quality relationship (OECD Tourism Committee, 1984). In particular there is concern over recent incidents in international terrorism involving airlines and other tourism sectors, most marked in 1986 by the large drop in Americans visiting Europe for fear of terrorist reprisals for the US raid on Libya. Competition between destinations, and between firms in the industry, can be expected to intensify.

The organisation of the tourism industry, particularly in the early post-Second World War years, was piecemeal, with private enterprise responsible for the operation of tourism enterprises and private associations, national and regional, attempting to ensure necessary co-ordination and regulation. The situation changed significantly during the 1960s with more and more governments setting up public or semi-public national tourist administrations to oversee the industry (Shackleford, 1979), although in market economy countries private enterprise has continued to play the leading role in the distribution of the tourism product. Governments are increasingly recognising the potential of tourism as a growth industry and their role in planning and facilitating tourism, in exercising supervisory control over the industry in their country, in promoting domestic and foreign visitors, (and even in direct ownership of important sectors of the industry) will be strengthened. Competition in the tourism industry will reach new levels as, for example, governments offer incentives to tour operators to include particular destinations in their programmes.

REFERENCES

Ashworth, G.J. & Bergsma, J. (1987) Policy for tourism: recent changes in the Netherlands, Tijdschrift voor Ekonomisch en Sociale Geografie, No. 2

British Tourist Authority (1985) British National Travel Survey, British Tourist Authority, London

Commission of the European Communities (1985) The Tourism Sector of the Community: A Study of Concentration, Competition and Competitiveness, Office for Official Publications of the European Communities, Luxembourg

Cowie, A. (1986) A room with a viewdata, The Guardian, 19 June

Craig-Smith, S. & Green, H. (1986) Tourist trade doubts, The Guardian, 25 April

Holloway, J.C. (1985) The Business of Tourism, 2nd edition, Pitman, London

Keynote Report (1985) Travel Agents/Overseas Tour Operators: An Industry Sector Overview, Key Note Publications, London

Matley, I.M. (1976) The Geography of International Tourism, Resource Paper No. 76-1, Association of American Geographers, Washington, DC

OECD Tourism Committee (1984) Tourism Policy and International Tourism: Evolution of Tourism in OECD Member Countries in 1983, Organisation for Economic Co-operation and Development, Paris

OECD Tourism Committee (1985) Tourism Policy and International Tourism: Evolution of Tourism in OECD Member Countries in 1984, Organisation for Economic Co-operation and Development, Paris

Pearce, D.E. & Grimmeau, J-P. (1985) The spatial structure of tourist accommodation and hotel demand in Spain, Geoforum, 16 (1), 37-50

Shackleford, P. (1979) Planning for tourism, Futures, 11 (1), 32-43

Simpson, A. (1968) The New Europeans, Hodder & Stoughton, London

Trade and Industry Committee (House of Commons) (1985) Tourism in the UK, HMSO, London

Webster, P. (1986) French take a break from sea, sex and sun, The Guardian, 5 August

Chapter 3

THE DEVELOPMENT OF TOURISM IN THE LEAST DEVELOPED COUNTRIES

Erlet Cater

The precise role of tourism in development has been the subject of much debate (see de Kadt, 1979). It remains a fact, however, that the development of tourism has been regarded as a panacea for the economic malaise of many of the Less Developed Countries (LDCs), which are faced with a narrow resource base and serious balance of payment difficulties. It is not surprising that tourism seems an attractive proposition in attracting much needed foreign exchange. Indeed, tourism has stimulated employment and investment, modified land use and economic structure, and made a positive contribution to the balance of payments in many of the developing countries (Mathieson & Wall, 1982).

At the same time, the growth of tourism has brought with it adverse economic, social, cultural and environmental effects. It is amongst the least developed of the LDCs (LLDCs) that these effects need most careful appraisal, particularly as they may more than offset the benefits to be gained from the development of tourism. The total environment, in terms of the interacting economic, social, cultural and environmental factors, is a very fragile one in these countries. The balance between the human and physical variables is a very fine one that is easily disturbed.

The LLDCs were first singled out for special attention, as far as development in general was concerned, in 1971 (United Nations, 1971). In terms of general indicators they are defined on a basis of three criteria: a per capita gross domestic product (GDP) of less than $350; a contribution of manufacturing to GDP of less than ten per cent; an adult literacy rate of 20 per cent or less. The designated 25 countries were added to over a ten-year period to arrive at a total of 31 (Weiss & Jennings, 1983) as shown in Table 3.1.

Tourism in the Least Developed Countries

Table 3.1: The 31 LLDCs - selected indicators

Country	Pop.1982 (millions)	GNP dollars 1982	% share manufact- uring in GDP 1982	Adult literacy rate % 1982
Afghanistan	16.8	-	-	20
Bangladesh	92.9	140	7	26
Benin	3.7	310	7	28
Bhutan	1.2	80	-	-
Botswana*	0.8	1010	-	-
Burundi	4.3	280	10	25
Cape Verde*	0.3	340	-	
Central African Republic	2.4	310	8	33
Chad	4.6	80	4	15
Comoros	0.3	320	-	-
Democratic Yemen	2.0	470	14*	40
Ethiopia	32.9	140	11	15
Gambia*	0.6	370	-	15
Guinea	5.7	310	2	20
Guinea-Bissau*	0.5	190	-	25
Haiti	5.2	300	-	54
Laos	3.6	80*	-	43
Lesotho	1.4	510	6	52
Malawi	6.5	210	-	25
Maldives	0.1	-	20*	82
Mali	7.1	180	5	10
Nepal	15.4	170	-	19
Niger	5.9	310	8	10
Rwanda	5.5	260	16	50
Samoa	0.1	-	-	-
Somalia	4.5	290	-	60
Sudan	20.2	440	7	32
Tanzania	19.8	280	9	79
Uganda	13.5	230	4	52
U.Volta (Burkina Faso)	6.5	210	12	5
Yemen	7.5	500	7	21

Source: World Bank Development Reports (1983 and
1984), Tables 1 and 3

*: 1981

It is the more detailed characteristics of these LLDCs that serve to complicate further the role of tourism in their development. These operate in two ways. First, they condition the country's actual potential for tourism: several of the LLDCs are so poor, economically, socially and physically that they will never attract anything other than the 'explorer' type of tourist.

Second, amongst the LLDCs that do succeed in attracting tourists, the impacts of tourism are likely to be even more complex and damaging. These two issues will now be examined in detail.

TOURISM POTENTIAL

A country's potential for attracting tourists depends on a wide range of interacting factors. It is not sufficient, for example, to possess outstanding scenery if the transport system of the country does not provide access to that scenery. Similarly political instability will deter potential visitors to an otherwise attractive destination. A systematic appraisal of the various types of tourism resources is essential. In order to make such an appraisal of the potential for tourism in LLDCs three resource categories need to be differentiated: physical, economic and socio-cultural. In defining these categories it must be remembered that none is mutually exclusive, and each will interact with and include aspects of the others. It is a useful categorisation in so far as it provides easy cross referencing with the same categories used in tourism impact studies.

Physical resources for tourism

This category covers a spectrum of characteristics including size, geographical position, climate, physiography, hydrology, flora and fauna. It is difficult to generalise about the potential for tourism among the LLDCs using these characteristics. Nevertheless, an attempt is made to draw attention to those natural features that individually, or in combination, influence LLDCs' potential for tourism.

The first consideration is the size of the country. It is no coincidence that 16 of the 31 LLDCs are under 200,000 km^2 in extent, 11 of these are less than 50,000 km^2 (Table 3.2). At its

Table 3.2:   Selected physical characteristics of
the LLDCs

Country	Area in thousands of km^2	Landlocked	Island state
Afghanistan	647	x	
Bangladesh	144		
Benin	113		
Bhutan	47	x	
Botswana	600	x	
Burundi	28	x	
Cape Verde	4		x
Central African Republic	623	x	
Chad	1284	x	
Comoros	2.2		x
Democratic Yemen	288		
Ethiopia	1222		
Gambia	11		
Guinea	246		
Guinea-Bissau	36		
Haiti	28		x
Laos	237	x	
Lesotho	30	x	
Malawi	118	x	
Maldives	0.3		x
Mali	1240	x	
Nepal	141	x	
Niger	1267	x	
Rwanda	26	x	
Samoa	2.84		x
Somalia	638		
Sudan	2506		
Tanzania	945		
Uganda	236	x	
U.Volta (Burkina Faso)	274	x	
Yemen	195		

Source: Geographical Digest (1983), pp 5-9

simplest size comes into play, as far as tourism potential is concerned, in terms of assessing the physical carrying capacity of an LLDC for the number of tourists. It is, of course, only one of the variables to consider in ascertaining this constraint. In more developed locations, for example Malta and Hawaii, size has not proved so critical. Ward (1975), however, points out how size militates against development from both a demand and supply point of view.

When size is considered in conjunction with other aspects of the physical regime it becomes evident how it conditions the strength of influence of these factors, in so far as it will dictate the diversity of environment found in that country. The movement of visitors in a mountainous country such as Nepal is severely constrained by the physiography. Similarly, where there is any lack of diversity in climatic regimes due to smallness of size, any marked seasonality in the climate will not be cushioned by the existence of an alternative climatic zone in the country.

Geographical location has an important role to play in attracting tourists. Location relative to the main tourist-generating regions is significant, although less so than hitherto with the advent of low-cost charter air travel. The increasing search for alternative destinations has brought previously peripheral locations into consideration. Many LLDCs are geographically well placed to increase their share of tourist movements. Certain countries are undeniably better located than others, proximity to already established tourist routes is a distinct advantage. Nepal is a popular stop-over on the route from Europe to the Antipodes. Other locations may be relatively disadvantaged. Location on or near a high-cost air route may serve as a distinct deterrent. Air fares within the South Pacific region are among the highest in the world with the cost/km of a typical scheduled economy-class fare from Los Angeles to Fiji being almost twice that of Los Angeles to Honolulu, (6.84 cents/km as opposed to 3.39 cents/km)(International Tourism Quarterly, 1977). Similarly location away from a high frequency air route acts as a disadvantage. Four of the LLDCs under consideration (Samoa, Maldives, Cape Verde and Comoros) are remote islands, at a distinct disadvantage in attracting all but the longer-stay tourist.

Those counties which are landlocked are even more susceptible to the actions of outside policy-makers, whether they be airline companies, tour operators or neighbouring countries. A total of 15 of the LLDCs are landlocked (Table 3.2), which has important repercussions for tourism potential since they lack a coastline and therefore beaches to attract the sunlust tourists. In exceptional cases this may be compensated for by the presence of large inland bodies of water, as in the case of resorts developed around Lake Malawi. Conversely those LLDCs which are endowed with attractive beaches along their coastlines, experiencing long hours of sunshine that follow from their tropical and sub-tropical locations, have a considerable advantage in attracting tourists. The Maldives and Gambia have been very successful in recent years in developing tourism.

Less easily defined under this heading is the country's location relative to the 'disaster' zones. The LLDCs are more prone to natural disasters, particularly those due to fluctuations in the atmospheric and hydrological elements such as typhoons, droughts and floods (Whittow, 1980). Due to their low level of development they are also less able to cope once such disasters strike, or even to ameliorate or prevent such occurrences.

Climate plays an important part in attracting tourists . As mentioned above the tropical and sub-tropical location of most LLDCs places them at a considerable advantage in attracting tourists from the More Developed Countries (MDCs) for at least part of the year. The search for alternative destinations pushes the demand to the more peripheral LLDCs. The rapid expansion of tourism in the Maldives in recent years (see Table 3.3) bears witness to this (International Tourism Quarterly, 1983a). Detracting somewhat from this advantage is the fact that, within these tropical and sub-tropical latitudes most of these countries experience a marked climatic seasonality. Heavy rainfall coupled with high temperatures result in excessive humidity levels unconducive to tourism for several months of the year.

The physiographic features of the LLDCs vary a great deal but they quite often contain extremes within their boundaries: Chad contains a desert area as large as the state of Texas, and many of the highest mountains of the world lie within the small Kingdom of Nepal. The complexity of the nature of tourism is highlighted by the fact that

Table 3.3: Maldives: number of visitors

Year	Total arrivals	Of which tourists
1978	29,325	16,846
1979	33,124	25,023
1980	42,007	34,695
1981	60,358	49,329
1982	68,685	52,595

Source: International Tourism Quarterly The
Maldives Special Report (1983)

what constitutes an attraction at one level, for
example the Himalayas in Nepal, may be an
impediment at another, constituting in this
instance a formidable barrier to transport and
communications.
The hydrological regime has already been
partially discussed above, with the threat of flood
ever imminent in the rainy season in low-lying
areas. In addition to this, and the generally
unconducive climate for beach activities during
several months of the year, the problem of water
supply must be mentioned. It is particularly
ironic that the contrast is often between either
too much or too little. In the rainy season there
is the ever-present problem of pollution of
supplies and the threat of water-associated
diseases, such as cholera and malaria. In the dry
season the shortages are such that local people may
be rationed to a bucket a day whilst witnessing
tourists casually showering on coming off the
beach.
Flora and fauna attract the tourist in terms
of both their diversity and distinctiveness.
Vegetation may be one of the major attractions of
many destination areas. The jungle flora of the
Terai of southern Nepal, or the thorn tree scrub of
Serengeti in Tanzania are so markedly different to
the temperate vegetation of the tourists' home
latitudes as to constitute major features of
interest in themselves. The hunting of animals
and, more recently, the viewing and photographing
of wildlife are also important tourist activities.
The rapid increase in patronage of East African
National Parks (30 per cent per annum over the past
fifteen years) bears witness to this fact.
Tanzania, in trying to attract the big game

hunters, may stand to gain considerable revenue from this source. The underwater attractions of the tropical seas also play an important role in developing tourism in such locations as Samoa and the Maldives. It is vital to take into account the fragility of such ecosystems in assessing the tourism potential of such localities. This will very much condition the impact of tourism as will be discussed presently and consequently will have important policy ramifications.

Economic conditions for tourism development

The economic conditions for tourism development in LLDCs must be viewed in both a national and international context. At a national level the mixture, quality and prices of the facilities and services being offered are of paramount importance. In addition to the more obvious features of hotels, restaurants and entertainment facilities, the infrastructural demands of tourism are very high. Typically, the LLDCs have poorly-developed transport and commmunication networks. As can be seen from Table 3.4 the only LLDCs to exceed 10km of all weather roads per 100km^2 are the island localities, which is a function of their smaller size. When the figures are contrasted with the UK provision of 141.6km per 100km^2 the low level of provision in the LLDCs becomes obvious.

The energy requirements of modern tourism are high (Soussan, 1985), with air-conditioned hotels and sophisticated services a prerequisite. Demands upon electricity generating capacity are particularly great, and the rapid expansion of a tourism industry frequently places a severe burden upon the electricity industry. The result is frequent blackouts or load-shedding, problems which many Western visitors regard as intolerable. Similar problems occur with water supply: water may only be turned on at certain times of the day.

Other economic bottlenecks that occur during the development of the tourism industry are the limited supply of skilled labour and managerial expertise. Although tourism creates relatively few jobs at a managerial and professional level, imported labour will have to be used if the demand cannot be met domestically. This will intensify the negative leakages as will be examined presently.

Table 3.4:   Density of transportation networks in
the LLDCs

Country	Km road per 100km^2	Km rail per 100km^2
Afghanistan	0.4	na
Bangladesh	2.6	0.5
Benin	1.8	0
Bhutan	0.9	0.1
Botswana	0.5	0
Burundi	6.1	0
Cape Verde	16.4	0
C.African Republic	0.3	0
Chad	na	0
Comoros	17.8	0
Democratic Yemen	na	0
Ethiopia	1.0	0.1
Gambia	4.1	0
Guinea	0.9	0.3
Guinea-Bissau	1.5	0
Haiti	na	0
Laos	na	0
Lesotho	9.2	0.01
Malawi	2.3	0.7
Maldives	na	0
Mali	0.6	0.1
Nepal	0.9	0.1
Niger	0.2	0
Rwanda	1.9	0
Samoa	10.6	0
Somalia	0.4	0
Sudan	0.1	0.2
Tanzania	0.6	0.3
Uganda	3.2	0.7
U.Volta (Burkina Faso)	1.4	0.2
Yemen	na	0

Source: Author's calculations based on data from
Europa Yearbook (1984)
na: not available

The shortage of capital to invest in tourism
severely inhibits its development in the LLDCs.
The workings of the world economic system (Hopkins
& Wallerstein, 1982) largely dictate the economic
fortunes of individual countries. Most poor
countries need external sources of capital to

supplement meagre domestic savings in order to
finance development projects. Exports of primary
products typically account for 60-75 per cent of
the annual flow of total foreign currency earnings
into the developing world. The LLDCs display all
the characteristics of a limited resource base
providing too few exports to pay for imports. The
falling real price of primary commodities has
resulted in a considerable decline in the
purchasing power of these countries. As they have
limited resources of their own to support tourism
the picture is bleak. The low level of domestic
savings and government finance limit the degree of
domestic involvement in the tourism industry. In
addition in such capital-scarce situations the
opportunity cost of investment in tourism is very
high. The same amount of investment applied
elsewhere in the economy may well bring more
significant and lasting returns.

It is not surprising, therefore, that the
LLDCs are very much at the beck and call of
patterns of foreign investment. If, for one reason
or another, they attract no such investment,
development of the tourism sector is unlikely.
Weiss and Jennings (1983) record that in 1977, 16
of the LLDCs attracted no net private capital
flows. Where such investment does occur, the degree
of foreign ownership carries with it an element of
loss of control, together with a reduction in
locally-realised benefits. Many of the
institutions involved with tourism in the LDCs are
foreign owned and/or operated, for example hotel
chains, tour operators, airline companies, car hire
firms and food chains.

When future economic prospects are considered
it is further evident that the international
economic system will continue to influence the
destiny of the tourism industry in the LLDCs.
Wahab (1975) has identified four major obstacles to
future tourism development. The first is economic
uncertainty stemming from inflation, fluctuating
currency exchange rates, unemployment and sudden
protective measures which are enforced on
international money markets (including revaluation
of currency, and the imposition of travel and
departure taxes). Second, there is the problem of
availability of energy resources at prices
affordable to tourists and operators of tourism
services. Third, inflation is increasing the
capital requirements and operating costs of the
tourism sector. Price changes will influence choice

of tourist destinations and spending behaviour within them. Last, increased pressure to incorporate environmental, social and cultural safeguards in tourism developments is likely to increase the cost of such developments. The overriding constraint is, however, that of demand. The role of domestic tourism and tourism from other LLDCs to the countries under consideration is negligible. Only in exceptional circumstances is the flow from LDCs in general of any significance. Indian nationals constitute 28.17 per cent of tourist arrivals in Nepal and 38.43 per cent in Bangladesh. This is due primarily to family and business ties, and in the former case also to religious pilgrimage. On the whole however the LLDCs are heavily dependent on tourist arrivals from North America, Europe, Australasia and Japan (Table 3.5). This fact illustrates their vulnerability to exogenous considerations. Mathieson and Wall (1982) document how tourism is a highly unstable export: 'It is subject to strong seasonal variations, to pronounced and unpredictable influences from external forces, to the heterogeneous nature of tourist motivations and expectations, and is highly elastic with respect to both price and income'.

Socio-cultural resources

The broad category of socio-cultural resources for tourism is perhaps the most difficult to evaluate as so many subjective considerations emerge. The peculiar mix of social, cultural and political factors experienced by each country may serve both to attract and deter tourists. The attraction of alternative cultures is of prime importance. Countries where there is a rich mix of art, crafts, music, dance, architecture, etc. are the most sought-after destinations. Amongst the LLDCs under consideration the rich cultural and architectural heritage of the Kathmandu Valley, Nepal is the most obvious example.
Several of the LLDCs do have considerable potential on this basis: on a cultural front the Polynesian island of Western Samoa and the Buddhist Himalayan Kingdom of Bhutan are two such examples. Others may have already tapped such resources for tourism but due to unfavourable political and economic climates are suffering a suspension of the

Table 3.5: Tourist Arrivals (1984) at selected LLDCs by origin (percentages)

LLDC Destination	North America	Europe	Austra-lasia	Japan	Total 1-4	Cent/S America	Africa	South Asia	SE Asia	Not stated
Bhutan	27	46	3	21	97	na	na	na	na	3
Nepal	12	35	3	4	54	1	.5	34	9	1
Maldives	2	75	4	9	90	.5	.5	8	2	1
Gambia*	na	91	na	na	91	na	na	na	na	9
Haiti	59	na	na	na	59	na	na	na	na	41

Source: World Tourism Organisation (1985), World Travel and Tourism Statistics 1983-84, WTO, Madrid
* For 1981: from International Tourism Quarterly (1983b)
The Gambia National Report 85.

Notes: na: not available as a separate figure. This data is included in final column.
Percentages do not always add to 100 due to rounding.

tourist trade. The early Christian heritage of Ethiopia has attracted a considerable number of tourists in the past.

The existence of social and cultural resources in themselves is insufficient to attract tourists if the willing participation of the population cannot be mobilised. The welcome that is extended to the tourist has considerable importance - this may be inherent or engendered; but if it does not exist, or is lost, tourism will suffer. This in itself is often a changing variable. Doxey (1975), in deriving his index of tourist irritation, describes how this changes over time through various stages between euphoria and antagonism on the part of the host community. Not only must the interrelationships between variables be considered therefore, but they must be set in a dynamic framework.

The politics of a country come into play as far as tourism is concerned not so much in terms of doctrine but in terms of stability. Countries actively promoting tourism have both capitalist and socialist regimes. Paradoxically Tanzania, despite its strong socialist principles, is attempting to attract the 'latter-day Hemingways'. Tourism is very vulnerable to disruption as has been made evident in recent years by the decline in the number of tourists to Uganda, Ethiopia and Afghanistan. A further illustration of the political dimension of tourism is offered by the Southern African countries of Malawi, Botswana and Lesotho. All three are heavily dependent on tourists from the same region, notably South Africa. In 1980 78 per cent of Malawi's visitors came from African countries south of the equator (International Tourism Quarterly, 1984).

It can be seen that a wide range of physical, economic and social factors condition a country's potential for tourism. Because of this, even within the relatively narrow category of the LLDCs, there will be considerable variation in terms of the number of tourists attracted (Table 3.6). It is not surprising therefore that amongst the group three basic types of country can be discerned. First, there are those countries with a low potential for tourism due to their own particular mix of variables outlined above. The landlocked sub-Saharan states of Chad and Mali, although both aspiring to develop tourism, face a barrage of constraints. The sheer level of poverty in both these countries militates against development,

Table 3.6: Tourist Arrivals in selected LLDCs, 1980

Country	Tourist arrivals (000s)	Growth (%) over last year	Over 5 years
Afghanistan	7	-81	-92
Bangladesh	64	12	0.3
Benin	41	20	125
Botswana	179	10	na
Burundi	35	3	36
C.African Republic	7	0	na
Chad (1978)	15	-6	na
Ethiopia	36	16	18
Gambia	35	-12	47
Haiti	155	15	96
Laos	28	4	na
Lesotho	162	6	na
Malawi	46	15	9
Maldives	49	55	193
Nepal	163	1	118
Niger	20	5	na
Samoa	23	0	18
Sudan	24	0	-22
Tanzania	175	12	78
Uganda	17	6	na
U.Volta (Burkina Faso)	38	-14	160
Yemen	39	11	144

Source: United Nations Statistical Yearbook (1979),
Table 144, and (1981), Table 194
na: not available

exacerbated by adverse physiographic and climatic regimes and a paucity of natural resources. The infrastructure in both countries is poor, and Chad has the added complication of civil strife over recent years. In terms of potential, Chad has the attraction of more varied scenery from the dense forests of the south to the deserts of the north, and has established two national parks and five game reserves. Mali, in addition to developing hunting and fishing, has the celebrated city of Timbuktu. None the less, for the above reasons tourism is largely undeveloped in both localities. A second group of countries comprises those LLDCs with considerably greater potential but where, for various reasons, tourism still remains at a relatively low level. This may be because it is in an embryonic stage of development, such as Bhutan, or because it may be in a temporary state of abeyance due to political factors. Ethiopia and Afghanistan have already been cited as examples of this latter category.

The final group contains those countries where tourism has developed very rapidly in recent years and figures as a mainstay of their economy. Bryden (1973) suggests that 'tourism countries' may be defined on the basis of tourism receipts constituting 5 per cent or more of national income, and those receipts furnishing 10 per cent or more of exports. Only six of the 31 LLDCs might be defined as 'tourism countries' on the basis of one or both of these criteria: Benin, Gambia, Haiti, Maldives, Nepal and Samoa (Table 3.7). Of the remaining countries Botswana and Tanzania are the strongest contenders to join this group. The need for caution in interpretation of this data is highlighted by the example of Gambia, where although tourism receipts constitute 58.1 per cent of total exports, net foreign exchange earnings are considerably reduced by leakages overseas (International Tourism Quarterly, 1983b).

It is evident from the above discussion that assessing the potential for tourism in an LLDC is not an easy task. However, whether the sector has been developed, is being developed or will be developed in the future it is essential to appraise what the likely impacts are.

TOURISM IMPACT

Many studies on tourism impact take a strictly topic-orientated approach. They have little or no regard to the spillover effects through the rest of the system other than those immediate to the topic under consideration. This is particularly true of the earlier studies where socio-cultural and environmental impacts were virtually ignored.

It is extremely difficult, and indeed unwise, to generalise about the nature of such impacts. Variations will occur over three dimensions: spatial, topical and temporal.

Spatial variations occur both between and within countries. Apart from the obvious physical and cultural differences that occur the wider developmental context will also condition the impact. An LLDC such as Nepal which never came

Table 3.7: The contribution of tourism to national income and exports 1980

Country	GNP (m $)	Exports (m $)	Tourism Receipts (m $)	Tourism as a % of GNP	Receipts as a % of Expts
Afghanistan	2809+	551	1	0.04	0.2
Bangladesh	11505	na	157	1.4	na
Benin	1054	54	7	0.7	12.9
Bhutan	104	na	1	1.0	na
Botswana	728	544.5**	24	3.3	4.4
Burundi	820	65	na	na	na
Cape Verde	90	na	na	na	na
C. African Republic	690	90	3	0.4	3.3
Chad	540	65	2^a	0.4	3.1
Comoros	120	na	na	na	na
Democratic Yemen	798	421^b	4	0.5	1.0
Ethiopia	4354	350	5^a	0.1	1.4
Gambia	150	31*	18	12.0	58.1
Guinea	82+	421	na	na	na
Guinea-Bissau	128	na	na	na	na
Haiti	1350	601	65	4.8	10.8
Laos	300+	21	na	na	na
Lesotho	546	na	na	na	na
Malawi	1403	317	6	0.4	1.9
Maldives	52	na	18.3^b	35.2	na
Mali	1330	200	9	0.7	4.5
Nepal	2044	97	45	2.2	46.4
Niger	1749	290	3	0.2	1.0
Rwanda	1040	140	na	na	na
W. Samoa	78+	na	6	7.7	na
Somalia	492+	141	5	1.0	3.5
Sudan	7667	543	6	0.1	1.1
Tanzania	5236	508	21	0.4	4.1
U. Volta (Burkina Faso)	1281	90.2*	7	0.5	7.7
Yemen	3010	na	72	2.4	na

Sources: Author's calculations based on data from United Nations Statistical Yearbook (1981), Table 194, and United Nations National Accounts Statistics (1981)
* United Nations International Trade Statistics Yearbook (1983)
** IMF International Finance Statistics (1982)
+: GDP;   a: 1979;   b: 1981

under direct colonial rule and remained cut off from Western influence until the mid-1950s, will have a considerably different experience to that of an ex-colonial country such as Malawi. Similarly within countries the impact will vary enormously according to whether the area being considered is in a relatively poor, remote and previously inaccessible location or in an already developed urban hub of the country.

Topical variations cover the vast range of tourism's social, economic and physical impacts. These arise from the nature of tourism and the types of tourists involved as well as the characteristics of the destination. The characteristics of tourists which have implications for the nature of tourism impacts include: the socio-economic characteristics of visitors; the level of use (the number of visitors and their distribution); their lengths of stay; and the types of tourist activity.

The temporal variations may be particularly relevant in the case of tourism, it is very easy to incur long-term costs for immediate short-term gains, and it is the long-term interests which are so often sacrificed. Short-term effects arise primarily through direct activity (and related multiplier effects), whereas long-term ramifications may affect the nature and fabric of a city or community. Very little research has been undertaken into the lag effects, obviously these will vary according to whether the development is large or small scale, and the characteristics of the destination.

Impact studies of all types are bedevilled by the difficulties of weighing up the relative costs and benefits as they occur over these dimensions. This is particularly well illustrated by the fact that the economic benefits of tourism have been over emphasized whilst there is a relative paucity of studies of environmental and social impacts. Furthermore the costs and benefits of tourism are not evenly distributed through society. The benefits to one group or individual in a community may be a cost to others in the same community. This is particularly true of the markedly skewed income distributions in the LLDCs: by enhancing the earning capabilities of one section of the population compared with those still engaged in subsistence activities the dualism between those two sections of the population will be further increased.

The complexity of such issues is also illustrated by the case of employment in tourism and tourism-related activities. The positive effect of increasing employment in services in certain instances may be more than offset by a countervailing negative impact of siphoning off labour from the agricultural sector, especially at times of peak need. Added to these conceptual problems are the practical difficulties of determining what are the actual impacts and then measuring them. The impacts may be absolute or relative, direct or indirect, quantitative or qualititive. The net impact of tourism may well be difficult to separate from the changes that would have occurred at any rate. The LLDCs are set in an ever-changing world and tourism is far from the only agent of that change. The complex nature of tourism makes it extremely difficult to devise a single measure of impact. Measures of economic impact, that is monetary measures, are inappropriate to the assessment of many of the qualitative considerations that emerge whilst considering social and environmental impacts.

Not only are the problems ones of definition or appropriateness, the LDCs as a whole are characterised by a shortage of reliable, timely and comparable data. The inadequate data sets relating to tourism present a particularly severe constraint. Few countries, for example, make a distinction between the business and leisure traveller, each of which have very different characteristics and needs.

Much has been written about the impact of tourism in developing countries, but because of the more extreme circumstances of the LLDCs the impact in those nations is likely to be that much more significant. It is the nature of the tourist activity itself together with the characteristics of the country discussed under the section on potential that will condition the nature of the impact.

The physical impact of tourism

The tropical or sub-tropical location of the LLDCs combined with the often severe topographical constraints discussed earlier result in extremely fragile ecosystems that are easily disrupted. Once disrupted the physical factors interact to cause rapid downgrading. This is perhaps most evident in examining the impact of tourist activities on vegetation cover. A variety of tourist activities impact upon vegetation. The most drastic is the wholesale clearance of vegetation, either for initial use of the site or for firewood. In the absence of other, or more costly, fuels wood is extensively used for cooking and water heating in the LLDCs. This is, of course, primarily a domestic phenomenon, but in fuel-scarce situations is added to by the demands of the tourism industry.

Pedestrian and vehicular traffic also impact directly on vegetation. In Nepal for example the large number of trekkers added to the local traffic scoring footpaths across the steep slopes has increased erosion. On the high plateau between Mawenzi and Kibo on Mt Kilimanjaro, Tanzania, any detour from the well-beaten path results in considerable impact on the fragile ecosystem at that high altitude.

Apart from problems of erosion, environmental pollution is a frequent problem. Excessive dumping of garbage is not only unsightly but ecologically damaging, and tends to be concentrated around sites of maximum usage. Those LLDCs with coastlines also have to pay particular attention to the threat of sea pollution, erosion, the destruction of habitats and the removal of shells and corals from reefs and beaches. The oceanic islands are especially vulnerable.

Mention must also be made of the impact of tourism on wildlife. The direct effects of tourist activity on wildlife depend largely on the intensity of tourism development, the resilience of the species to the presence of tourists, and their subsequent adaptability. Added to the threat of extinction posed by uncontrolled hunting and killing are the problems of disruption of feeding and breeding patterns. These impacts are most evident, and have consequently been well documented, in the case of big game in the national parks of East Africa. It is less obvious but still of considerable importance in the case of smaller species throughout the LLDCs. There are significant indirect effects due to the complex relationship that exists between tourism development and the needs of wildlife as well as those of the local inhabitants. This conflict is very much in evidence on the margin of national parks where the population is increasingly forced to seek alternative areas for cultivation and grazing.

Much has been written in recent years of the importance of 'bushmeat' as a valuable source of protein in an otherwise deficient local diet. This further illustrates the complexity of tourism, as what is a potential area of conflicting interests (the viewing needs of tourists versus the killing of game by locals), could be turned to a potential advantage. The controlled management of wildlife in Zimbabwe has benefited not only the local population but also has contributed to varied tourist menus in hotels including impala, warthog and crocodile meat.

The ability of wildlife to withstand an influx of tourists will obviously vary from species to species and region to region. It is primarily a function of the size of national parks. In the smaller national parks such as Lake Manyara and Ngoro Ngoro the concentration of tourists is likely to be more of a problem than in the case of a larger expanse such as the Serengeti.

There is, however, a distinct danger of being overtly pessimistic regarding the environmental impact of tourism. Mathieson and Wall (1982) emphasize that tourism can give rise to a positive impetus towards conservation, the need being to conserve that which attracts tourists in the first place. There are environmental limits to the development of tourism, but having recognised such limits it should be possible to defend the environment from adverse tourism impacts (Cohen, 1978).

The economic impacts of tourism

During the 1960s tourism was acclaimed as generating a multitude of beneficial effects upon such economic indicators as balance of payments, income, employment, regional equality, tax revenues, improved infrastructure, etc. However, not only are there the considerable environmental and social risks to be considered, but in addition the positive economic effects may be counterbalanced or even exceeded by negative considerations of the same ilk.

Although tourism may be seen as a useful agent in earning foreign exchange this may be offset in many cases in the LLDCs by considerable leakages. With a narrow resource base it becomes necessary to import many of the requisite materials and products for tourism, a procedure exacerbated by the

centralised purchasing procedures of the larger
hotel chains. In addition the repatriation of
profits by foreign workers increases this leakage.
In the case of the Gambia it is estimated that only
10 per cent of gross earnings are retained, in
Tanzania 40 per cent. Even if there is a net rise
in GNP it does not mean development for all, the
distributional benefits are likely to be very
skewed.

Tourism, because it is a labour intensive
activity, is often acclaimed for its employment-
generating capabilities, both direct and indirect.
Typically speaking, however, the employment is low
paid, and of low skill levels. In addition, as
tourism is in its infancy in many of the LLDCs,
tourism-related employment remains very limited as
a contributor to development. Farver (1984) for
example concludes that the tourism industry in
Gambia has not employed many Gambians, nor has it
provided sufficient wages to allow them to improve
their standard of living. Furthermore employment
in tourism is very vulnerable to fluctuations due
to downswings in the world economy, changing tastes
and seasonality. The indirect employment generated
may be particularly vulnerable, for example when
construction of tourism facilities is completed.
In addition there is the danger that in some
instances scarce labour may be diverted from the
rural sector.

The widening of employment and earning
opportunities for both young people and women has
been attributed to tourism development by several
writers. Reynoso y Valle and de Regt (1979) found
significant changes in the employment of women in
their Mexican case study. However, whilst this
might be true of the Latin American situation,
conditions are somewhat different amongst the
LLDCs, especially in Africa. These differences can
be attributed to a number of factors, quite often
it is the sheer level of poverty and lack of
alternative employment opportunities that mean that
such vacancies are taken up by male workers, as in
Malawi. In other instances, such as the Muslim
countries of Yemen and Bangladesh, there will be
cultural restrictions against the employment of
women. In countries where tourism is significant
in widening female employment opportunities there
is the added complication, documented by de Kadt
(1979) that, although this will decrease their
dependence on traditional family ties, it will
coincidently strain intra-familial relations.

59

Inflationary pressures often result from the development of tourism: consumer prices, land and house prices usually rise considerably. Any infrastructural improvements have to be paid for and are unlikely to benefit the entire population since they are concentrated in the urban areas and it is the tourists who will be the most intensive users.

The social impacts of tourism

In an ideal world contact between different peoples should promote wider understanding and remove national prejudices. In addition pride in culture may be engendered by tourism to such an extent that preservation or even renaissance of traditional arts and crafts should occur. In reality it has frequently been noted that tourism may play a more disruptive role in socio-cultural relations. The most obvious way in which this occurs is through the sheer pressure of numbers. As noted in the introduction many of the LLDCs are small in size, both in terms of land area and population. It follows that a large influx of visitors can have a considerable demographic impact (Table 3.8). The presence of large numbers of tourists in particular places at specific times will mean congestion of facilities and services as well as having a considerable impact on the local community. Many writers have pointed to the workings of the demonstration effect, where so-called superior consumption patterns are likely to be adopted. The effect is stronger the wider the gap between the more and less developed, and the greater the extent and awareness of that gap. Obviously, although not the only agent publicising this gap, tourism is the most immediate and tangible. For most residents of destination areas the symbols of affluence remain tantalisingly beyond reach (Rivers, 1973). It is not surprising that, quite often, the ostentatious presence of the tourists results in resentment on the part of the indigenous population, as documented in Tanzania by Shivji (1975). They see yet further evidence of neo-colonisation as they are priced out of their own markets by foreigners. As Young (1973) points out this resentment can have a backlash in deterring tourists from visiting because of the local hostility generated.

Tourism in the Least Developed Countries

Table 3.8:   Tourism density in selected LLDCs, 1980

Country	Tourists/100 pop.	Tourists/km^2
Afghanistan	0.4	0.01
Bangladesh	0.06	0.44
Benin	1.17	0.36
Botswana	22.37	0.31
Burundi	0.79	1.26
C. African Republic	0.35	0.01
Gambia	5.83	3.10
Haiti	3.16	5.59
Laos	0.77	0.12
Lesotho	12.46	5.34
Malawi	0.79	0.39
Maldives	32.88	164.4
Nepal	1.19	1.16
Niger	0.38	0.02
Samoa	15.33	8.12
Sudan	0.13	0.01
Tanzania	0.97	0.19
Uganda	0.09	0.09
U.Volta (Burkino Faso)	0.57	0.14
Yemen	0.67	0.20

Source: Author's calculations based on data from World Development Report (1982), Table 1 and United Nations Statistical Yearbook (1981), Table 194

Amongst the other disruptive socio-cultural effects is the commercialisation and consequent cheapening of cultures. Turner and Ash (1975) refer to 'deep-frozen folklore'. Other disruptive influences include those on moral conduct and the breaking up of traditional community and kinship bonds. The forces of modernisation would bring about change without tourism, but tourism, inevitably, accelerates that change.

CONCLUSION

There is a definite danger of being unduly pessimistic about the role of tourism in the development of the LLDCs. They do have special

61

problems and they are more likely to be susceptible to the adverse effects of tourism given the very delicate balance that occurs between people and resources in those localities. However, with better-informed tourism planning, there is no reason why the positive effects should not be maximised and the negative ones minimised. It must be remembered that these countries have little else to turn to in attempting to accelerate their rate of development.

The first essential is perhaps the most difficult, that is to appraise the country's potential for tourism and from it determine how large a role it could or should play in the economy within the constraints of carrying capacity. It must be recognised that there will be an upper limit to the number of tourists a country can admit: if this limit is exceeded then the costs will outweigh the benefits. The limit itself will be dictated by the type of tourists being considered and the characteristics of the area and its people as outlined in the section on potential. Research into the carrying capacity of countries and localities is still very much in a formative stage, but recognition of its importance was indicated several years ago when limits were set to the number of daily visitors to national parks in Tanzania (Young, 1973).

Having decided on the role and relative size of the tourism sector a myriad of other policy decisions then have to be made. It is essential that tourism should not be planned for in isolation but should be integrated with the rest of the economy both sectorally and spatially, it should be co-ordinated with regional planning and fit in with overall economic and social planning policies. Similarly these wider social and economic policies will, in turn, have ramifications for tourism. As de Kadt (1979) points out: 'Planners of tourism can do little to provide greater equality in the distribution of the benefits of that industry, if the forces making for inequality are left a free rein in their society, and if policies aimed at the eradication of poverty are not rigorously pursued'.

Decisions will have to be made as to the type of tourist to attract; if a mismatch between the type of tourist and what the country has to offer occurs the impact will be adverse. An interesting approach along these lines is the attempt, mentioned earlier, by Tanzania to attract the 'white hunters', recognising that the country does not have the infrastructure of her neighbour Kenya to support the mass (charter) type of tourism. The Bhutan government (Ray, 1983; Richter & Richter, 1985) has adopted an unusual policy towards tourism, in an attempt to keep the Bhutanese religious and cultural heritage intact. Visitors have to be members of a guided group and the costs of tours are prohibitively high to all but the 'elite' type of tourist (Smith, 1977). Similarly Western Samoa has adopted a cautious attitude towards the promotion of tourism, fearing that the Samoan way of life might be disrupted by such an influx (International Tourism Quarterly, 1982).

Further debate concerns the scale and location of tourist activities. Rodenburg (1980) argues that the objectives of development are best met by smaller-scale tourism enterprises, arguing that it is necessary to adapt the scale of tourism development to the realities of the local situation. Jenkins (1982), however, argues that large-scale developments are likely to be inevitable because of external economies of scale and market structures in international tourism. Similar discussion concerns the location of tourist activities in a country. One view suggests that they should be localised in tourist enclaves in order to confine adverse effects. The Maldives have consciously restricted tourist resorts to the central Male and Ari atolls. The alternative is to attempt to disperse development, perhaps as an instrument of regional policy, in order to spread beneficial effects. These issues are perhaps not contradictory but complementary: it is essential that decisions concerning the size, role and location of tourism should be set within a dynamic framework. It is inevitable that in the earlier stages of tourism development, because the prime concern will be to attract tourists, the emphasis will most likely be on large-scale, localised developments. The degree of foreign investment is likely to be highest at this stage of development, bringing with it considerable knowledge and experience of the pattern of demand, marketing channels and product identity. However, as indigenous firms gain knowledge the degree of foreign involvement decreases. McQueen (1983) found that 'the ownership advantages of MNE (multi-national enterprise) hotels, while possibly substantial in the initial period of the development of the international tourism sector, decrease over time'. As development proceeds government planners can begin to co-ordinate investment in infrastructure with the needs of small-scale entrepreneurs and the needs of local communities. Thus the focus changes over time, from initially concentrating on the needs of the tourist, to seeking methods by which tourism can contribute to the development of an area. It is essentially therefore a gradual process, as de Kadt (1979) suggests 'the negative socio-cultural effects are likely to be reduced if the growth of tourism facilities is neither rapid nor massive, and if there is time for local populations to adjust to this activity and for tourism to fit itself to the local society'. This gradualist approach is particularly endorsed for the LLDCs.

It is also pertinent to draw attention to the fact that the impact of tourism needs as careful appraisal in the least developed regions of the LDCs as a whole. Indeed the very designation of the LLDCs as a special category of LDCs met with considerable resistance from the Group of 77, as documented by Weiss and Jennings (1983), for the very reason that gross discrepancies within their own boundaries may thus be neglected.

Once more a plea is made for a systematic approach to the potential for and impact of tourism amongst the least developed nations and regions, recognising the complexity of interlinkages that occur, and setting such an approach in a dynamic framework. This latter requisite is all the more vital given the fact that tourism is still in its infancy in many of the LLDCs. Clearly flexibility of approach is necessary, and comprehensive monitoring an essential of tourism planning. Such monitoring of course depends very much on a flow of timely and reliable information, which in turn is likely to provide just as severe a constraint as any.

Finally it is essential to consider the wider context in which tourism planning in the LLDCs must be set. To bring about more balanced development requires much more than improvement in tourism planning, it requires a national, and indeed international, commitment to a greatly modified development programme in which equality occupies a much more dominant position. At present too much blame is laid at the door of tourism for those impacts which arise as a result of the very nature and fabric of the social and economic milieu, both intra-national and international, in which it is operating as a process.

REFERENCES

Bryden, J.M. (1973) Tourism and Development: A Case Study of the Commonwealth Carribean, Cambridge University Press, Cambridge

Cohen, E. (1978) The impact of tourism on the physical environment, Annals of Tourism Research 5, 215-37

de Kadt, E. (1979) Tourism: Passport to Development?, Oxford University Press, Oxford

Doxey, G.V. (1975) A causation theory of visitor-resident irritants: methodology and research inferences, 195-8 in The Travel Research Association, The Impact of Tourism, Proceedings of 6th TRRA Conference, Salt Lake City

Farver, J.A. (1984) Tourism and employment in the Gambia, Annals of Tourism Research, 11 (2), 249-65

Hopkins, T.K. & Wallerstein, I. (eds) (1982) World Systems Analysis: Theory and Methodology, Sage, Beverly Hills, California

International Tourism Quarterly (1977) Fiji, National Report 41, 20-33

International Tourism Quarterly (1982) South Pacific Islands, Regional Report 12, 14-34

International Tourism Quarterly (1983a) The Maldives, Special Report 45, 59-69

International Tourism Quarterly (1983b) The Gambia, National Report 85, 17-26

International Tourism Quarterly (1984) Malawi, National Report 95, 9-15

Jenkins, C.L. (1982) The effects of scale in tourism projects in developing countries, Annals of Tourism Research, 9 (2), 229-49

McQueen, M. (1983) Appropriate policies towards multinational hotel corporations in developing countries, World Development, 11 (2), 141-52

Mathieson, A. & Wall, G. (1982) Tourism: Economic, Physical and Social Impacts, Longman, London

Ray, N. (1983) Mountains and monasteries, Geographical Magazine, 55 (12), 645-50

Reynoso y Valle, A. and de Regt, J.P. (1979) Growing pains: planned tourism development in Ixtapa-Zihuatanejo, 111-34 in E. de Kadt (Ed) Tourism: Passport to Development?, Oxford University Press, Oxford

Richter, L. & Richter, W. (1985) Policy choices in South Asian tourism development, Annals of Tourism Research, 7 (2), 177-96

Rivers, P. (1973) Tourist troubles, New Society, 23, 250

Rodenburg, E. (1980) The effects of scale in economic development: Tourism in Bali, Annals of Tourism Research, 7 (2), 177-96

Shivji, I.G. (1975) Tourism and socialist development, Tanzanian Studies 3, Tanzania Publishing House, Dar Es Salaam

Smith, V.L. (1977) Hosts and Guests: An Anthropology of Tourism, University of Pennsylvania Press, Philadelphia

Soussan, J. (1985) Energy in small island economies, Ambio, 15 (4), 242-4

Turner, L. and Ash, J. (1975) The Golden Hordes: International Tourism and the Pleasure Periphery, Constable, London

United Nations (1971) Special measures in favour of the least developing countries, United Nations, New York

Wahab, S.E. (1975) Tourism Management, Tourism International Press, London

Ward, M. (1975) Dependent development: problems of economic policy in small developing countries, pp 115-131 in P. Selwyn (ed.), Development policy in small countries, Croom Helm, London

Weiss, T.G. and Jennings, A. (1983) More for the Least: Prospects for the Poorest Countries in the 80's, Lexington, Lexington

Whittow, J.B. (1980) Disasters: The Anatomy of Environmental Hazards, Penguin, Harmondsworth, Middx

World Bank (1981) World Development Report, Oxford University Press, Oxford

World Bank (1983) World Development Report, Oxford University Press, Oxford

Young, G. (1973) Tourism: blessing or blight?, Penguin, Harmondsworth, Middx

Chapter 4

THE ROLE OF TRAVEL AGENT AND TOUR OPERATOR

Maurice Buck

SETTING THE SCENE

It would be fair to say that the travel agent is dependent, for his livelihood, on the tour operator; but the converse may not necessarily be true.

The travel industry in the United Kingdom is a dynamic environment in which a change in one part of the system necessitates adjustments elsewhere. The multiplicity of changes which have taken place over the last ten years have created an environment in which the supplier of travel products, the distribution system for those products, and the consumer are in a continual state of open hostility.

This may seem dramatic, but not altogether surprising in a situation where the objectives of each component of the total system are not in accord. For instance:

(i) The tour operator brings together the various sources of both UK and overseas suppliers of goods and services into a package in order to sell to the consumer at a profit. The tour operator may sell direct to the public or via travel agents. Some tour operators use both methods.

(ii) The travel agent has no product of his own to sell, only the quality of his service. Thus, the travel agent is to a large extent dependent on the tour operator for his continued existence. Any changes in the trading arrangements between operator and agent such as withdrawal of product, pricing policies, terms of trade and methods of distribution will cause considerable pressure on the agent. These pressures will manifest themselves to a greater or lesser extent

depending on the inherent profitability of the agent.
(iii) The consumer, generally, requires a travel product at the lowest price and of the highest quality - consistent with his own value judgement and preferences. It is quite evident to travel agents that there is a minority group of travellers whose value judgements are so out of line with the norm that their expectations could not be satisfied in any economic way. Within society, there are other pressure groups supportive of the rights of the consumer which tend to react to and lobby for this minority group.

Consequently, both travel agent and tour operator need to react to this new pressure in such a way that ultimately quality is improved at a minimal increase in price.
This brief synopsis may suggest an air of disenchantment with the tourism industry. It is categorically not so. This scenario is suggested if only to emphasize that the industry is organised and controlled by people for people; and that all those involved seek to maximise their own profit and pleasure from participation.

THE ROLE OF THE TRAVEL AGENT

A travel agent's perception of his role will vary according to his organisation's position in the structure of the tourism industry. Broadly speaking there is a dichotomy of roles between the single independent who must concentrate on service and skill and the multiple chain which adopts a 'supermarket approach' to retailing travel products.
The independent, on the one hand, usually provides an in-depth service in three main areas:

pre-sales service,
the sales situation,
after-sales service.

The multiple chain, on the other hand, will allocate more resources and give greater priority to the period during which active selling takes place within the agency.

Pre-sales service

How are these differences manifested in practice? The independent travel agent is more sensitive to the individual consumer's wishes than the multiple chain. In respect of pre-sales service independents maintain longer opening hours than multiple chains which keep standard shop opening hours. At this stage the independent is in much closer contact with his local market and develops this through local promotional activity whereas the multiple chain relies on mass media advertising to bring in customers. The independent is particularly aware of local market segmentation and the needs of special interest groups. Cost comparisons across a wider range of holiday and travel-associated services are provided at this stage by the independent. These differences between independent and multiple chain at the pre-sales stage are summarised in Table 4.1.

Table 4.1: Pre-sales service

Independent Travel Agency	Multiple Chain
Increased accessibility through longer opening hours	Standardized opening hours
Closer contact with specific market segments through local promotions	Blanket market coverage through press and TV advertising
More efficient local information gathering/ dissemination activities for special interest groups	Very little effort expended in this area
Cost comparisons across wide range of alternatives	Little effort made to compare alternatives

The sales situation

Table 4.2 compares the roles of independents and multiple chains during the sales situation. Again the independent has a greater awareness of the consumer's wishes and exercises greater care in matching the holiday package sold to the customer's needs. The multiple chain is less likely to consider as wide a range of alternatives and more likely to offer packages which maximise their commission earnings. The independent travel agent therefore establishes a more personal relationship with clients, which is likely to be reflected in their repeated use of that agency. Independents, however, are at a disadvantage compared to multiples in respect of capital investment in information technology. The latter is being widely adopted as a means of searching for travel information, making holiday bookings, etc.

Table 4.2: The sales situation

Independent Travel Agent	Multiple Chain
Greater degree of questioning client in order to match the product commission earnings to client's needs	Proclivity to sell product which maximises commission earnings
Advisory role on best choice or range of alternatives	Advisory role restricted since product range offered restricted
Personal relationship established with client/ increases credibility	Less chance to develop relationships as throughput is paramount
Limited financial resources available for technological developments	Considerable investment in new technology to increase throughput

After-sales service

Feedback from clients on the success of a holiday (or lack of it!) is actively sought to a much greater extent by the independent travel agent and the information thus gathered concerning travel modes, accommodation, resorts, etc. is evaluated for possible future use. Where holidays are not wholly successful and problems arise the independent agent may proffer more assistance as a 'trouble-shooter' both during the holiday and subsequently, e.g. in supporting complaints and insurance claims. The differences between independents and multiple chains at the after-sales stage are summarised in Table 4.3.

Table 4.3: After-sales service

Independent Travel Agency	Multiple Chain
Receiving, noting, using information provided by clients on resorts and hotels	Activity dependent on each individual travel clerk
Supportive role in dealing with clients' complaints and insurance claims	Some effort expended in this area
Problem solving, e.g. clients requiring additional funds in resort/arranging for clients' repatriation when return flights have been missed - both inside and outside office hours	Help mainly during office hours only

Changing structure and practices

It is not difficult to understand why the above distinctions occur. Most of the multiple retail chains are subsidiary companies of larger organisations. Thomas Cook belongs to the Midland Bank, Pickfords to the British Transport Services, Lunn Poly to Thomson Holidays and Hogg Robinson to the massive insurance company of the same name.

The acquisition policy and continued expansion of these retail chains had very little to do with customer service. The rationale stemmed mainly from the cash-generating characteristics of the retail agent. Cash which could be utilised either for further investment in more cash-generating outlets or for use in the parent company's existing business. The expansion of the major retail chains, for whatever reason, has had a significant effect on the travel industry.

In the last three years, it is suggested that the major chains have probably reached a market penetration of between 20-25 per cent of outlets, and 40-45 per cent of sales. Their strength in the distribution network is such that they can force tour operators into providing 'override commissions' in excess of the generally accepted 10 per cent. Whilst there is an argument that productive agencies should be rewarded through increased commission levels, it is not in the public or tour operators' interest to have retail chains forcing the issue for all of their outlets whether these are productive or not.

The Midlands tour operator, Horizon, withdrew its product from the Pickfords's chain during 1984/5. It was reported that this action stemmed from differences over the amount of 'override commission' which should be paid. Despite the fact that Horizon was then the third largest tour operator in the UK, the company found that the loss of more than 200 retail outlets for the distribution of its product could not be tolerated for more than one season. One could argue that this represents misuse of power in the market place. There are many examples that could be quoted where multiple chains 'buy' commercial business accounts through heavy discounting; thus increasing the size and growth rate of the multiple chains.

The irony of the situation for the remaining 75 per cent of retail agents was that this practice was as rife under the period before 'Stabiliser' was dispensed with as it is now. Operation Stabiliser, introduced by ABTA (the Association of British Travel Agents) in 1965, was the reciprocal booking arrangement, which amounted to a closed shop, whereby travel agent members of ABTA sold only the services of ABTA tour operators and the latter offered their products only via ABTA travel agents. ABTA had over the years developed a code of conduct, part of which was that tour operators' products should be sold to the public at the price set by each tour operator. This policy was generally accepted by the trade as a form of retail price maintenance necessary for the preservation of retail margins and thus the tour operators' distribution network.

Current developments indicate that the recent banning of the 'Stabiliser' by the Restrictive Practices Court has created an environment in which discounting has become the norm. The consequence

of such a policy will be to increase polarisation
in the retail area - the large will get larger and
the smaller less profitable - units will close down
or merge with larger organisations.

The effect that this will have on the consumer
is quite clear. Since most retail chains sell only
a 'preferred' list of tour operators consumer
choice will diminish. It is the single independent
outlet which provides a wider range of tour
operators' products and they are usually the only
means that small specialist tour operators have to
distribute their product and reach the market
place.

THE AGENT AND THE TOUR OPERATOR

The discussion above concentrates on one
aspect of the relationship between agents and tour
operators. There are many other facets of this
relationship which have been initiated by the tour
operator and which are also leading to internal
tension within the industry.

Growth in the overseas holiday market is
primarily a function of the marketing efforts of
tour operators. For the majority of the public a
package holiday is the only means by which they can
afford to reach 'guaranteed' sunshine. In the UK
there are in excess of 600 tour operators licensed
by the Civil Aviation Authority for charter air
holiday packages. A proportion of these tour
operators will also be licensed for charter flights
only.

In the last two to three years there have been
significant changes in the number of major
operators in the market place. Mergers between
secondary operators have created several large
companies at the top, viz. Thomson, Intasun,
Horizon, Rank and Cosmos, with a myriad of small
operators below.

Under the ABTA rules all ABTA tour operators'
products could be sold through all ABTA agents'
outlets. However, major operators, in their quest
for cost savings, have invested heavily in computer
reservations systems and begun to reduce their
telephone reservations facility. Pressure has been
exerted on retail agents to install computer
terminals in their agencies in order to access the
tour operators' reservations systems. Thus, tour
operators are passing part of the reservation costs
down the distribution chain. This development has

reached the point with Thomson Holidays that the telephone reservation system for its summer sun/winter sun packages was withdrawn from 8 December 1986.

Parallel with this development are moves to service only the most productive of retail agents. The effect on small retail agents will be quite significant - reduced sales from a lower level of service. Add to this the diminution of sales as a result of multiple chain discounting, and the closure of many independents becomes self evident.

For those operators and agents who remain in business the future looks bright. The number of passengers travelling overseas is increasing steadily each year. Shifts in demand patterns are followed closely by the market, as illustrated by the trend towards increasing numbers of self-catering holidays and flight-only arrangements. Tour operators have reacted quickly and expanded their range of products to satisfy this growing market: as indeed they must if they are to protect, and certainly enhance, their share of the market. Travel agents are not in the forefront of this development but responding to it through increased awareness of the sources of inexpensive charter flights to satisfy their clients' requirements.

The introduction of new destinations arises from tour operator innovation. Travel agents can help stimulate demand following familiarisation visits and educational programmes. It is possible that the scenario for the future will result in restricted opportunities for the marketing of new products and resorts through conventional retail agents. Thought should then be given to marketing the product directly to the public via tourist offices or organisations. This policy could be marginally successful until the industry, as a whole, recognises the product or resorts' potential.

Chapter 5

THE ROLE OF THE TOURIST BOARD

Stan Bowes

TOURIST BOARDS IN THE UNITED KINGDOM

Tourist boards in the United Kingdom exist in a variety of guises. There are the statutory boards which include England, Wales, Scotland and Northern Ireland and the British Tourist Authority as well as the non-statutory boards which include 12 Regional Boards in England. There are also three Regional Tourism Councils in Wales plus the Scottish network of Area Tourist Boards and a number of 'off-shore' boards, like the Isle of Man Tourist Board. The status of the Guernsey Tourist Board and of the Jersey Tourist Board, Sark Tourism Council, the Alderney Tourist Board, and a number of 'Trade Associations', which call themselves sorts of tourist boards should also be acknowledged.

Tourism in the UK is remarkably free from legislation. The 1969 Development of Tourism Act is the only piece of legislation in the entire post-Second World War period devoted to tourism. Astonishing in its brevity (14 pages), it is really an enabling Act which left all of the details to be filled in by the Secretary of State as and when he saw fit. It actually came out of the Harold Wilson government's response to the interminable problem with the balance of payments. No Conservative government could have produced a better piece of legislation from the viewpoint of the private sector. The 1969 Act contained quite sweeping powers, some of them so sweeping that no government has yet dared to use them. For instance the compulsory registration of accommodation, which needs only an Order in Council, and from this it would be an easy step to introduce grading and classifications, then it would be one more easy step to introduce price controls.

The English Tourist Board

Enlarging on this latter theme the English Tourist Board has recently introduced for 1987 an accommodation classification system called the Crown Classification. For a long time in this country the Automobile Association with its star ratings has been the sign for the consumer to recognise that standard hotel accommodation has arrived and the English Tourist Board's Rose classification or Rose Category never gained widespread acceptability. The Crown Classification is having an awful struggle to gain acceptance by a fairly large majority of the accommodation sector in this country at this moment in time, but it is something that is practicable. As previously mentioned, it only needs an Order in Council and it could become mandatory, but at the moment it is voluntary.

The English Tourist Board, created under the 1969 Act, got going around 1970, with Sir Mark Ungar as its first chairman: at the time he was leader of Leicester City Council. He felt there should be a partnership between the English Tourist Board, local government and trade interests.

The Regional Tourist Boards in England

The 1970s was a period in which regionalism was very much the vogue in England - the Regional Sports Councils, Regional Arts Association, Regional Orchestral Associations, Regional Tourist Boards all being established during this period. The various regional tourists boards and councils in England and Wales are shown in Fig. 5.1. There is a striking variation in the spatial extent of tourist board areas and the regions covered are frequently unique. For example, the Thames and Chilterns Tourist Board comprises five counties - Bedfordshire, Berkshire, Buckinghamshire, Oxfordshire and Hertfordshire - a spatial grouping not recognised for any other government function. These regions also differ markedly in terms of the number of tourists, both domestic and overseas, who visit. The West Country attracts most domestic tourists, whilst London is the focal point for tourists from overseas. The London Tourist Board tried changing its name to the London Visitor and Convention Bureau (for reasons best known to themselves) for a period of two years but reverted to its original name in 1987.

Figure 5.1: Regional Tourist Boards and Councils in England and Wales

In most cases the Regional Tourist Boards were easy to set up because there were already local organisations which could be absorbed or developed: for instance, the English Lakes Travel Association became the Cumbria Tourist Board. The Yorkshire Travel and Tourism Association became the Yorkshire Tourist Board. The London Tourist Board had in fact already been in existence for six years when the 1969 Act was passed. Some boards were immediately successful. The East Midlands Board was able to find a local politician of standing who was favourable to the new tourist boards - Alan Yates in Nottinghamshire, who was chairman of the East Midlands Sports Council, chairman of Nottinghamshire County Council and a Manpower Services Commissioner, and who rapidly gathered political and cash support for the East Midlands Tourist Board. However, other Regional Tourist Boards were seen as a menace: the Thames and Chilterns, for instance, was met with indifference from Oxfordshire and Berkshire County Councils, neither of whom would put up an initial subscription, and with outright hostility from Buckinghamshire who felt that it would lead to 'brutalisation' of the Chilterns. Buckinghamshire in actual fact only joined the Thames and Chilterns Tourist Board in 1986, some 14 years after the inaugural annual general meeting.

Differing roles of tourist boards

Right from the outset different tourist boards had different roles to play, which reflected the great differences in tourism on the ground in different parts of England. The four Northern Boards (Cumbria, Northumbria, North West, Yorkshire and Humberside) play a very important role in stimulating tourism development partly through Section 4 of the 1969 Act. Section 4 is that part of the Act which gives the government powers to grant money for capital investment in tourism projects as long as the private sector contributes a fair amount. The Northern Boards adopted this role, in part, because of the famous Peter Shore tourism growth point experiments, e.g. Scarborough and the North East, and many other coastal boards have had very great involvement with their resorts: the infamous problem of the resorts! Some resorts are flourishing, like Blackpool, whereas others are in the final throes of death, like Hunstanton in north-west Norfolk. The reasons for this have not been fully established but probably reflect the local political and social structures. Table 5.1 summarises the grants and loans received by the boards over their first 15 years of life and also indicates their current sources of income. There is more than a ten-fold variation in the amount of grant aid received by boards over this period, with well over half the total amount being spent in peripheral regions. Similarly there is wide variation in Regional Boards' dependence upon different sources of income. Most receive about a fifth of their annual income in the form of a subvention from the English Tourist Board whereas local authority contributions vary from a low (if London discounted) of 4 per cent (Thames & Chilterns) to a high of 48 per cent (Northumbria). Likewise there is considerable variation in the proportion of income deriving from commercial interests (4 per cent in North West to 44 per cent in London) and other private sources (25 per cent Northumbria to 70 per cent Southern).

Table 5.1: Regional Tourist Boards - Tourism Development Grants (1971-86) and Sources of Income (1985-86)

Tourist Board	Gov.Grants/ Loans recd 1971-86	Total £'000s	Income Sources % from			
			ETB	LAs	Comm	Other
Cumbria	6,502	437	23	14	13	50
Northumbria	4,839	479	23	48	5	24
North West	4,982	703	17	15	4	64
Yorks & Humberside	8,586	619	21	25	8	46
East Midlands	2,288	385	30	15	6	49
Heart of England	1,654	518	22	20	14	44
East Anglia	1,322	524	22	12	7	59
Thames & Chilterns	825	484	22	4	12	62
London	1,195	1,361	19	-	44	37
West Country	10,164	783	18	13	11	58
Southern	3,012	700	15	9	6	70
Eastern	1,752	463	26	19	12	43
Totals	47,121	7,456	21	14	15	50

Source: English Tourist Board (1986) Annual Report

The Role of the Tourist Board

It must be stressed, however, that the boards are first and foremost marketing agencies, although in addition some are seen as having development roles, and yet others are seen as having to manage tourism (in so far as it is manageable).

GOVERNMENT GUIDELINES

Amidst all of this the central government policy has been far from clear, or indeed consistent. The Shore guidelines, written in the back of a taxi, talked of the need to get tourists out of London, and any scheme which involved tourists and work on the periphery of the metropolis or beyond was entirely acceptable. In Lord Young's Pleasure, Leisure and Jobs published in August last year, and due to be launched in the mark II edition later this year, this body of policy was described as a mistake (Cabinet Office, 1985). It is now recognised that about two-thirds of all visitors to Britain start their holidays in London. This is not expected to change and there may well be a hotel shortage there, certainly in the foreseeable future.

Some of the government's own schemes have shown this same ambivalence over policy. The hotel development incentive scheme appeared highly successful and open-ended, but ran only from 1970 to 1973, during which time it produced an incredible rush of hotel building and extension- some of it unnecessary, some of it poor quality, but it got Britain ready for the great tourist boom of the late 1970s. A whole range of investment promotion schemes have been tried since: one scheme, subsidising the interest that entrepreneurs pay on loans as the base rates rose, has proved almost impossible to administer. Section 4 of the 1969 Act permitted grants or loans to be made, but the loan part has never been used, just grants only. In some ways Section 4 is a misconceived scheme since applicants must pass a test of financial need yet simultaneously pass a test of financial viability! These are mutually exclusive. It would be much better to pay a standard rate of grant, say 25 per cent or whatever. In practice the average grant runs at just under 20 per cent.

FUTURE OUTLOOK FOR TOURIST BOARDS

Looking more towards the future it is accepted that Regional Tourist Boards will need to generate more and more of their own money if they are to continue to grow. By the late 1980s there will be several Regional Tourist Boards with budgets of well over one million pounds, with the average probably approaching two million pounds and a staff of around 50. Central government funding will probably drop as a proportion of the total: which for the Thames and Chilterns at the moment is around 22 per cent. In the case of the Thames and Chilterns Board we feel we will remain very much a marketing organisation but we are also looking at major new development initiatives (as are other tourist boards). For instance, bringing water-based tourists from The Netherlands.

The Thames and Chilterns and English Tourist Boards are working together to try and create new products in the tourism scene - budget accommodation, inns with bedrooms, high quality self-catering complexes. Given the rise in the self-catering field, this latter tourism need is quite significant, especially at this moment in time. This is a general synopsis of the tourist board as seen by a participant: we see ourselves as principally a marketing operation and we have a commercial membership as well as a local government membership of the Board. The director of the Thames and Chilterns Board, Christopher Jennings, has an academic and town planning background and has been with the Board for fourteen years. We have a research and development officer who administers Section 4 grants for the region as well as advising and giving consultations on development in the areas of accommodation and tourism attractions. The management structure of the Thames and Chilterns Board is shown in Fig. 5.2.

The Board itself has set up a self-catering agency which is self-supporting and covers 120 people who have self-catering cottages throughout the Thames and Chilterns which are now administered by the Board. We also run, on behalf of the West Oxfordshire District Council, three tourist information centres.

Tourist information centres are a bane, if not the bane of our existence, because they are so often unprofessional. There are, however, some very good ones. Information centres are, in the main, run by district councils and they are as good

Figure 5.2: Management structure of the Thames and Chiltern Tourist Board

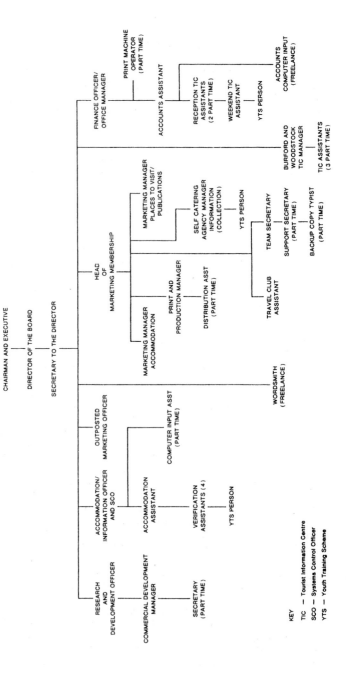

KEY

TIC — Tourist Information Centre
SCO — Systems Control Officer
YTS — Youth Training Scheme

as the people that are employed in them - employees are poorly paid, and centres' opening hours are not really the right hours in terms of what the tourists need. It is an area infested with difficulties and one worthy of further research. The association with tourist boards is generally limited, although not appreciated by the general public or the tourists. The Thames and Chilterns Board operates several information centres for the county councils, e.g. the one we run for the Vale of White Horse, which is our head office in Abingdon and is considered to set a good example. All tourist information centres should be run to guidelines set down by the English Tourist Board (1984). The actual way they run varies between district councils because the latter pay and provide the space.

MARKETING STRATEGIES

Turning to marketing, our overall objectives are to increase the emphasis on overseas markets particularly towards the long-haul English-speaking markets. We work with the British Tourist Authority on that, where there are many opportunities for overseas promotions. We are particularly interested in the European market and are conscious of the fact that 3-4 million visitors come from The Netherlands every year to this country (33 per cent of them on business). But we need to cultivate the Western European market much more. The private or commercial sector amongst our members in the tourist board seems to concentrate on the North American market: perhaps not solely but they have devoted a lot of finance and energy marketing opportunities in North America. It is only this year they suddenly realised that they have put all their eggs in one basket and that they need to cultivate the Western European market a great deal more than they have done. So at least the lesson was learned by the people in the tourism business as such: the early part of 1986, during which American visitor numbers dropped dramatically, served as a salutory warning. We need to encourage a wider range of availability in the accommodation sector. There is a general feeling, both amongst people in the tourist boards as well as more generally, that the accommodation sector prices itself too highly in this country and we are seeking what is known as 'budget-priced' accommodation, or to use the AA Handbook analogies, '2 Star' (but good two Star). Such provision would complement the earlier concentration on the higher priced luxury accommodation, and hopefully reduce the extent to which consumers are turning to a self-catering operation rather than spend a lot of money on hotel accommodation. We are working on this: for example, the inn style accommodation by publicans, who have suddenly developed an interest in providing accommodation in their licensed premises. We are working with about three breweries: Charles Wells brewery in Bedfordshire comes to mind as they have two or three properties available at this moment and are transforming their licensed premises into more than a pub - an inn for accommodation with a nice restaurant associated. Marketing is designed to attract family business rather than the old-style beer drinker for which the English pub is rather well known.

Encouraged by the government, the tourist boards are supporting better signposting of usually by-passed, historic communities, scenic routes and certainly instructions on hard-to-find hotels (and there are many tucked away in the rural communities - those very nice hotels that people never seem to find). The extension of signposting follows on from the successful tourist attraction signing experiments in Kent and Nottinghamshire in the summer of 1985. The scheme is now recommended for use throughout England (Department of Transport, 1986).

The role of tourist information centres as an aid to marketing must be improved. What we would like to see is the development of new 'key' centres: the British Tourist Authority themselves have just developed one such centre in London's Regent Street. We feel that provided the finance can be found this would be a good tool in terms of marketing tourism, but it is likely to be complicated by local political overtones.

Support is also needed for proposed schemes that would make the region a better place to visit. We are committed in various ways to help improve the quality of the local environment for the visitor (in so far as we are able). We are encouraging as many projects as we can through the job creation scheme. In line with the national opinion we are trying to encourage attractions within the region to open longer and to develop all-weather facilities where appropriate.

Opportunities exist which would qualify for a
Section 4 grant, but we have found a reluctance,
certainly on the historic house side, for them to
extend their season any further than they are doing
at the moment. This needs more persuasion by the
Board. We want to encourage amongst employees
within the travel industry and in particular those
who have front-line contact with tourists, such as
hotel receptionists, an awareness of the range of
leisure facilities that exists throughout the
region in order that visitors are better briefed to
prolong and enjoy their stay within the Thames and
Chilterns area.

Specific areas of marketing that we are
looking at are waterways, self-drive hire and short
off-season breaks. The Board itself is committed
to the promotion of waterway holidays on the
Oxford, Grand Union, and Kennet and Avon Canals,
the Lee and Stort Navigation and especially the
River Thames. We are seeking to ensure that the
self-drive hire market sustains the maximum season
and to develop this wherever possible in
conjunction with the trade. We also recognise the
vast importance of past performance but we have in
our region the River Thames which is a very
important tourist attraction and capable of further
development. On the accommodation front we are
continuing to market short breaks, which are of
vital importance in improving occupancy levels
throughout the season and especially out of season.
The scheme that the English Tourist Board has run
for the past four or five years called 'Let's Go'
(which is a free publication, some two million
copies of which are now in circulation) is a
marketing tool for motoring short breaks throughout
the whole country. The 'shoulder-month' promotions
and other peaks and troughs of occupancy may not be
as great in the Thames and Chilterns as in certain
other regions, but there is little room for
complacency. Many of the region's accommodation
establishments remain vulnerable, July through to
September, and are heavily dependent upon the
strength of the overseas market at a particular
time. We are seeking to develop a marketing
programme for this peak period, perhaps using the
theme 'luxury at budget prices'. To further this
the Thames and Chilterns Tourist Board is a member
of a consortium of regional boards which is called
'London Plus': this incorporates in addition the
London Tourist Board, East Anglian Tourist Board,
South East Tourist Board, and the Southern Tourist

Board. It seeks to market tourist accommodation and tourism attractions, within 100 to 130 km of London.

Our other marketing strategy concerns conferences. Conference business is a rising trend in tourism as such. In essence it is business based but closeness to London, the major airport, the motorway and rail networks, and the strength of the business economy, makes the Thames and Chilterns area a popular choice for conferences. The Board is fully supportive of the business travel segment on the grounds that it builds upon strengths rather than weaknesses and the region's conference hotels and conference centres may provide a basis for developing the incentive market, again for a North American as well as a Western European clientele. For example, I was in Copenhagen in February 1987 promoting particularly conferences to the Scandinavian countries.

Joint promotions, with commercial board members such as hotel groups, for developing specific marketing themes are under investigation: these will cover gardens, historic houses, zoos, scenic railways, as well as geographical sub-regions. The 'Beautiful Berkshire' Campaign is one which the Board initiated in co-operation with Berkshire County Council and this has developed a momentum of its own. Another joint promotion deals with 'houses and gardens in the Vale of the White Horse'; others exist with St Albans and Hatfield House. The Board has recently joined with the Beautiful Berkshire campaign to help provide them (on a fifty-fifty basis) with a marketing employee, and we are intending to do the same in Hertfordshire where the county has suddenly realised that the M25 has opened up new avenues for tourism.

Under the 'joint print' programmes with the British Tourist Authority (for standard format brochure prints for overseas distribution) the Board produces well over one million brochures each year and this represents another marketing area of importance. As part of this programme the brochure 'Oxford: City of Dreaming Spires' has been produced in five languages (Dutch, French, German, Italian and Spanish) in addition to English. Such promotional literature deals with excursions throughout the region although there is a certain wariness of the 'days-out' promotion because of the volume of day visitors already received in parts of the Thames and Chilterns region, e.g. Windsor. But

throughout much of the region, apart from those
areas that benefit especially from this day-trip
market, most of the tourism industry is indifferent
as to whether it sells to the day or staying
visitor in terms of attractions.
The 'day-out of London campaign' was
dovetailed with an excursions workshop. The
excursions workshop is to be held again under the
aegis of the London Plus consortium in London, with
all the tourism attractions concentrating on one
exhibition area to which are invited all the
various organisations, institutions, etc. who are
planning days out through a club or society. We
are intending to develop this market even further,
for example, by running, a schools fair, because
tourism attractions need business all the year
round and all through the week. The Board also
works with the recognised language schools and from
our research in Oxford we have found that schools
there have a great part to play in this context. So
we are maintaining a helpful attitude to these
schools and are working with them in their own
marketing groups as well as with the British
Tourist Authority serving their interests overseas.
Our final marketing exercise is to become more
adventurous in the identification and promotion of
the geographical sub-areas of the region. Less
attention should be paid to county boundaries and
more to the geography of the region, highlighting
the internationally known areas such as the River
Thames Basin and the Cotswolds.

CONCLUSION

Having described the Board's role in marketing
tourism its relationship with national
organisations must be understood by way of
conclusion. The British Tourist Authority has
recently announced its marketing strategy for the
late 1980s and the Thames and Chilterns Board will
dovetail into the national marketing strategy and
plans over the next three to five years. That
general strategy concentrates on the following
objectives. First, the maximum net national
benefit is sought from tourism, notably in terms of
export earnings, which is the prime factor in
encouraging tourism. Second, all possible steps
should be taken to spread overseas visitors to
destinations throughout Britain, emphasizing the
attractions of Scotland, Wales and the English

regions, whilst continuing to recognise London as Britain's principal gateway as well as being a major visitor attraction. Despite statements to the effect that visitors do not need to go to London, or they can visit London from another area, 80 per cent of foreign tourists go to London. This is a fact, and you cannot change it to any significant extent. Third, there is a need to create demand for periods of low occupancy, since nearly 50 per cent of tourism accommodation, attractions and transport are unused much of the year.

Obviously we, as well as the British Tourist Authority and the English Tourist Board are looking for increased support through joint activity with the trade. More money cannot be anticipated from government sources, even though government support for tourism is a minute proportion of total government expenditure. Tourist boards will therefore have to generate their own finance (as in part we do already). As a consequence tourist boards will become more and better integrated with the activities of tourism and the travel trade as a whole and will play a significant role in ensuring a continuous flow of tourists.

REFERENCES

Cabinet Office (Enterprise Unit) (1985) Pleasure, Leisure and Jobs: The Business of Tourism, HMSO, London
Department of Transport (1986) Traffic Signs to Tourist Attractions in England, Circular Roads 3/86, Dept of Transport, London
English Tourist Board (1984) Tourist Information Centres: Operating Guidelines, English Tourist Board, London
English Tourist Board (1986) Seventeenth Annual Report, 1985-86, English Tourist Board, London

Note: The views expressed in this chapter are the personal views of the author and do not necessarily represent the policy of the Thames and Chilterns Tourist Board.

Chapter 6

PLANNING OF TOURIST ROUTES: THE GREEN COAST ROAD IN THE NORTHERN NETHERLANDS

Jan R. Bergsma

CONTEXT

Before describing the procedures and discussing the results of a research project carried out in the first half of 1986 on the planning of a specific kind of tourist route in the northern Netherlands, some remarks are in order about the wider context in which this study must be considered. Using tourism as a tool for regional economic development remains one of the prime objectives of studies of the Recreation Research Group in Groningen (Bergsma, 1983 & 1986a). It was also the main topic of the joint Groningen-Reading Recreation and Tourism Workshop of 1985 on 'the impact of tourism in disadvantaged regions' (Ashworth & Goodall, 1986). If tourism is to be used as a vehicle for regional and economic development purposes, we not only need knowledge about the intrinsic physical, socio-cultural and economic potentials for developing a regional tourism product, but we also need to know what possibilities there are for promoting, distributing and finally selling the product.

This can be linked with more general questions: namely to what extent and in what way is it possible for the localised tourism industry, the intermediary organisations and the government to direct and manipulate tourist flows and more particularly tourist behaviour and tourist spending? Actually this poses the question of the degree of autonomy of tourist behaviour, in terms, for example, of travel patterns. Of course this will vary with the kind of tourism that is involved and especially with the transport mode that is used. In particular those kinds of tourism where a complete package is sold, including not only the travel to and from the destination area, but also overnight accommodation and organised excursions, offer the greatest possibility to direct tourist flows and tourist behaviour. The role for example of the tourist guide in determining tourist behaviour and spending in a coach full of Americans 'doing Europe' is considerable. More detailed understanding of the structure and the meaning of all kinds of organised, inclusive tours or package deals are very important in this context, as Goodall has already emphasized at the 1985 Groningen-Reading Workshop in his contribution about the role that package tourism can play in the tourism development of less favoured regions of the EEC (Goodall, 1985).

Besides the possibilities offered by package tourism, however, there is a completely different way of generating and directing tourist flows, which is by the planning and promoting of tourist routes.

TOURIST ROUTES

A simple distinction can be made between two kinds of tourist route:

(i) Most tourist routes have a circuitous character, without a clear point of origin or a clear point of destination. Normally such routes are planned in an attractive landscape and allow for stops to be made at points of interest. For the tourists the 'travel on the route' is part of the tourism experience itself (Clawson & Knetsch, 1966). There is no such thing as distance minimising behaviour, because the tourist is seeking to maximise satisfaction and because of the absence of a clearly identifiable destination. Most scenic circuit routes have a total length that does not exceed a certain value, and most are intended to be used by day trippers.

(ii) Other tourist routes, also planned through attractive landscapes, are linear and are often destination linked.

The planning of this second type of tourist route was the subject of a research project carried out by the Recreation Research Group of the University of Groningen in 1986.

THE GREEN COAST ROAD

Planning objectives and problems

The Green Coast Road more or less follows the coastline from Bergen in Norway, via Sweden, Denmark, northern Germany and The Netherlands to Belgium and the coast of northern France. The route is primarily intended for tourists travelling by car from the Scandinavian countries or from the northern part of Germany, who want to go to the Dutch, Belgian or northern French coastal resorts (Schut, 1970). As early as the 1950s the Green Coast Road was signposted and promoted by leaflets, advertisements and so on. To date the number of users and in particular the way the route is used is disappointing. This low level of usage underlies the efforts of an international foundation over a number of years to improve the situation. The Dutch representatives especially play a very active role. They are giving the Green Coast Road careful attention and are trying to promote increased awareness of its existence and therefore the use made of it by tourists. Of course they are primarily concerned with the Dutch part of the route, leading through the provinces of Groningen and Friesland (see Fig. 6.1). The Dutch part of the foundation has two main objectives. Besides attracting more tourists there is the aim of encouraging tourists to stay longer in the provinces of Groningen and Friesland, with the expectation that this will result in an increase of regional tourist expenditure. In order to realise these objectives it has been suggested that a new route for the Green Coast Road through the northern Netherlands should be planned, which opens access to other and probably more attractive places. The Recreation Research Group of Groningen was commissioned to design a new route for the Green Coast Road through the provinces of Groningen and Friesland, taking into account both of the above mentioned objectives.

In carrying out the research, the first problem to come to terms with was the very specific type of tourist traffic which the route had to cater for. Most of the tourist traffic was destination linked. In fact this kind of tourist traffic cannot be distinguished from business or freight traffic in the sense that it is characterised by the minimising of time, money or distance involved in the journey. Previous

Figure 6.1: The Green Coast Road

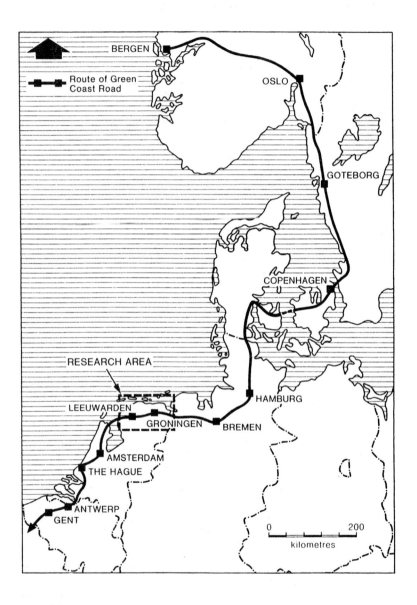

research on this topic made clear the importance of
time-minimising in particular as the main factor in
the explanation of route choice behaviour
(Hamerslag, 1979; Bovy, 1981).

The Green Coast Road as a destination-linked
route should generate a type of tourist traffic
that lies somewhere in between the above mentioned
extreme of minimising time or cost and the other
extreme where there is no minimising behaviour at
all, as is the situation on circuitous routes. On
the one hand the potential users and the target
groups of the Green Coast Road are tourists who are
on their way to a certain destination point or area
(like a seaside resort or a big city). On the
other hand, in order to realise a longer stay in
the northern Netherlands, tourists have to be
seduced to a travel behaviour that is not fully
characterised by minimising distance, time or cost.

The main planning problem that emerged was to
plan a route that was attractive and gave rise to
local tourist expenditure, for example on overnight
accommodation and catering, but at the same time
was not too long in order to maintain the essential
destination-linked function. We were therefore
dealing with the realisation of two objectives,
which were pulling in opposite directions.

The research phases

The research project was carried out in four
phases:

(i) determination of the spatial variation in
attractiveness,
(ii) analysis of the infrastructure,
(iii) determination and assessment of
alternative routes,
(iv) choice of the optimal route.

First we had to consider the attractiveness of
the area of the provinces of Groningen and
Friesland. In order to determine attractiveness
the area was divided into 240 localities, each
containing several features likely to attract
tourists. The data base comprised tourist
information brochures of the provincial tourist
boards of Groningen and Friesland (VVV's Groningen
en Friesland, 1985). Using a set of criteria
(covering not only the intrinsic attractiveness but
also the accessibility and the character of

facilities) it was possible first to assign an individual 'attraction value' to each attraction point and later, taking into account the so-called synergism effect and the existence of the tourism industry, to assess the attractiveness of each of the 240 places. Although it was acknowledged that the spatial pattern of attractiveness may vary for different target groups among tourists, this was not taken into account in this research project.

Figure 6.2: The potential (attraction) surface of Friesland and Groningen

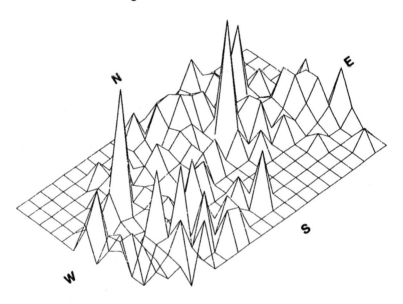

Figure 6.2 presents a computerised three-dimensional attraction surface calculated as a result of the assessment process described above. The highest attraction values are to be found in the south western part of Friesland, together of course with the towns of Groningen and Leeuwarden.

The second phase of research was concerned with the infrastructure. The new track of the Green Coast Road will necessarily comprise sections from the existing road network. For the purpose of this research the complete road network of

Groningen and Friesland was divided into nearly 1600 road sections, all between two recognised nodes or places. Length and attractiveness was determined for each of these sections. Road section attractiveness was directly related to the attractiveness of the immediate environment, established in phase (i). Every place that could be reached within 3 km driving distance from any point on a certain road section was taken into account.

It would take too long, as well as not being necessary, to analyse every possible route through the provinces of Groningen and Friesland. Hence a selection was made of a limited number of alternative routes representative of as much of the area as possible. For this purpose the area of the provinces of Groningen and Friesland was divided into three parts: the area between Nieuweschans and Groningen, the area between Groningen and Leeuwarden and the area between Leeuwarden and the Afsluitdijk (see Fig. 6.3). A number of alternative routes were determined for every sub-area. Because every alternative was made up from a number of already analysed and assessed road sections, it was easy to determine for every alternative:

(i)   the route attractiveness, by adding up the attraction values of every road section that was part of the route,
(ii)   its total length, by adding up the lengths of the individual road sections.

The last phase of the research was the most complicated one, because it gave rise to severe methodological and technical problems. How to choose, out of a number of alternative routes, the best one with regard to the objectives mentioned above? We have already noted that the alternative that unlocks the most attractive parts of the area and receives the highest route attraction value is not necessarily the best choice, because if it is too long the main, destination-linked character cannot any longer be maintained. A trade-off therefore existed between attractiveness of a place and the length of detour the tourist would be prepared to accept.

Figure 6.3: The Green Coast Road – sub-areas within Friesland and Groningen

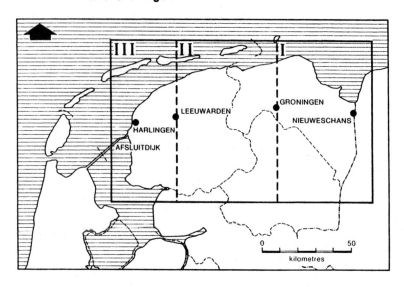

The optimal route

Figure 6.4 relates to the problem of making the right or optimal choice out of a number of alternatives. The curve in Fig. 6.4 can be called an 'iso-willingness curve' (Bergsma, 1986b). Actually this is a specific interpretation of the well-known distance-decay function. With an increasing length of route we need more and more extra route attractiveness in order to maintain a given number of tourists that is willing to use and follow the route.

The theoretical curve had to be operationalised. Because of the lack of available empirical data on this matter, the basis of the operationalisation adopted is shown in Fig. 6.5. Each of the dots in Fig. 6.5 represents one of the route alternatives, all characterised by a certain length and associated attraction value. Route number one is the shortest. It is self-evident that route alternatives that would have less attractiveness than the shortest one are not interesting. The theoretical curve shown in Fig. 6.4 has therefore been operationalised in the following way:

Figure 6.4: Theoretical relationships between route length and attractiveness

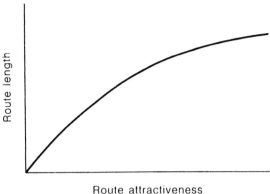

(i)   we assumed that in all those cases where route alternatives have a length less than twice the length of the shortest route, length does not operate as an increasing constraint. So in all these cases the assumption is made of a linear relationship between attractiveness and length,

(ii) when route alternatives are longer than twice the shortest possible one, the assumption is that length becomes more and more a constraint on the intensity of use of the route,

(iii) the last assumption made is that every route alternative longer than three times the shortest route is not of interest, because the difference in the distance that has to be bridged and therefore probably in time and cost is considered as too large. In these cases the characteristic function as a route meant for people on their way to a holiday destination does not exist anymore.

A correct interpretation of Fig. 6.5 makes clear that the route alternative that is characterised by the greatest deviation from the operationalised curve in the 'bottom direction' of the figure is the best and optimal choice.

Figure 6.5:   Length-attractiveness ratios for eight alternative routes

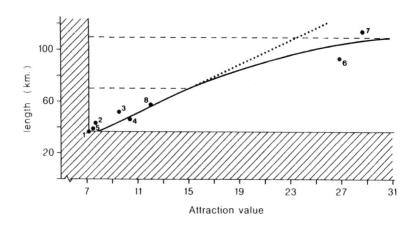

By applying this procedure a decision could be reached for a new course of the Green Coast Road through the Northern Netherlands as shown in Fig. 6.6. The optimal route leads from the eastern part of Groningen via Groningen town, the attractive Lauwersmeer area, Leeuwarden town to the Afsluitdijk. It is characterised by a length twice, and an attraction value almost three times, that of the shortest possible route. Consequently the Dutch part of the international Green Coast Road Foundation will in the near future promote this particular alternative as the new route for the Green Coast Road. At the same time they will try to stimulate and activate the private tourism industry that is located along this route into taking initiatives for a further development of this specific kind of a regional tourism product.

CONCLUDING REMARKS

The method of planning a destination linked route through a certain area, in such a way that regional economic benefits can be optimised, described above, has to be considered as only a first step in developing a more elaborate and generally applicable method of route planning. The method can be criticised in several ways and further research is needed to refine the methodology. For the purpose of a better

Figure 6.6: The recommended route for the Green Coast Road in Friesland and Groningen

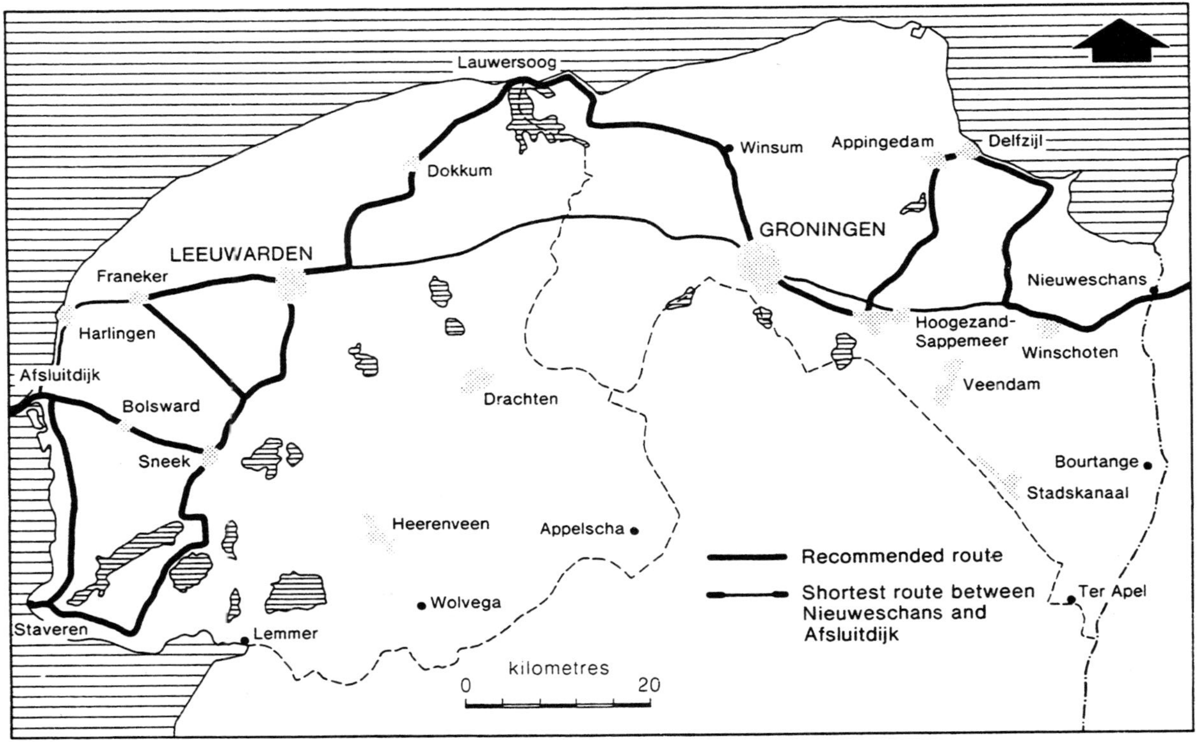

operationalisation we especially need more
empirical data about the willingness of tourists,
on their way to or from a holiday destination to
travel and behave like non-distance/cost/time
minimisers. Moreover we have to establish how the
localised regional tourism industry can take
advantage of the existence and the use of an
international tourist route. The research reported
above will hopefully function as an incentive for
more academic and non-academic attention for this
particular topic in tourism research.

REFERENCES

Ashworth, G.J. & Goodall, B. (1986) The impact of
tourism on disadvantaged regions, Sociaal-
Geografische reeks no 35, GIRUG, Groningen
Bergsma, J.R. (1983) Recreatieonderzoek
Geografisch Instituut R.U.G./Activiteiten
Werkgroep Recreatie 1977-1983, GIRUG,
Groningen
Bergsma, J.R. (1986a) Vaarrecreatie in Noord
Nederland, een voorbeeld van toegepast
geografisch onderzoek, pp 319-28 in
Proceedings Nederlandse Geografendagen 1986,
Utrecht
Bergsma, J.R. (1986b) Groene Kustweg, het plannen
van een toeristische doorgaande route, pp 69-
76 in Proceedings Nederlandse planologische
Diskussiedagen 1986, Delft
Bovy, P.H.L. (1981) Het kortste-tijd
routekeuzeprincipe: een toetsing van de
voorspellende kwaliteit, Verkeerskunde no 6,
291-96
Clawson, M. and J. Knetsch (1966) Economics of
Outdoor Recreation, Johns Hopkins Press,
Baltimore
Goodall, B. (1985) Some initial thoughts about the
role of package tourism in the economic
development of less favoured regions, GIRUG,
Groningen
Hamerslag, R. (1979) Onderzoek naar routekeuze met
behulp van een gedisaggregeerd logitmodel,
Verkeerskunde no. 8, 377-82
Schut, H.J. (1970) De Groene Kustweg, NWIT, Breda
VVV Friesland (1985) Gids voor Vakantie en Vrije
Tijd, Leeuwarden
VVV Groningen (1985) Gids voor Vakantie en Vrije
Tijd, Groningen

RECREATIONAL DEVELOPMENTS IN GRAVEL WORKINGS:
THE LIMBURG EXPERIENCE

Henk Voogd

INTRODUCTION

Central Limburg in The Netherlands, originally
an area with few water resources and with a
predominantly agricultural landscape, is in the
process of an unprecedented restructuring of its
regional economy. This is a geographical revolution
of historic proportions as well as a rather unique
socio-economic process through which a very
intensive recreation infrastructure is being
developed. The commercial exploitation of the
lakes, beaches, mooring places and ports, the
establishment of small- and large-scale hotel and
restaurant facilities, sailing and boardsailing
courses and the organisation of water sports
associations will no doubt evoke an entirely new
regional economic structure.
    The main cause of this restructuring process is
gravel. It is an indispensable building material,
used in large quantities for purposes of civil
engineering and housing. Almost 95 per cent of the
Dutch production of, on average, almost 11 million
tons of gravel per year is won by private firms in
wet mineral workings in the most southerly province
in The Netherlands: Limburg.
    The total surface area of Limburg is only
220,000 hectares (550,000 acres). The quarrying of
gravel is limited to a relatively small area along
the floodplain of the river Maas, a stretch of
about 20 km near the city of Roermond in Central
Limburg. Almost 25 per cent of this area is being
excavated to a depth of 10-15 metres so as to leave
a landscape covered in lakes (see Fig.7.1). It is
obvious that such quarrying activities offer great
opportunities for large-scale recreational
developments with an emphasis on water sports (see
also Goodall, 1986). This chapter will examine
these developments and discuss some consequences
with respect to recreation and tourism.

Figure 7.1: Central Limburg

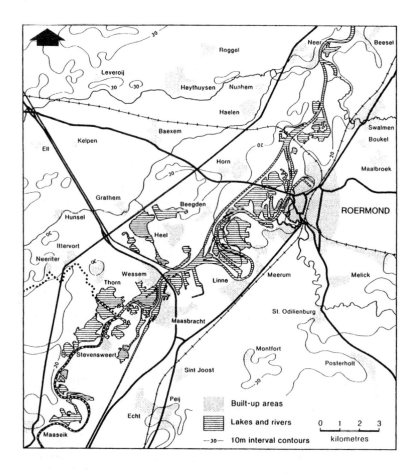

THE HISTORICAL AND GEOGRAPHICAL BACKGROUND

Over the ages the river Maas, with its source
on the Plateau de Langres (France), carried along
large quantities of stone rubble (mainly gravel and
sand) from the Ardennes mountains. In many places
in South and Central Limburg, a layer of gravel
averaging 10 metres in depth was formed. In the
north of the province, a considerable quantity of
sand piled up, thus protecting the deeper layers
for commercial exploitation today.

The first impetus for gravel quarrying was given by the canalisation of the Maas in 1929, making this river navigable for larger ships. The building industry's demand was very modest in the pre-war period: less than two million tons annually. However, this increased explosively after 1945 when post-war rebuilding began. In 1971, almost 19 million tons of gravel were quarried in Limburg (Dutch domestic requirements totalled 25 million tons). In 1976 the Limburg production fell back to 11 million tons and now the gravel companies in this area extract approximately 10 to 11 million tons each year.

At first, gravel was quarried from the areas exposed as the river shrank in summer and later from the lower river terraces. Before 1969 the gravel workings were mainly small-scale pits in the winter bed of the Maas. As Fig. 7.2 shows, the impact of these pits on the regional structure of Central Limburg is considerable. Until now, an area of approximately 3,500 hectares (8,750 acres) has been involved. The fact that the Dutch building industry is almost totally dependent on this region for its gravel supply makes extension of the quarry area in the future economically essential and, therefore, very likely (see also Bennema, et.al., 1985).

In order to avoid a further uncontrolled deterioration of the landscape, the Provincial Government decided in 1969 to concentrate future gravel production in a limited number of areas. The reasons for concentration were very similar to those advanced by Yeoman (1986) who advocated a big 'superquarry' in Glensanda (Scotland): less nuisance, competitive prices, security of supply over many years, etc. In the years after 1969 a new big pit has therefore been created near Panheel-Beegden, an area outside the winter bed of the Maas. Local citizens, municipalities and environmental organisations protested vigorously against this project. Major objections were, among others, imminent isolation of small villages which are more or less permanently surrounded by open water, the disappearance of the characteristic landscape and the loss of environmental and agricultural qualities in the vicinity of the quarry due to hydrological changes. Last but not least, criticisms were focused on the emphasis in the restoration plans on the creation of water recreation instead of aiming at a dry restoration. The total amount of land directly involved in the

103

Figure 7.2: The spatial impact of gravel pits in Limburg

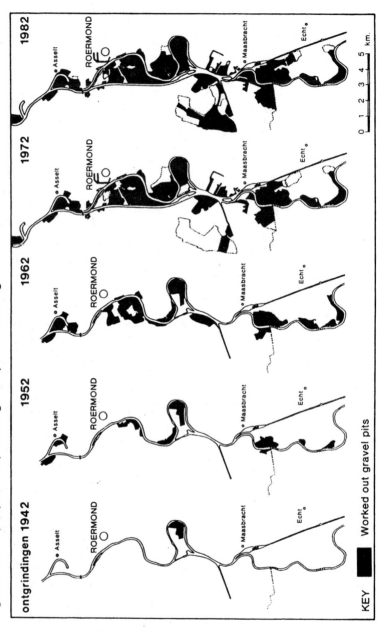

Panheel-Beegden project was 464 hectares (1,160 acres). By comparison, the Scottish 'Mammoth Concept' quarry Glensanda, in its first 20 or 25 years, will occupy about 240 hectares (600 acres) (Yeoman, 1986).

WET RESTORATION: MAKING A VIRTUE OF NECESSITY

Fig. 7.3 compares the amount of wet versus dry restoration of the Limburg gravel pits over time. It shows that in earlier days approximately 40-50 per cent of the quarries were filled for 'dry' reuse (mainly agriculture). However, due to the lack of suitable filling materials the percentage of wet restoration has increased considerably, up to 80 per cent in recent years. In comparison in England, on average, 27 per cent of sand and gravel workings have undergone wet restoration, with South West England as a high exception where 48 per cent of the workings have been left as water areas (Neville, 1985).

In earlier days mine-stone, a waste product from the old coal mines, was often used as filling material. However a more thorough chemical investigation of this mine-stone in the 1970s revealed some undesirable environmental characteristics that may cause, in the long run, groundwater pollution. Besides, due to the closure of all coal mines in the 1960s, mainly as a result of the discovery of large reserves of natural gas in the northern part of The Netherlands, the production of mine-stone stopped. Consequently, this kind of filling material is no longer used.

The top layer of sand above the gravel, has, until recently, mostly been used in building and other civil engineering works. However, the rules in recent planning permits now make it impossible for the gravel firms to sell this top layer, since it may also be used as a filling material. Therefore, the sand above the gravel is nowadays used to restore the pit, but obviously this enables only a partially dry restoration.

Filling material costs money, if only for transporting it to its final destination. This was one of the reasons why in 1969 the provincial government entered into a contract with the joint gravel producers. According to this contract the firms have to restrict until 1990 their applications for new production sites to areas which are assigned by the provincial government.

Figure 7.3: The progress of gravel pit restoration

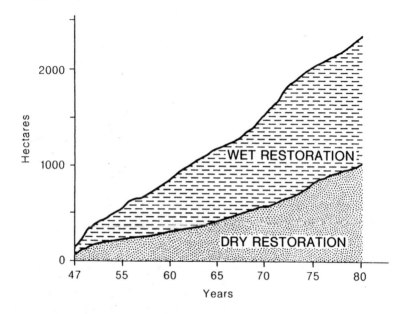

The provincial government, in return, had to
guarantee gravel production until 1990, amongst
others by means of the previously mentioned
Panheel-Beegden 'superquarry'. Besides, it was
agreed that after closure of a quarry, the
ownership rights are transferred to the province
without payment. The cost of restoring the land
will be covered by a special rehabilitation fund.
To this end, the gravel companies have to pay 1.87
guilders per ton of quarried gravel and 0.86
guilders per ton of sand into this fund.

ASPECTS OF RECREATION PLANNING AND POLICY

The recreational use of the Limburg gravel
lakes started in the early 1960s and has developed
rather haphazardly. A total of 13 yacht harbours
were built during this time, as well as various
small-scale facilities for water and land
recreation. The area enjoys a growing reputation
both within and beyond The Netherlands as a very
water-rich province. Over 25,000 water sports
enthusiasts visited the Central lakes area in 1983.

In the provincial 'restoration plan' for the gravel pits, several reuse functions are considered. The 12 projects in this plan include 1,930 hectares (4,725 acres) of water and 1,540 hectares (3,850 acres) of land, of which approximately 85% is now owned by the province of Limburg. In the plan a distinction is made between 'major' and 'important additional' reuse functions. In Table 7.1 an overview is given for the 12 (major) restoration projects.

Table 7.1: Proposed recreational projects in Limburg and their functions

Project	Major function	Additional functions
Ohe en Laak	sailing/motorboats	boardsailing/ nature
Stevensweert	intensive day recreation	angling/water- sports
Thorn	nature	angling
Wessem	intensive day recreation	angling/board- sailing
Panheel	nature/angling/ water basin	boardsailing
Pol	sailing/motorboats	agriculture/ nature
Molengreend	boardsailing	day recreation
Osen	sailing/motorboats	nature
Oolerveld	sailing/motorboats	angling/day recreation
Roermond	intensive day recreation	boardsailing/ angling
Asselt	sailing/motorboats	nature/water sports
Rijkel	nature	angling

Source: Herinrichtingsnota, Provincie Limburg, 1985

For each project a separate project plan has been designed, in which the various functions are spatially elaborated. Generally, these project plans should be approved by the various governmental authorities before the quarrying begins. But given the fact that the plans often have to deal with geographical situations 15 or 20 years later, they do not have a legally binding status.

At the moment 2,170 hectares (5,425 acres) is still being exploited by the gravel companies. When finally worked out - in the early 1990s - it will encompass 1,750 hectares (4,375 acres) of water and 420 hectares (1,050 acres) of land. The cost of restoring the land and facilities of this area is estimated at around 220 million guilders, to be covered by the rehabilitation fund, mentioned before. The physical restoration of the pit itself (i.e. filling, creation of shores, etc.) is estimated at 136.4 million guilders; the rest is necessary for completing the Panheel-Beegden project (fl.34.3 million), planning and management (fl.17.5 million) and maintenance costs (fl.15 million).

According to their policy of optimising the recreational benefits of the Central Limburg water lakes, the provincial government decided a few years ago to sell the entire lake area to a single private organisation. Several candidates showed interest, in particular:

(i) the joint gravel companies, who realised that, in order to gain the goodwill of the population, a satisfactory restoration could mean continuity of employment;
(ii) the 14 municipalities in the area, who, on the one hand, not only feared the negative consequences of a fully commercial development for their own inhabitants, but, on the other hand, also relished the likelihood of financial profits if the subsequent exploitation of the lake area could be entirely in their hands;
(iii) project development groups, who saw the lake area simply as a profitable object for investment.

The municipalities were not really considered as serious candidates by the province because of their inability to finance the whole operation. The gravel firms, however, were well able to raise the money, but they were not acceptable as buyers because of their 'possible conflict of interests'. In March 1985 the decision was made to sell the lake area for 6.5 million guilders to an international investment group Lanera (with the British carpet firm Tredford an important participant) and the Dutch project developer

Wyckerveste. Today the group already exploits several restored projects under the name Aqua Terra and the first signs of a more commercial approach can already be seen (e.g. fencing to enclose the lakes).

The present situation is obviously viewed with mixed feelings by the local communities. According to the present plans by 1995 there will be room for 6000 motorboats and yachts. With an average of almost three persons per boat, these figures imply almost 20,000 boat-tourists, most of them Germans. Presently every sunny weekend, many people from Mönchengladbach, Köln and Dusseldorf drive to the Central Limburg lake area for a few hours sailing or boating, and then drive back home. Consequently, the desired local economic impact is not great as yet, although the presence of the Germans is very obvious. Many watersports clubs in the area seem to survive only by having many German 'guest members'. German guests, however, only need this membership in order to obtain a place in one of the many harbours. In the Touristic and Recreational Overall Plan of Limburg (TROP, 1981) it is estimated that approximately 60 per cent of the boats in the harbours of Central Limburg are owned by Germans. Where a harbour is combined with camping facilities, this participation rate may be up to 90 per cent (TROP, 1981).

CONCLUDING REMARKS

The Dutch experience in Limburg shows that mineral extraction may play a significant role in providing a basis for the development of various kinds of water recreation. Despite the fact that the gravel companies have to hand over the exhausted quarries to the provincial government without payment, the eagerness of several parties to buy this 'derelict' or 'idle' land nevertheless clearly demonstrates its intrinsic economic value.

The final consequences of the large scale privatisation of the Limburg water lakes is not yet fully discernable. The province stresses the fact that the sale of the area to one single firm, Aqua Terra, enables a better control of the developments than in the case where many individual developers are involved. The provincial authorities expect that Aqua Terra, having determined the recreation activities that can be accommodated, should set a market rent appropriate to encouraging viable tenants and the growth of recreation, rather than trying to charge unrealistic rentals that encourage nobody. The municipalities, however, are very concerned about the present developments. Not only because their influence on the whole process is rather limited, but also because privatisation implies for their inhabitants a restriction on the use of (or in practice, a fence around) the water areas - the same inhabitants who also had to suffer yesterday from the nuisance of the gravel workings. This addresses the fundamental planning problem of efficiency versus equity: the 'oil' and the 'water' of policymaking (Miller, 1985). The case of Central Limburg illustrates that they do not mix well in most operational contexts!

REFERENCES

Bennema, S.; Hoen, H.'t.; Setten, A. van & Voogd, H. (1985) Studying Gravel Extraction through Multicriteria Analysis, 179-88 in: A. Faludi & H. Voogd (eds), Evaluation of Complex Policy Problems, Delftsche Uitgeversmaatschappij, Delft

Goodall, B. (1986) Outdoor Recreation and Environmental Improvement, Department of Geography, University of Reading (mimeographed)

Miller, D.H. (1985) Equity and Efficiency Effects of Investment Decisions, 35-50 in A. Faludi & H. Voogd (eds), op.cit.

Neville, B. (1985) Wet restoration, Mineral Planning, 24, 24-32

Provincie Limburg (1985) Herinrichtingsnota, Maastrict

TROP (1981) Toeristisch en recreatief ontwikkeling plan voor Limburg, Eindrapport, Netherlands Institute of Tourism Development Consultants, Arnhem

Yeoman, J. (1986) The Mammoth Concept, Mineral Planning, 27, 4-8

Chapter 8

THE ECONOMIC EFFECTS ON DESTINATION AREAS OF FOREIGN INVOLVEMENT IN THE TOURISM INDUSTRY: A SPANISH APPLICATION

Thea Sinclair and Charles Sutcliffe

The tourism industry is currently receiving increasing acknowledgement for its role in promoting the development of tourist destination areas. However, differences in the degree of foreign relative to domestic ownership and control of the tourism industry can lead to considerable differences in the effects which tourism has on a destination area. Such effects can be divided into five main categories: the balance of payments, the distribution of public and private revenue, the value of foreign expenditure on tourism and the associated income multiplier effects in the destination area, the techniques of production utilised and the level of employment, and the degree of control which the host area can exercise over the development of the tourism industry and destination area. This chapter will use empirical evidence for the Spanish tourism industry to examine the ways in which alternative degrees of foreign and domestic participation in the tourism industry can lead to differing effects on tourist destination areas.

THE BALANCE OF PAYMENTS

Foreign tourism plays a very important role in the economy of many destination countries (Erbes, 1973; United Nations, 1973). The tourism industry in Spain, for example, developed into one of the most important sectors of the Spanish economy in an extremely short period of time. Table 8.1 shows that whereas in 1951, 1.3 million tourists visited Spain, by 1985 43.2 million tourists arrived (Ministry of Information and Tourism, 1964-77; Ministry of Commerce and Tourism, 1978-83). The rise in tourist arrivals which occurred during the 1960s was due particularly to the intervention in the travel trade of foreign tour operators who

111

Economic Effects on Destination Areas

Table 8.1: Tourist arrivals in Spain (000s)

Year	With pass-port	In tran-sit	24hr Excurs.	Span. resid. abroad	Total
1951	676	325	189	72	1,263
1952	776	430	196	81	1,485
1953	909	545	172	83	1,710
1954	993	679	177	102	1,952
1955	1,383	765	244	129	1,522
1956	1,560	731	277	157	2,728
1957	2,018	719	220	227	3,187
1958	2,451	661	152	327	3,593
1959	2,863	715	283	332	4,194
1960	4,332	837	256	686	6,113
1961	5,496	827	319	813	7,455
1962	6,390	762	573	942	8,667
1963	7,941	855	1,113	1,022	10,931
1964	10,507	1,094	1,309	1,193	14,103
1965	11,080	1,013	979	1,180	14,252
1966	14,443	1,051	366	1,392	17,252
1967	14,810	1,132	328	1,589	17,859
1968	16,238	1,182	282	1,482	19,184
1969	18,879	1,220	240	1,343	21,682
1970	21,267	1,109	281	1,448	24,105
1971	23,738	1,139	443	1,439	26,759
1972	29,438	1,131	428	1,509	32,506
1973	31,606	1,050	209	1,694	34,559
1974	27,364	1,001	172	1,806	30,343
1975	27,359	968	75	1,721	30,123
1976	27,389	922	72	1,631	30,014
1977	31,597	959	119	1,592	34,267
1978	36,943	832	481	1,715	39,971
1979	33,860	994	2,112	1,937	38,903
1980	32,925	903	2,689	1,510	38,027
1981	35,569	882	1,943	1,735	40,129
1982	37,651	815	1,462	2,083	42,011
1983	37,089	741	1,379	2,054	41,263
1984	39,004	732	1,175	2,051	42,962
1985	39,672	792	780	1,991	43,235

Source: Ministry of Information and Tourism, 1964-77 and Ministry of Commerce and Tourism, 1978-83, Madrid

Table 8.2:   Foreign currency receipts from tourism
in Spain

Year	Receipts ($ million)
1952	58.4
1953	94.2
1954	90.0
1955	90.7
1956	94.8
1957	76.9
1958	71.6
1959	128.6
1960	297.0
1961	385.0
1962	513.0
1963	679.3
1964	918.6
1965	1,156.9
1966	1,138.5
1967	1,126.8
1968	1,178.9
1969	1,310.7
1970	1,680.8
1971	2,054.5
1972	2,607.6
1973	3,091.2
1974	3,187.9
1975	3,404.3
1976	3,083.4
1977	4,003.0
1978	5,488.0
1979	6,483.8
1980	6,967.7
1981	6.715.9
1982	7,126.1
1983	6,836.1
1984	7,716.7
1985	8,150.8

started to provide low-priced package holidays on a
massive scale.

The growth in demand for Spanish tourism has
caused the tourism industry to be of prime
importance in the Spanish economy. As Table 8.2
demonstrates, the absolute value of foreign
currency receipts from tourism is considerable.

Table 8.3: Tourism and the balance of payments, 1984 (millions of SDRs)

Country	(1)	(2)	(3)	(4)	(5)
Industrialised Countries					
Austria	4,376	25,964	16.9	-26,628	16.4
France	7,409	144,504	5.1	-141,615	5.2
Italy	8,369	96,752	8.6	-100,658	8.3
Netherlands	1,499	81,823	1.8	-76,035	2.0
UK	5,393	138,585	3.9	-134,656	4.0
US	11,110	353,700	3.1	-441,200	2.5
Southern European Countries					
Cyprus	351	1,352	26.0	-1,592	22.0
Greece	1,288	7,162	18.0	-10,828	11.9
Portugal	929	6,970	13.3	-9,588	9.7
Spain	7,572	36,133	21.0	-35,003	21.6
Turkey	535	9,517	5.6	-12,952	4.1
Third World Countries					
Jamaica	413	1,327	31.1	-1,753	23.6
Jordan	440	1,857	23.7	-3,755	11.7
Kenya	205	1,584	12.9	-1,860	11.0
Mexico	3,198	31,529	10.1	-28,085	11.4
Philippines	358	7,837	4.6	-9,426	3.8
Singapore	1,944	30,998	6.3	-31,773	6.1
Thailand	1,182	9,337	12.7	-12,413	9.5
Tunisia	491	2,728	18.0	-3,782	13.0

Source: IMF Balance of Payments Statistics, Vol.36, Yearbook, Part I, 1985
Key: (1) Travel Receipts, (2) Goods,Services and Income: Total Receipts,
(3) 1 as % of 2, (4) Imports of Goods, Services and Incomes, (5) 1 as % of 4.

Spain's tourism receipts are also high relative to the amounts received by other countries, as is shown in Table 8.3. Of all the countries included in the table, Spain received the third highest value of travel receipts. The value of travel receipts is also high in most industrialised countries, followed by Mexico, Singapore, Greece and Thailand.

Additional measures of the importance of tourism receipts to a country's development process are tourism receipts relative to total receipts, and to payments for imports. Column 2 in Table 8.3 gives the values of total receipts from goods, services and income, column 4 the values of imports and columns 3 and 5 travel receipts as percentages of each of these categories. Column 3 shows that Spanish travel receipts constituted 21 per cent of total receipts, the percentages for Cyprus, Jordan, Greece and Tunisia being 18 per cent or higher. Ten of the 13 southern European and Third World countries included in the table obtained over 10 per cent of their total receipts from tourism.

The final column in Table 8.3 provides travel receipts as a percentage of the value of expenditure on imports and indicates the importance of tourism receipts as a source of foreign exchange for financing imports, which are frequently necessary for a country's development process. The calculated percentages again tend to be higher for the southern European and Third World countries included in the table than for the industrialised countries. Of the latter, travel receipts only constitute over 10 per cent of expenditure on imports in Austria, whereas eight of the southern European and Third World countries have percentages of over 10 per cent, with three over 20 per cent. In Spain, tourism receipts were 22 per cent of the value of imports. The value of expenditure on travel by Spaniards who have travelled abroad has been low relative to the value of receipts, constituting only 11 per cent of the value of travel receipts in 1984. Thus current receipts from foreign tourism greatly exceed expenditure abroad by Spanish tourists and the sector appears to make a large positive contribution to the economy in terms of supply of foreign exchange. However, before concluding that this is definitely the case, it is necessary to examine the amount of expenditure on inputs which are imported to meet the requirements of the tourism industry. Such imports include goods and services consumed by

115

tourists and capital goods required for providing accommodation and infrastructure.

Third World countries which have an established tourism industry but a limited industrial base often import large quantities of both the goods and services which are directly purchased by the tourists who visit them and the goods and services which indirectly meet the tourists' needs. Thus a high proportion of gross receipts from tourism can be lost from the destination country in the form of payments for imports from foreign firms. Foreign ownership or control of tourism facilities (hotels, flats, etc.) in the destination area can lead to higher payments for imports if foreigners have a policy of importing goods and services with which they are familiar from their own country. Foreign firms also benefit from increased purchases of imported goods and services by local residents who receive higher incomes as the result of local tourism development, or who increase their expenditure on imported goods as a consequence of the demonstration effect of consumption by foreign tourists. The relatively developed nature of the Spanish economy with its diversified range of economic activities means that a considerable proportion of the products which are required by the tourism industry are produced within Spain. A study carried out by the Spanish Institute of Tourism has shown that the total value of goods imported to meet the requirements of the tourism sector amounts to approximately 1.5 per cent of GNP and 2.8 per cent of the total value of imports into Spain (IET, 1978a, 222-23).

Foreign participation in the tourism industry also leads to losses from the destination country in the form of factor payments abroad. For example, foreign ownership of tourism facilities such as hotels, flats, restaurants, etc. in the destination area usually results in remittances of rent, profits and dividends. In addition, income is earned by foreigners who sell their expertise to the destination country, for example via management contracts involving the management of hotels, blocks of flats or other tourism facilities. Income is also paid to foreigners who are employed in the destination area or who train residents of the destination area.

In the case of Spain, factor payments abroad which are associated with foreign tourism are relatively low. Outflows in the form of investment income constitute approximately 3 per cent of total outflows, while wages and salaries paid to foreigners are negligible owing to the country's strictly enforced laws prohibiting the employment of foreigners when Spanish nationals are available to carry out the work. Expenditure by the Spanish government is only approximately 2 per cent of total outflows. The total value of outflows which occurs as a direct consequence of foreign tourism in Spain is 13 per cent of the total value of receipts from tourism. However, it should be borne in mind that outflows from particular sub-national tourist destination areas are of far greater relative importance than outflows at the national level; for example, the propensity to import, resulting in considerably lower income multiplier values for the former than the latter. The importance of outflows in the form of payments for imports which are associated with tourist expenditure in the Spanish province of Malaga will be discussed below.

THE DISTRIBUTION OF PUBLIC AND PRIVATE REVENUE

The development of a tourist destination area is considerably affected by the distribution of the revenue obtained from tourism between the destination area and elsewhere and, within the destination area, between the public and private sectors. It was argued above that, for a given total value of tourist spending, such as might occur in a country with a stable, well-established tourism industry, an increase in the extent of participation in the tourism sector by origin countries can lead to a notable increase in the proportion of tourist spending received by origin countries and a corresponding decrease in the revenue received by the destination area owing to payments for imported goods and services, factor payments abroad, etc. The decrease in the revenue received by the destination will, in turn, affect the private sector by lowering profits. It will also affect the public sector by decreasing the value of tax receipts - both of direct tax and indirect taxes such as sales tax, customs revenue, tourist arrival or departure tax etc.

Foreigners can increase their control over the tourism industry in the destination area in two ways (Dunning & McQueen, 1982):

(i) direct foreign investment in tourism facilities in the destination area, resulting in partial or total ownership;
(ii) the drawing-up of contracts between foreign tour operators and the indigenous owners of tourism facilities.

In the case where there has been considerable direct foreign investment in the destination area, some local policy makers have attempted to increase the proportion of revenue from tourism which is retained within the destination area by increasing the rate of taxation on the profits generated by the tourism industry, or by imposing restrictions on the amount of money which can be remitted abroad. Multinational enterprises (MNEs) can circumvent such restriction by the manipulation of transfer pricing. This can occur because, in the case of MNEs, a large number of transactions take place within the firm, so that the traditional theory of pricing does not apply. Buyers and sellers do not try to maximise their individual profits. Instead, their aim is to maximise the joint profits of the firm as a whole.

If, for example, the rate of taxation in the destination area exceeds the rate of taxation elsewhere, the MNE will wish to decrease the proportion of its profits which it declares in the destination area. An example will clarify how this occurs. If an international hotel chain finds that there is a relatively high tax rate on profits in the foreign country and a relatively low rate on profits in the home country, it will attribute a relatively high accounting price to accommodation in the foreign country. This results in a fall in the value of declared profits in the foreign country and an increase in the home country, giving rise to a decrease in the total value of tax payments. Accommodation in the foreign country is said to be 'over priced' relative to the 'arm's length price'; i.e. the price which would occur in the open market, between unrelated units. Thus MNEs can use transfer pricing to decrease or increase the value of revenue from tourism in the tourist destination country. A decrease will lower receipts from taxation.

It is obviously extremely difficult to obtain data to ascertain the extent to which transfer pricing occurs, and there is a lack of evidence concerning the extent to which it takes place in the Spanish tourism industry. However, there has

been a tradition of tax evasion via the under-
declaration of profits in Spain and the tax rate on
declared profits has been 20 per cent. Hence it is
unlikely that large amounts of money have been
transferred out of Spain for the motive of tax
avoidance. Further motives for transfer pricing
include the aim of decreasing payments to local
shareholders, the avoidance of an effective tax on
profits via the existence of multiple exchange
rates, currency speculation and decreases in the
level of risk associated with political
instability. These are unlikely to apply in the
case of Spain, where payments to local shareholders
are of relatively low importance, there is only one
exchange rate which has not been prone to a high
level of fluctuation and there has been relative
political stability. However, it is likely that
the foreign owners of tourism facilities in Spain
wish to retain a high proportion of their profits
in their home countries, and a common way of
attaining this objective has been by requiring
tourists to Spain to pay for the use of ownership
of these facilities in their home countries. For
example, many newspapers commonly advertise the
sale of Spanish villas for which payment can be
made in the purchaser's country of origin. By this
means a considerable proportion of the profits from
tourism in Spain never reach the destination area,
and the distribution of profits is switched towards
the tourists' countries of origin.

The second means by which foreigners gain
control over the tourism industry in the
destination area, where tour operators make
contracts with indigenous owners of tourism
facilities, which is very common within the
international tourism industry. The tour operator
is the prime mover in the provision of the product
of package holidays. Since the tour operator
decides which hotels or flats, in which countries
and which airlines or other form of transport are
used, the tour operator has a vital role in
determining the structure of the tourism industry.
It is likely that a lower level of demand for
tourism would be forthcoming in the absence of the
tour operator's intervention, implying a lower
level of expenditure on tourism in the destination
area. This, in turn, would result in a lower value
of income generation in the area, as will be
explained below. However, if an equivalent level
of demand for tourism could be attained without the
intervention of foreign tour operators, it is

likely that the value of expenditure on tourism in the destination area would be higher. This is because tourists who purchase package holidays from tour operators pay for their holidays in their country of origin, so that part of the purchase price fails to reach the destination area.

Tourists who purchase inclusive tours to Spain almost invariably pay for their holidays in their country of origin. Thus, a proportion of the amount which they pay for their holidays remains in the origin countries in the form of profits, and the tour operator does not have to face the problem of repatriating these profits from Spain. Since a high proportion of tourists arrive in non-Spanish airlines, further amounts are siphoned off before payment is made for accommodation. In the case of accommodation which is owned by a foreign MNE, foreign companies or individuals, a further proportion of tourist expenditure is lost to Spain. Finally, considerable pressure is often placed upon both indigenous and foreign accommodation owners to charge extremely low prices to tour operators, almost all of which are foreign. Original survey data obtained by Sinclair and Sutcliffe (1979) showed that the maximum legally permitted discounts of 30 per cent off the officially established accommodation prices are common, particularly during the low season, and informal conversations with numerous participants in the tourism industry, including employees of foreign tour operators, showed that much larger discounts are often obtained. Thus, of the initial cost of the holiday to the tourist, a considerable proportion never reaches the Spanish economy.

THE VALUE OF EXPENDITURE ON TOURISM AND ASSOCIATED MULTIPLIER EFFECTS IN THE DESTINATION AREA

Tourist expenditure in a given destination country induces increases in the value of national income. The changes in the value of income which result from tourist expenditure can be quantified by means of various techniques such as export base multipliers, input-output analysis and simultaneous equations models, as has been explained by Sutcliffe (1985). One of the most useful ways of estimating the income generation effects associated with tourist expenditure is via the use of the Keynesian income multiplier model. The technique requires a smaller quantity of data than would be required for the formulation of an input-output table or a simultaneous equations model but provides a large amount of information which is of use to policy makers by permitting the estimation of the multiplier values and income generation associated with a range of different types of tourist expenditure.

Multiplier values can also be estimated in order to calculate the changes in income which are generated by changes in tourist expenditure in the different regions or other sub-national areas where tourists are concentrated. Multiplier formulae for sub-national areas have been derived by Sinclair and Sutcliffe (1982) for changes in GNP and disposable income. The formula for the long run GNP multiplier is:

$$\Delta Y'/\Delta E = K*(1+\bar{K}K) \qquad (1)$$

where $\Delta Y'$ = the change in GNP at factor cost, resulting from an initial change in tourist expenditure in the area, which occurs over all rounds of the multiplier process;

ΔE = the initial change in tourist expenditure in the area;

$K*$ = the propensity to generate GNP during the first round of the multiplier process and $K* = (1-L_1)$ where L_1 is the first round propensity to withdraw for the area;

$\bar{K}$ = the propensity to generate GNP during the second round of the multiplier process;

K = $1/(1-K_s)$ and is the subsequent round multiplier for GNP where K_s is the propensity to generate GNP during subsequent rounds of the multiplier process.

As shown in Sinclair and Sutcliffe (1982), the formula which is appropriate for calculating the GNP multiplier, including separately estimated first and second round propensities is:

$$\Delta Y'/\Delta E = (\Delta EK* + \Delta EK*\bar{K}K)/\Delta E \qquad (2)$$

The formula for the long run disposable income multiplier is:

$$\Delta Y'_d/\Delta E = \Delta EK_oK'/\Delta E \qquad (3)$$

121

where $\Delta Y'_d$ = the change in disposable income, resulting from an initial change in tourist expenditure in the area, which occurs over all rounds of the multiplier process;

K_O = the propensity to generate disposable income during the first round of the multiplier process and $K_O = (1-L^*)$ where L^* is the first round propensity to withdraw for the area;

K' = $1/(1-Q)$ and is the subsequent round multiplier for disposable income where Q is the propensity to generate disposable income during subsequent rounds of the multiplier process.

The total change in GNP or disposable income which results from a change in tourist expenditure is simply obtained by multiplying equations (1) to (3) by ΔE.

A high degree of foreign ownership and/or control of the tourism industry can have particularly important effects on two variables within the multiplier formulae: the change in tourist expenditure, ΔE, and the first round propensities to withdraw from the area, L_1 and L^*. In the case of ΔE, as was explained above, a high degree of foreign ownership and/or control will often result in a lower level of tourist expenditure than would have occurred if the facilities had been owned by local residents and the demand for tourism had remained the same. The effect is to decrease the value of income generation within the destination area.

Partial or total foreign ownership of tourism facilities decreases the value of local income generation by increasing the value of the first round propensity to withdraw profits from the area, either directly if there are no controls on profits remittances, or indirectly via transfer pricing. This results in the loss of potential income multiplier effects in the area. Considerable first round withdrawals also frequently occur in the form of payments for imports of goods and services which are required by the tourism sector and are purchased from firms and industries in other areas - either in other countries, if the national income multiplier is being estimated, or in both foreign countries and other areas within the same country, if the local income multiplier is being quantified. Such payments can lead to a considerable decrease in the value of the multiplier associated with tourist expenditure and to a corresponding fall in the value of income generation resulting from such expenditure.

In the case of Spain, as was shown above, outflows in the form of payments for imports into Spain are relatively low. The latter conclusion is supported by survey evidence in which managers of both nationally owned hotels and hotels which form part of a non-Spanish MNE stated that they purchased virtually all of their inputs from Spanish sources. However, regions and other sub-national areas are far more open than national economies and so have a higher propensity to import, including 'imports' from other parts of the same country as well as from abroad. This can be seen by examination of the income multiplier values calculated for different types of tourist expenditure in the Spanish province of Malaga, which are given in Table 8.4.

Table 8.4: Long-run multiplier values for changes in different types of tourist expenditure in the Spanish province of Malaga

Types of tourist expenditure	Long-run GNP multiplier	Long-run disposable income multiplier
Accommodation	0.66	0.50
Food, drink and entertainment	0.53	0.40
Expenditure by tourists staying in flats & villas	0.47	0.36
Tourist expenditure on miscellaneous items	0.99	0.75
All tourist expenditure	0.72	0.54

The way in which the values included in the table should be interpreted is that, for example, for every £1 which tourists spend on accommodation in Malaga, the values of GNP and disposable income which are generated in the province are £0.66 and £0.50 respectively. The main reason why the multiplier values are fairly low is that a large proportion of the change in tourist expenditure in Malaga is lost to other areas in the form of profits remittances and expenditure on inputs which are purchased from outside the province. For example, the values of the long-run first-round propensities to remit profits which are associated with the change in tourist expenditure on accommodation are 39 per cent for the GNP multiplier and 51 per cent for the disposable income multiplier, and the first round propensities to 'import' inputs into Malaga are 74 per cent and 78 per cent respectively (Sinclair, 1981). The extremely high values of the first round propensities to import indicate that one policy which could increase the value of income generation in the province would be a policy of import substitution, in which the aim could be to increase the value of local production of those items for which imports are particularly high. Similarly, an increase in the value of local production of those goods and services which local residents purchase using additional income generated by the tourism industry would result in further increases in the value of local income generation.

TECHNIQUES OF PRODUCTION AND THE LEVEL OF EMPLOYMENT

The degree of foreign ownership of tourism facililites in the destination area may include both the techniques of production which are used in the tourism industry via the transfer of technology to the destination country and the level of employment. For example, partial or total foreign ownership is often accompanied by access to foreign as well as domestic capital markets, permitting a larger scale of operations to occur and hence a higher level of employment. However, foreign ownership may also lead to increased employment of foreigners relative to domestic residents.

Foreign owners and managers of tourism facilities may also have greater knowledge about and access to labour-saving techniques of production than local owners and managers. The use of such techniques results in higher levels of productivity per employee and lower levels of employment per unit of output. In some cases, beneficial spread effects occur in the destination area as foreigners' knowledge of alternative techniques of production is transferred to domestic suppliers, and an increasing demand for tourism is sufficient to compensate for any falls in the level of employment which the use of alternative techniques of production might otherwise generate. However, in some cases foreign suppliers have unique knowledge about alternative techniques of production and there is an absence of spread effects. Foreign ownership may result in greater training of the labour force if the foreign owners or managers have greater access to training facilities than locals.

Table 8.5: The level of employment in Spanish and foreign-owned hotels

Ownership	Location			
	Coastal area		Cities	
	Average employment	Employment per bed-place	Average employment	Employment per bed-place
Spanish-owned	141	0.30	243	0.68
Foreign MNE	180	0.29	285	0.49

Survey evidence obtained by Sinclair and Sutcliffe (1979) for both Spanish and foreign-owned hotels permitted investigation of the potential effects. Table 8.5 shows the average level of employment and employment per bed-place in hotels which are owned by residents of Spain and hotels which are part of MNEs. It demonstrates a higher average level of employment in hotels which are part of a foreign MNE and which are located in both coastal areas and cities, although the average level of employment for both types of hotel is greater in cities than in coastal areas. The level of employment per bed-place is similar for the two types of hotel in coastal areas, but is higher for Spanish-owned hotels located in cities, although it is possible that the figure 0.68 is a slight over-estimate of the true value. Owing to the strict Spanish legislation concerning the employment of foreigners, there were few foreign employees in either type of hotel. There was little difference in the wages and conditions of employment of the employees in hotels in a given province because these are determined by negotiations for all hotels at the provincial level.

Knowledge concerning labour-saving techniques was not found to be significantly greater for hotels forming part of an MNE than for Spanish-owned hotels. Any specialist knowledge which the MNE-owned hotels may have possessed concerning the equipment or related techniques of production utilised in hotels appears to have been transferred to local enterprises, and there was some tendency towards increasing productivity levels and decreasing levels of employment in both types of hotel in coastal areas. The only area in which the MNE-owned hotels seemed to possess greater expertise was in the area of marketing. The only hotels which incurred limited expenditure on training courses for employees were Spanish-owned hotels located in cities. Thus it appears that Spain, unlike some Third World countries, has a supply of labour which is sufficiently skilled to meet the needs of the hotel sector.

THE DEGREE OF CONTROL WHICH THE HOST AREA EXERCISES OVER THE DEVELOPMENT OF THE TOURISM INDUSTRY AND THE DESTINATION AREA

There are a number of ways in which foreign participation in the tourism industry can decrease the degree of control which the host area can exert over the development of the tourism industry and the associated development of the destination area. First, if foreign capital promotes the development of the tourism industry in the absence of alternative forms of economic activity, the destination area will become increasingly dependent upon the tourism industry for the provision of foreign exchange and associated generation. The figures in Table 8.3 show that Spain receives 21 per cent of its total receipts from goods, services and income from tourism and that its dependence upon earnings from tourism to provide the foreign exchange necessary for financing its imports is also high, receipts from travel constituting 22 per cent of the value of imports. Although the income generation effects resulting from tourist expenditure in particular destination areas such as the province of Malaga are relatively low, Spain as a whole benefits greatly from the income multiplier effects originating from rising tourist expenditure (IET, 1978b). The interrelations between the tourism industry and other sectors of the Spanish economy mean that a decline in expenditure on Spanish tourism generates a considerable downward multiplier effect on the level of income in the economy. Moreover, the extremely high level of dependence of a number of Spanish provinces upon tourism and related activities, such as the construction industry, causes these areas to experience particularly large falls in income and increases in the level of unemployment when tourist demand declines. The province of Malaga is one example of this effect, with 25 per cent of the active population becoming unemployed in the immediate aftermath of the 1974 oil 'crisis' and the consequent drop in foreign tourism.

Second, dependence upon a limited number of foreign tour operators for maintaining the demand for tourism entails a high level of risk since tour operators have the possibility of switching the tourists to alternative destinations if the level of wages and other local costs increases. In Spain some increases in wages have occurred, as limited increases in trade union strength in the hotel and catering sector have taken place. However, increases in wages have tended to result in falls in the level of employment as labour-saving techniques such as self-service have been introduced, particularly in coastal areas.

Third, dependence upon foreigners for promoting the tourism industry increases foreigners' ability to pressurise the government of the destination country to provide a large amount of costly infrastructure, e.g. airports, which is necessary to meet the requirements of the tourists who arrive at the peak of the season. Such pressure can be exerted via the explicit or implicit threat of switching demand to other destinations. Government provision of infrastructure can be argued to constitute a hidden subsidy to the foreign owners of tourism facilities, to foreign operators and the tourists themselves. The infrastructure which has been provided for the tourism industry in Spain has been financed from revenue obtained by taxing the Spanish population, principally in the form of indirect taxation. Thus the costs of developing the sector have been borne by the population as a whole, whereas a large proportion of the benefits has been received by a small proportion of Spanish nationals.

Fourth, dependence upon foreigners for promoting the tourism industry enables them to exert pressure on the government to ensure that the development of the sector is in accordance with their requirements. Pressure from both foreign and Spanish business interests for the development of the Spanish tourism industry to cater for mass tourism at the fastest possible rate has entailed numerous social costs in the tourist destination areas. The destruction of the environment which has occurred along much of the Mediterranean coastline is obvious to the most casual observer. Large areas of the coastline have been taken over by huge hotels or blocks of flats, inadequate provision of sewerage and waste-water disposal facilities has led to serious pollution of the sea, and many beaches are extremely dirty, resulting in skin infections. The 'demonstration effect' produced by the 40 million tourists who arrive in Spain every year has led to noticeable changes in the values and traditions of the local population. Although it is extremely difficult to place monetary values on these phenomena, this does not lessen the significant costs which they entail.

It is thus clear that as well as benefiting the Spanish economy, tourism has brought about considerable adverse effects. Although some of the damage which has occurred to the Spanish environment is probably permanent, the Spanish authorities could implement stricter planning controls to limit any further damage. The provision of vital infrastructure such as sewerage and waste-water disposal facilities could be further improved, and the method of financing such provision could be made more egalitarian. This has already started to occur, as recent changes in the Spanish taxation system have decreased the level of tax evasion and made the tax system more progressive. The government could also consider increasing the rate of taxation on profits obtained from the tourism sector and imposing an arrival or departure tax on the tourists themselves.

Fifth, many host areas have limited possibilities of increasing their degree of control over the development process because of their high degree of dependence on foreigners, and particularly on foreign tour operators, for maintaining the demand for tourism in the area. It is difficult for domestic policy-makers to challenge this situation because they are dealing with tour operators who often operate on a massive scale and have internalised a large quantity of information and expertise. In contrast, the domestic tourism sector which provides accommodation, etc. for foreign tourists frequently consists of a large number of independent units competing with each other, and which have a very low level of bargaining power. In the case of Spain, it is not possible for the fragmented Spanish accommodation and catering sector to bargain successfully with oligopolistic tour operators. Hence the government could consider the various mediating roles which it could play.

CONCLUSION

Using data for Spanish tourism, this chapter has argued that increases in the level of foreign relative to domestic participation in the tourism industry have a considerable impact on the role which tourism plays in the development of the destination area. Examination of countries' balance of payments accounts shows the importance of receipts from tourism as a percentage of total receipts from goods, services and income, and as a percentage of payments for imports. Foreign tourism can also be associated with considerable outflows in the form of payments for imports and factor payments abroad. In Spain, most of the inputs which are purchased for use in the tourism industry originate from domestic rather than foreign sources so that the value of outflows which are related to the tourism industry are relatively low. However, a large amount of tourists' expenditure on holidays never reaches Spain because tourists usually pay for their holidays in their country of origin, and a considerable proportion of the profits which are made are retained abroad. Such losses to the destination country do not feature in the balance of payments figures. Direct foreign investment and intervention by foreign tour operators tend to reduce the share of tourist revenue received by the destination area. In the case of foreign investment in the tourism industry by an MNE, profits can be remitted from the destination area by means of transfer pricing. However, it is unlikely that transfer pricing for the purpose of evading tax has occurred on a large scale in Spain since under-declaration of profits and tax evasion has been common throughout the country. It is possible that the main means by which profits are retained within the countries of origin of tourists is via the operation of foreign tour operators, from whom the vast majority of tourists to Spain purchase their holidays. Since the tour operators often use carriers from their own country and also obtain large discounts from the suppliers of tourism facilities such as accommodation within the tourist destination area, only a limited proportion of the tourists' total expenditure on package holidays ever reaches the destination country. One effect is to decrease the values of profits and tax revenue in the country.

Since tourist expenditure in the destination area generates rises in the local level of income via the income multiplier process, limitations in the value of expenditure reaching the destination area result in correspondingly lower levels of local income generation. The value of income generation also depends on the values of the propensities to withdraw which are included in the multiplier equation, and in particular on the value of the first round propensity to import into the area. If the national level of income generation resulting from tourist expenditure in Spain is being considered, the value of the first round propensity to import is relatively low since participants in the Spanish tourism industry, unlike those in many Third World countries, purchase most of the goods and services which are required from domestic sources. However, if the value of income generation is estimated for different sub-national areas where tourism is concentrated, the first round propensity to 'import' is high since a large proportion of inputs originate from outside the destination area. This results in a considerably lower value for the local income multiplier and a decrease in the value of local income generation.

Foreign firms which invest in the tourism industry tend to have greater access to international capital markets and to available expertise in the tourism industry than domestic firms. They often generate a higher absolute level of employment per tourism establishment than domestic firms, while their greater access to labour-saving techniques of production tends to result in a lower level of employment per unit of output. In the case of the Spanish hotel sector the average number of employees in hotels forming part of an MNE was greater than in Spanish-owned hotels. The average number of employees per bed-place was found to be similar in hotels located in coastal areas, but was lower for hotels forming part of an MNE in cities than for Spanish-owned establishments. The level of knowledge about available techniques of production, with the exception of marketing, was found to be similar in both types of hotel, indicating the developed nature of the Spanish hotel sector.

The growth of the tourism industry can lead to increasing dependence upon tourism as a major source of foreign currency and domestic income generation. Such dependence increases the ability of foreign participants in the tourism industry to exert direct or indirect pressure on local policy-makers to maintain low levels of wages, provide the infrastructure required by the tourism sector and develop the destination areas in general accordance with foreigners' interests. In the case of Spain, tourism is one of the country's main sources of foreign exchange and means of financing imports. It also leads to considerable income generation in the country. The high level of dependence upon the tourism industry and reliance upon a limited number of foreign tour operators to channel tourists to Spain entails a high level of risk, since a decrease in tourism demand would result in pressure on the balance of payments, a considerable decrease in the level of income and a large rise in the level of unemployment.

Both foreign and domestic pressures for the rapid development of the tourism industry have resulted in considerable costs - both direct monetary costs such as the cost of providing the infrastructure required by the tourism industry, and non-monetary costs such as adverse environmental effects. It is thus clear that foreign participation in the tourism industry has had a wide range of effects, both beneficial and adverse, upon the tourist destination areas and that such effects should be taken into account by analysts and policy-makers who are concerned with the development of both the tourism and the destination area.

REFERENCES

Dunning, J.H. and McQueen, M. (1982) Multinational corporations in the international hotel industry, Annals of Tourism Research, 9, 69-90

Erbes, R. (1973) International Tourism and the Economy of Developing Countries, OECD, Paris

Instituto Espanol de Turismo (Research Team of the Spanish Institute of Tourism: coordinated by M. Figuerola Palomo)(1978a), La Balanza de Pagos Turistica de Espana en 1976, Estudios Turisticos, 57/58, 1/2, 205-32

Instituto Espanol de Turismo (Research Team of the Spanish Institute of Tourism: coordinated by M. Figuerola Palomo)(1978b), Determinacion y Valoracion de la Estructura Economica del Turismo Espanol, Estudios Turisticos, 59/60 3/4, 301-65

International Monetary Fund (1985) Balance of Payments Statistics, 36, Part I, Washington DC

Ministerio de Transportes, Turismo y Comunicaciones (Ministry of Transport, Tourism and Communications) (1964-86) Anuario de Estadisticas de Turismo, Ministry of Transport, Tourism and Communications, Madrid

Sinclair, M.T. (1981) 'The Theory of the Keynesian Income Multiplier and its Application to Changes in Tourist Expenditure in the Spanish Province of Malaga', PhD Thesis, University of Reading

Sinclair, M.T. and Sutcliffe, C.M.S. (1979) The Role of Transnational Corporations in the Tourism Industry of Spain, Report submitted to the United Nations Centre on Transnational Corporations, New York

Sinclair, M.T. and Sutcliffe, C.M.S. (1982) Keynesian income multipliers with first and second round effects: an application to tourist expenditure, Oxford Bulletin of Economics and Statistics, 44, 4, 321-38

Sutcliffe, C.M.S. (1985) Measuring the Economic Effects of Tourism on an Underdeveloped Region, in G. J. Ashworth and B. Goodall (eds) The Impact of Tourist Development on Disadvantaged Regions, Girugreeks No. 35, Geografisch Institut, Rijksuniversiteit, Groningen

United Nations (1973) Elements of Tourism Policy in Developing Countries, Report by the Secretariat of the United Nations Conference on Trade and Development, TD/B/C.3/89/Rev.1, New York

CHAPTER 9

THE IMAGE OF DESTINATION REGIONS: THEORETICAL AND
EMPIRICAL ASPECTS

Michael J. Stabler

INTRODUCTION

This chapter has arisen out of field research
conducted in Languedoc-Roussillon, where resorts
developed since the mid-1960s on the northern half
of the coast of Golfe du Lion were studied.   The
fieldwork consisted of three main parts: mapping of
the land-use functions; a survey of visitors
covering their recreational patterns and attitudes;
the study of tourist recreation promotional
publications produced by official and commercial
organisations.

Image, the aspect of the study considered
here, was investigated by analysing promotional
material produced by the tourism industry in the
destination region.   In a limited way tourists'
images of each resort and the region were obtained
in a survey of visitors.

The role of image in determining consumers'
tourism choices, particularly their destination,
and the influence of suppliers' promotional
operations, has not been widely studied by either
economists or geographers, since it has been seen
as being more the province of social psychologists
and sociologists. Lip service has been paid to its
importance but usually the problems of establishing
exactly what image is, and how it enters the
decision-making process, is uncertain. This study
attempts to provide some insights into the
phenomenon, and a method of identifying key
attributes of tourist regions and resources is
offered.

Since it holds implications for the economic
analysis of tourism, image is first examined within
the context of consumer behaviour and supply theory
and then related to tourism development.   A review
of previous studies is undertaken to establish the
key attributes of tourism resources which have been
identified as influencing the image of destination

regions. Next an outline of the research project in Languedoc-Roussillon, and the method of investigating image, is given. Subsequently both the method and results are considered in relation to the theoretical framework and their contribution to this particular field of research assessed. Finally, possible future lines of research are indicated.

IMAGE AND ITS RELEVANCE TO TOURISM

A dictionary definition of image is 'mental conception, perception or idea'. This accords quite closely to that adopted by Murphy (1985) in his examination of demand for tourism in which he equates images to mental maps of the world and argues that they consitute perceptions. Lawson and Baud-Bovy (1977) consider image to be: 'the expression of all objective knowledge, impressions, prejudice, imaginations, and emotional thoughts an individual or group have of a particular object or place'. Images, therefore, form part of consumers' decision-making processes in that they will influence the choices they make. Basic psychological, physical, cultural, social and economic motivators govern behaviour and these are conditioned by experiences, information and individual preferences to create images of reality.

With respect to recreation and tourism, certain general images might arise such as expenditure, travel, excitement, hedonism, relaxation and social interaction. More specific ones, related to particular countries or regions, might be climate, landscape, culture, activities and facilities. Some researchers, Ehemann (1977), Hunt (1975) and Mayo (1973) indicate that images are both positive and negative but that the overall view of a region might be favourable or unfavourable. Moreover, because of certain events, images can change radically. For example, for UK residents, the image of Spain has been of an inexpensive, sunny, friendly country with an attractive coastline and beaches. Publicity concerning muggings and the activities of ETA have tarnished this image somewhat though a recent survey indicated visitors' unconcern about possible violence, so that the general image appears to be still favourable.

It is not clear, indeed there is some controversy among researchers, whether the choice of tourist trip is person-determined or destination-determined. This uncertainty reflects lack of empirical evidence on the role information plays in the creation of image. Is it via personal experiences or that of others or via the supply side communication network? Undoubtedly the image built up is influenced by all three sources of information as indicated in Fig. 9.1, based largely on Murphy (1983).

From the point of view of the supply side, especially the intermediaries, it is desirable to establish the importance of media sources since it will obviously dictate marketing strategies in general and promotional material in particular. Indeed, as Mathieson and Wall (1982) suggest: 'the

Figure 9.1: Tourist demand and supply and the creation of image

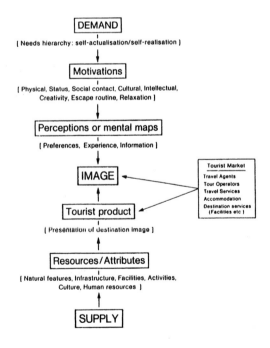

larger the difference between image and reality, that is between expectations and experience, the more likely is a tourist to be dissatisified'. In theory, it may equally be argued that tourists' expectations were exceeded and so they were more than satisfied. However, in practice, given suppliers' tendency to indulge in 'advertisement puff' the assertion by Mathieson and Wall is likely to hold true. Either way this observation is the foundation of an implicit hypothesis of the fieldwork carried out in Languedoc-Roussillon, namely to test that the image presented in promotional material corresponded to that held by visitors. Clearly the study did not consider completely the correspondence of supply side information to tourists and how it influenced their formation of their images, because it covered only tourists experiencing the destination region. A more comprehensive project would include the impact of the information on potential tourists in countries of origin, particularly how media material is transmitted to consumers via what has become known in marketing circles as 'the two-step communication flow'.

Another aspect of the interaction between consumers and suppliers is the acknowledgement by destination regions that individuals have different images of tourism. This makes it possible to segment markets by appealing to specific nationalities or groups of tourists of differing socio-economic status, ages or interests. It is also possible to differentiate the image according to seasons and activities and facilities offered.

What emerges from this brief discussion of image is that, with other determinants, it influences consumers' demand for commodities and services and thus the level and pattern of their expenditures. Consequently, it is of significance to economic consumer behaviour theory to which attention is now turned.

IMAGE IN THE CONTEXT OF ECONOMIC THEORY

Demand

Traditional deterministic economic theory would consider the price of the commodity, the price of substitutes and complements, income and tastes, habits and preferences as the most important determinants of demand. Other variables, for instance population, age, education, occupation, paid annual leave, weekly hours of work, etc. could be included. These variables form the foundation of mathematical, econometric and statistical models which attempt to forecast demand.

When applied to tourism the variables which emerge as significant are price and income, though more comprehensive models have attempted to include qualitative aspects such as consumer attitudes and the intuitive insights of experts. Though motivations and preferences, in which images are embodied, are acknowledged as being important, they tend to be ignored by 'main stream' economists, because they are either assumed to be relatively stable and therefore do not influence the model, or are considered too complex to cope with.

However, there are other, more fundamental reasons why tourism is not easily analysed within the standard conceptual framework of consumer price theory, or trade theory, in the case of foreign travel and tourism. Price theory is unsuitable because it cannot encompass multiple commodities, the introduction of new commodities, quality changes or generated demand. Trade theory is inadequate because it assumes factor immobility, and, in a spaceless model, usually omits transport costs which are a significant proportion of tourism travel.

Economists working in recreation and tourism, needing to assess demand for non-priced resources and externalities, are more aware of the restrictions imposed by traditional theory and the necessity of including more qualitative determinants. Lancaster (1966) expressed dissatisfaction with classical theory by recognising, in addition to the new commodity and quality problems, that commodities are not the object of utility by themselves. Lancaster pointed out that they possess characteristics or attributes from which utility is derived. More correctly, he assumed that commodities combine with one another to generate activities which in turn generate the characteristics. This allows for a particular commodity to possess more than one characteristic depending on with which others it is combined. In effect Lancaster saw demand emanating not so much from consumers' characteristics but from their perception of commodities. This is the keystone of the theory which allows it to accommodate new products, quality changes and advertising.

It is apparent, therefore, that Lancaster's theory is potentially useful as a means of assessing tourist demand and one of the earliest attempts to apply it in such a context was Rugg (1971). He found, however, that although it could be adapted to tourism, it was difficult to formulate workable travel demand functions directly because they tended to be in unwieldy non-linear form. Rosen (1974) also makes this point when considering Lancaster's theory in relation to product differentiation in highly competitive markets. Rugg used statistical equations, proposed by Quandt and Baumol (1966) and which approximated to Lancaster's formulation, to identify the main determinants of, and demand functions for, choice of foreign travel destination and transport mode. Rugg's results suggested that, subject to income, cost of travel and accommodation and time constraints, the most significant travel-destination variables were climate (temperature, rainfall and sunshine), population in the generating and destination countries and attractions, especially historic artifacts and museums. In addition he referred to but did not include in his model what he called geographical features, such as mountains, beaches, lakes, rivers and forests; cultural phenomena like theatres, exhibitions and architecture; recreational facilities and inhabitant characteristics, namely language and religion. Thus, Rugg, in considering destination attributes which influenced tourists' choices, implicitly incorporated in his thesis, image as it is examined in this chapter.

In the middle to late 1970s, Lancaster's ideas have been incorporated into economic analysis as 'hedonic pricing' which has been used in recreation research, e.g. Brown et.al. (1978), but mostly applied in empirical studies on housing and environmental economics, e.g. Freeman (1979). Pearce (1981) defines hedonic pricing as: 'the implicit or shadow price of a characteristic of a commodity. The quantity of a commodity may be resolved into a number of constituent characteristics which determine its quality. Part of the price of that commodity may be associated with each characteristic and variations in quality may thus be valued'. This can perhaps be more succinctly summarised as a measure of implicit prices not explicitly traded but which are characteristics of traded goods.

The wide use made of the hedonic method in

housing research has been in connection with the
impact of the attributes of the dwelling itself, or
the neighbourhood, on the price of a specific
house. Housing is seen as a complex multi-
dimensional demand for a flow of services, for
example, position, size of plot, number of rooms,
etc. with respect to the dwelling and physical
environment, socio-economic mix of the
neighbourhood, access to the transport network,
employment, schools, amenities, etc. with regard
to location. To paraphrase Freeman (1979) in the
context of recreation, reflecting the housing
market which, in terms of the appropriate analysis
it closely resembles, the hedonic method would
recognise that there are attributes in a particular
activity which differentiate it in the eyes of a
potential participant. If such differences matter
to the consumer (participant) and they vary for a
given array of activities then, with a specified
level of supply, these preferences will influence
the pattern of prices.

To construct what might be termed an
'attribute demand function' necessitates the
estimation of the implicit prices of
characteristics, using the hedonic technique, and
then it is possible to derive the demand function.
The technique, following the Lancaster thesis, is
that for a satisfaction maximising consumer, the
attributes or characteristics of one or more
commodities generate utility. In the exposition of
theory, the terms 'characteristics' and
'attributes' are used as synonyms, but in
applications it is apparent that some authors
confuse the reader by equating 'attributes' with
'commodities', arguing that 'characteristics' are
generated by them from which consumers derive
utility. Here, the terms are considered as
interchangeable in the theoretical sense but
echoing tourism literature the word 'attributes'
tends to be used.

Where more recent developments of the hedonic
approach depart from Lancaster's original thesis is
that the former is attempting to establish how
prices, rather than the level and pattern of
demand, are influenced by characteristics. By the
very nature of the context in which it has been
applied, the hedonic approach has also been more
concerned with problems of estimating prices for
non-traded commodities in public sector investment,
as well as those of the attributes of traded
commodities.

Conceptually the Lancaster/hedonic method can assist in the construction of tourist demand models since it reflects rather more realistically, than traditional economic theory, the structure of the market. It is, for example, marked by innovation in the type of holidays offered (new commodities) and by improvements in transport and accommodation (quality changes). Also, as has been suggested in Fig. 9.1 and earlier, it is a multi-dimensional product. Finally, it is characterised by vigorous promotion likely to lead to changes in the pattern of tourism in addition to extending demand (generated demand).

To focus the foregoing discussion on tourism, it is of value, first, to identify those attributes which are significant, especially those appertaining to the destination region, and, second, to relate attributes to image.

(i) The attributes of a destination region. It is possible, a priori, to identify likely image-forming attributes, both in general terms and applicable to a particular destination. To an extent these attributes are equivalent to resources. A listing, suitably categorised, is presented in Table 9.1. It is of course an empirical question to establish which are significant. As indicated earlier Rugg (1971) has identified a number for US tourists and Murphy (1985) presents an amalgamation of those from several earlier writings. The evidence from the Languedoc-Roussillon study given below is necessarily sketchy because of the nature of the consumer survey.

(ii) Attributes, image and analysis. The linkage of destination attributes, image and demand theory has been broadly indicated in Fig. 9.1. The impact of image on demand is not sequential, stemming from signals from the supply side only, as implied in the diagram, but subject to a two-way process with feedbacks from and to suppliers and to and from consumers. As shown in Fig. 9.2, transmission of information from supply through the marketing of tourism and the media, previous experience and opinions of other consumers, combined with motivations and socio-economic characteristics form perceptions, the images of tourism and tourist destinations.

The study of image makes it possible to identify the attributes from which, as a first step, a utility or prices function is derived for

Table 9.1:   Tourist destination attributes

Climate	Natural resources	Infrastructure
Sunshine	Beaches	Water supply
Temperature	Lakes/shoreline	Drainage
Rainfall	Rivers/waterways	Energy supply
Humidity	Forests	Telecommunications
	Mountains	Roads
	Flora	Railways
	Fauna	Ports/marinas
		Airports

Tourist/rec. amenities	Cultural	Econ./Political/Social
Accom.	Historic features	Indust. structure
Restaurants	Theatres	Govt. structure
Tourism organs	Concert halls	Planning system
Shopping	Art galleries	Language
Sports facs.	Museums	Religion
Rec. parks	Architecture	Mores/customs
Zoos	Exhibitions	Gastronomic
Entertainment	Festivals	Hospitality

Key elements for tourism development:

    climate
    access
    amenities (esp. accommodation)
    cultural

Attributes cited from Languedoc-Roussillon regional development documents:

    sand
    sea
    sun
    wine
    architectural/artistic/historic features
    language
    custom
    hospitality

each attribute. The second step is to incorporate as many of these functions in the final demand equation as are relevant to consumers in making their decisions on choice of vacation and destination.

It is possible that in a number of instances consumers might consider a specific attribute as synonymous with the image held of a specific destination. Indeed to spell out an earlier point, resources, attributes and images may not be separated in tourists' perception of a particular type of holiday or destination. For example, for a 'sunlust' tourist the resources of a seaside resort - beaches, sunshine, clear blue sea, water-based facilities, etc. - may be the attributes which in turn form the image of the destination.

If such notions truly reflect tourists' perceptions then analysis should not be too

Figure 9.2: Factors influencing the information of consumers' tourist image

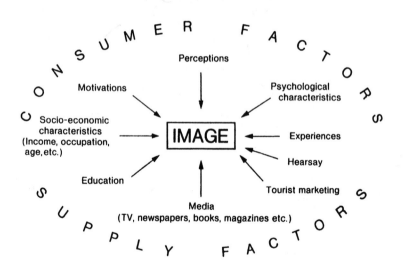

concerned to separate the three; it may well be better to adopt a pragmatic approach. In any event it is probably more important to consider the different images held by individual, or groups of, tourists of the same destination, especially if possibilities of extending a market are contemplated. Another feature of market extension is the separation possible by the identification of tourist types; for example the 'wilderness seeker' and the 'socialiser'.

In essence, looking at it from the demand side, at a practical level, but within the Lancaster/hedonic framework, the identification of tourists' images constitutes the characteristics which explain demand and price. Whether then the approach can be made operational is uncertain, given the present state of the 'art'. Inspection of the research literature in which the Lancaster/hedonic technique is referred to tends to show discussion being confined to a theoretical level. As applied in the housing market the approach has been subject to much criticism. Maclennan (1982) takes a somewhat jaundiced view, considering that citations of the Lancaster theory are so much window dressing with no real effort to examine the model empirically. However, it does emerge, in his critique, that it is the structure of the housing market which makes the technique inappropriate rather than its inherent flaws.

It would appear that the structure of the tourist market is very different from that for housing, and for the reasons given earlier, the Lancaster/hedonic framework is a feasible vehicle for analysis. Furthermore, if nothing else, it does help to clarify issues, offering insights into tourist behaviour in the development of a workable demand theory.

Since, in this chapter, it is asserted that tourist demand in general and image formation in particular cannot be fully understood in isolation from supply, attention is now turned to considering that side of the tourist market.

Supply

Reference to Fig. 9.1 indicates that supply is based on the resources of the destination region and that formation of tourism capital combines with these resources to yield the tourism product. However, this product in being marketed, where the intermediaries play a decisive role, gives rise to the tourist image as perceived by the consumer. More correctly perhaps, resources, capital and marketing activity all create the image but the marketing intermediaries give it focus and it is this aspect on which discussion is concentrated.

The tourism industry in a particular region can adopt one or both of two main strategies. It can differentiate itself from other destinations in terms of resources (natural, capital and human) and/or it can appeal to specific origins and/or types of tourists, perhaps accentuating climatic, seasonal and accessibility differences as part of the strategy, i.e. it can segment its market. Thus having assessed its own resources and identified its market, the industry then should, on the basis of meaningful attributes, concentrate promotion, supply and price on exploiting that market.

Sophisticated marketing approaches, for example, psychographic segmentation which attempts to identify linkages or homogeneity of tourists not obviously belonging to the same market, cut across traditional views rooted in socio-economic characteristics - age, sex, income, education and occupation. McIntosh (1972) refers to tourist market orientations based on interests such as agriculture, business, sport, science and education. Recent developments in activity holidays, ranging over wildlife specialisms, sport, historic buildings, language, geology, etc. are in line with this kind of approach.

Another dimension to segmentation, alluded to earlier, is of tourist types. Murphy (1985) reviews the different classifications adopted by researchers, but suggests there are two main categories of tourism - 'interactional' and 'cognitive-normative'. An interactional approach emphasizes the interaction between visitors and tourist regions whereas the cognitive-normative category concentrates on travel motivation. Some tourists are happiest in an organised structure while others abhor such an experience. Another way of classifying tourists is to distinguish the explorer, perhaps wilderness, type at one end of the scale to charter/mass type at the other.

Related to such typologies might be perceptions of a destination and the possible conflicting or complementary nature of tourist activities. Backpackers and some walkers seek isolation in wilderness recreation whereas touring caravanners tend to be more sociable, viewing attractive scenery as a backdrop to their main objective. Those wishing to participate in competitive sport may find that more passive tourists as spectators are desirable, if not essential, for them to afford and enjoy their activity. In some cases activities are simultaneously conflicting and complementary, for instance waterway boating and fishing. Spatial segmentation may also be appropriate for example, power boating, sailing and swimming. Yet another differentiation might be temporal, for instance skiing in winter and walking in summer in the Austrian, French and Italian Alps.

This brief examination of segmentation indicates the complex nature of tourist markets and that many different dimensions enter into the marketing process and consequently influence the way in which the image of a particular tourist region is promoted. Indeed, that promotion will undoubtedly be in many forms and adopt different methods of transmission according to its specific function. With regard to both forms and methods which in many cases are inseparable, it may be through media such as films, videos, television advertisements, radio, magazines and newspapers, or via leaflets, brochures, posters, signs, or by diffuse means such as education or through official bodies or agencies. The differing functions include promotion directed at potential foreign or domestic tourists, or information for visitors actually in the destination region.

Analysis of promotion from an economic viewpoint is embodied in the theory of the firm and is concerned with the impact on the level and structure of costs and revenue in the usual marginality analysis in which incremental changes in total revenue are related to those in total costs, i.e. promotion would be undertaken to the point where marginal revenue equals marginal cost.

An associated area of theoretical analysis would be the influence of promotion on the market structure of the tourism industry. Though tourism advertising to an extent may have an informatory role, there is no doubt that most of it is directed at increasing a particular destination's and/or intermediary's share of the market. As a result there may be a change in the scale of operations and the competitive structure of the firms involved. Following this line of thought, it might be possible to connect promotion to the diseconomies of tourism in terms of both private and social costs.

Observations on both demand and supply and image

An attempt has been made to set image into both sides of economic theory. Drawing the threads of the argument together with respect to demand it has been suggested that images are conceived through the interaction of needs, motivations and preferences on the one hand and experience, knowledge and personal characteristics on the other, to influence the decision process of selecting tourist activities and destinations. A crucial element in the information available to the consumer is the images as perceived and promoted by the supply side. In this, image is founded on the resources and attributes of the destination region. Successful promotion of the destination's image results in a higher level of tourist activity with consequences for its economic socio-cultural and environmental structure.

EMPIRICAL IMPLICATIONS

Some reference has already been made to the evaluation of the Lancaster/hedonic technique as applied in housing, recreation and tourism. Though it is theoretically acceptable the researcher faces a formidable task empirically in securing objective measures of characteristics generated by different tourist 'commodities'. Almost certainly the identification of these will involve social surveys, either through self-completed questionnaires or interviews in both tourist origin and destination regions. It is possible that respondents will have difficulty in conceptualising the attributes of the destination in general and specific cities and towns in particular, especially if they have had limited experience of it, as illustrated in Hunt's (1975) study of four American states. Such a survey, in order to be comprehensive, would need to be multiphased and be conducted over a fairly long time period to identify temporal (seasonal) differences in tourist types and perceived attributes of a region.

Prima facie a supply approach would appear to be easier since it largely involves the collection and analysis of promotional material. The main problem would be to get a complete coverage over all forms of promotion. Rugg (1971) indicates the magnitude of the task, including the analysis of material and derivation of a meaningful set of

attributes. The analysis is made
the separation of material targ
tourist origins (foreign and dom
to that aimed at those already
region. An added complicatior
publications, particularly ι.
informatory nature, are used in bo.
destination regions.
A complete study would clearly .
approaches from both the demand and supply si..
order to test hypotheses, such as t..
correspondence of tourists and the tourism
industry's images. Moreover, in a study
concentrating on the supply side only, for example
the consideration of the impact of promotional
effort on revenue, it would also be necessary to
study the demand side. It would be very difficult
to associate intensification of promotional effort
directly with increased revenue, even if proxy
variables like the change in the number of tourists
or occupancy were used, as other factors are likely
to contribute to changes in revenue. Thus it may
be necessary to resort to more qualitative measures
- such as ascertaining the number of tourists
stating that they were influenced by specific
promotions - and in a more sophisticated analysis
the negative as well as the positive impact. In
the following section the contribution to the
identification of image of a preliminary study of
it in the Languedoc-Roussillon region is outlined.

THE LANGUEDOC-ROUSSILLON STUDY

The area

The Languedoc-Roussillon regional development,
incorporating five tourist units along the coast of
the Golfe du Lion from Aigues Mortes in the north
east to Collioure in the south west, reflected a
desire by the French government to relieve
pressures on the Riviera and to encourage the
population to take holidays in France. The
objective of the tourist resorts was to assist
employment and raise incomes in the province as
part of a policy of regional growth.
The five units (see Fig. 9.3) comprise:

(i) Le Grau du Roi, Port Camargue, La Grande
Motte, Carnon, Palavas des Flots

(ii)   Sete, Cap d'Agde, Grau d'Agde
(iii) Valras, Narbonne, Gruissan
(iv)   Port Leucate, Port Barcares
(v)   Canet, St Cyprien, Argeles.

Of these, the resorts in the first three units were
included in the fieldwork undertaken in the late
spring of 1986.

The fieldwork

The programme consisted of three main projects
undertaken by student groups located for the whole
of the study period in the eleven resorts given in
units (i), (ii) and (iii) above. Three groups were
assigned to Sete, it being a much larger settlement
than any of the others.
The main project was concerned with mapping
land use functions. The second was a survey of
visitors, combined with an observational exercise
of cars to assess the total number and their
department (for France) or country of origin. The
third element in the programme was a study of the
image of the resorts as represented in official and
commercial promotional publications.
The visitor survey was conducted over four
days to include two weekdays and a weekend.
Interviewers were assigned to beaches, car parks
and streets in each resort and approached visitors
as they passed a given survey point. On completion
of an interview the next visitor to pass was
approached and so on, interviewing taking place
throughout the day. The survey concentrated mainly
on the origin, party size, holiday duration, trip
patterns, accommodation, travel mode and
expenditure patterns. Three questions on the
interview schedule covered respectively the use of
publications, and opinions of the specific resort
and the Languedoc-Roussillon coast in general. The
investigation of tourists' image was not central to
the programme and was somewhat tentative because of
the difficulties of the students being required to
interview in a foreign language and the problems of
employing appropriate adjectives in translations of
the questionnaire.
The study of image on the supply side was
partially structured in the interests of
consistency of approach at each resort. It was
confined to analysis of publications emanating from
the following sources:

Figure 9.3:   Languedoc - Roussillon study area

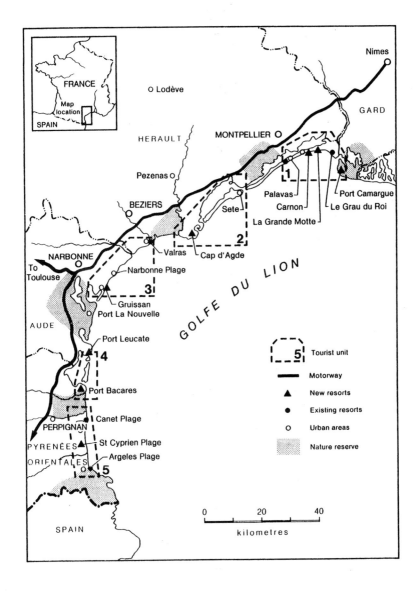

    (i)   central and local government,
    (ii)   tourist offices,
    (iii)   trade organisations,
    (iv)   commercial sector,
    (v)   voluntary organisations, including clubs
    (vi)   other bodies.

The attractions or attributes were identified, in both illustrations and text, and the proportion each constituted of the whole publication calculated. The 13 predetermined categories covered accommodation, shopping, entertainment, culture and architecture, etc. The calculation of the proportion of each category of attractions for all publications would enable a ranking of attraction to be established and facilitate comparison of one resort with another. Also taken account of were any changes in publications, and their content, at different times in the year and in different languages. Supporting the more objective analysis was the collection of evidence on changes in the presentation of the image as the resort has developed and a report on the relationship between image and the resort's functional structure.

The results

At the time of writing only a preliminary analysis of data arising from the visitor survey and image study had been possible. Moreover, comparative analysis of the results from the individual resorts has been confined to those parts of the project relevant to visitors' impressions and the textual and photographic material made available at those resorts.

The visitor survey

There were 964 respondents to the survey from the eleven resorts. The smallest number was 37 at Carnon and the largest 246 at Sete. The sample sizes were sufficient to be statistically reliable for all resorts. As far as is allowed by the constraints placed on respondents by the structure of the interview schedule, it is possible to gain some insights to visitors' image of the resorts and region and the relationship between this image and that promoted by the supply side.

Table 9.2:   Use of a brochure or guide: all resorts

Publication/Source	Frequency	%
None	793	82
Michelin	49	5
Tourist Office	19	2
Other	97	10
No response	6	1
	964	100

Table 9.2 on the use of publications shows that over 80 per cent of visitors did not make any use of published material. Thus their impression of resorts and the region must have been formed by observation and experience. However, it is not clear whether the responses reflected consultation of literature during the visit as opposed to before it. Another point of uncertainty is how respondents interpreted the words 'brochure/guide'. It is possible that many did not consider information booklets, leaflets and maps as guides. These factors would require clarification in any future survey.

Table 9.3 shows, for the resorts and region respectively, that there is no very marked distinction between visitors' views of the resorts and the region, most variation being explained by differences in non responses or indifference responses. However, the results do show quite significant variations in visitors' impressions of individual resorts. What emerges is a distinction between the newly developed and traditional resorts. Cap d'Agde, Carnon, Gruissan, La Grande Motte, Port Camargue, Grau du Roi are effectively new resorts whereas Agde, Grau d'Agde, Narbonne, Palavas, Sete and Valras have largely maintained their traditional character. Statistics for an example of each type of resort are presented in Table 9.4. La Grande Motte has a distinctive style of modern architecture while Valras, which originally served local populations of towns such as Beziers and Narbonne, is very much a traditional resort. These examples were chosen because the resorts are very similar in area and the number of respondents in each sample was identical.

Table 9.3:   Opinions of resort and Languedoc-
Roussillon region: all resorts

Opinion		Resort		Resort	
		Frequency	%	Freqency	%
(i)	Beautiful	768	80	793	82
	Indifferent	130	13	75	8
	Ugly	53	6	36	4
	No response	13	1	60	6
(ii)	Historic	210	22	311	32
	Indifferent	282	29	242	25
	Modern	447	46	323	34
	No response	25	3	88	9
(iii)	Vulgar (Unspoilt/simple)	572	59	485	50
	Indifferent	185	19	205	21
	Sophisticated	170	18	177	19
	No response	37	4	97	10
(iv)	Exciting (Lively)	421	44	479	50
	Indifferent	415	43	341	35
	Boring (Relaxing)	83	8	52	5
	No response	45	5	92	10
(v)	Noisy	136	14	183	19
	Indifferent	143	15	183	19
	Peaceful	649	67	507	53
	No response	36	4	91	9

        Visitors did consider La Grande Motte to be
very modern but did not necessarily find Valras
historic (see the responses to Table 9.4 (ii)).   It
would appear that a high proportion of respondents
were indifferent but it is more likely that they
were undecided as to how to categorise the resort.
This is to an extent also true of attitudes towards
La Grande Motte in Table 9.4 (iii) and both resorts
in 9.4 (iv) with regard to the characteristics of
simple/sophisticated and exciting/boring
respectively.   The data for other traditional
sites, such as Narbonne and Sete (not given in the
table) reveal similar results.   In certain
questions the level of non response was higher
which interviewers reported was a consequence of

Table 9.4: Opinions of resort and Languedoc-Roussillon region at a modern and traditional resort

	Opinion	La Grand Motte Resort (%)	Region (%)	Valras Resort (%)	Region (%)
(i)	Beautiful	74	81	71	80
	Indifferent	7	4	23	5
	Ugly	19	13	4	4
	No response	-	2	2	11
(ii)	Historic	5	23	6	32
	Indifferent	-	24	59	32
	Modern	95	52	31	20
	No response	-	1	4	16
(iii)	Vulgar	29	45	77	50
	Indifferent	26	20	10	25
	Sophisticated	45	31	9	9
	No response	-	4	4	16
(iv)	Exciting	58	71	29	38
	Indifferent	31	16	58	44
	Boring	11	9	9	4
	No response	-	4	4	14
(v)	Noisy	15	19	10	15
	Indifferent	10	14	14	18
	Peaceful	75	64	74	52
	No response	-	4	2	15

two factors: the critical tone of questions at one end of the scale and the change in the nature of the question in translation, particularly into French. For example, 'vulgar' in English has been translated as 'simple' in French, implying the resort is unspoilt, and 'boring' was translated as 'relaxing'. Given that a high proportion of respondents were French, the translation has clearly changed the character of the question. In general, reservations concerning the survey method and structure of the questions notwithstanding, visitors found the Languedoc Region and its resorts beautiful, largely unspoilt and peaceful.

Table 9.5: Respondents' use of specific facilities: all resorts and La Grande Motte and Valras

Facility	All resorts %	La Grande Motte %	Valras %
Beach	87	86	94
Food Shops	70	61	75
Restaurants	60	55	55
Souvenir Shops	28	19	34
Sports Facilities	23	20	20
Other Facilities	21	32	12

In some respects data presented in Table 9.5 on what visitors did at the resorts gave more information about their reactions, which could be related to the image promoted by suppliers, than any of the attitudinal questions. With the exception of the use of souvenir shops and other facilities at La Grande Motte, there is a good correspondence between all resorts and the two examples for the proportion of visitors using the facilities about which they were questioned. Of some significance is the very large proportion of visitors undertaking beach activities and the relatively low proportion using the sports facilities which does not match suppliers' views of the resorts, examined below. Over two-thirds of visitors used food shops, ranked second in the table which is almost certainly a reflection of the importance of self-catering holidays in the area.

The image study

Results were obtained for nine of the eleven resorts at which fieldwork was conducted. It was found that there was insufficient information on Grau d'Agde and Narbonne for a study to be of value. Because they are in close proximity to each other, almost all the promotional literature for Port Camargue and Grau du Roi has been jointly produced, no attempt was made to distinguish them in the analysis. An additional image study was done of Agde, which is a short distance inland from Cap d'Agde and Grau d'Agde. As its character is very different from Cap d'Agde, the analysis for

Agde is presented separately. The photographs and text in each publication were analysed separately, under the 13 categories to which reference has been made above. Photographs were analysed for each category by the proportion of the publication they occupied. Text was considered by the number of lines as a percentage of the total number of lines in the publication, for the same 13 categories. The results for the eight resorts for which it was possible to complete the analysis, plus Agde, are given in Table 9.6 for text and Table 9.7 for photographs. Average percentages for all resorts are shown in the last column of each of the tables. The predetermined categories do not appear to have put an undue constraint on the analysis. The proportion of text and photographs in the 'other' categories can be explained by specific facilities at certain resorts, which were identified but have not been presented in the table. For instance, the large proportion of this category for Cap d'Agde is explained by the conference centre and the naturist facilities.

What is striking is the ranking of the images presented by the resorts. Sport is given two and a half times the exposure of the next category of promotion, historic architecture, the ranking of which has been boosted by the results for Agde. The beach and natural history came equal third but as relatively small proportions of the total image promotion. Surprisingly, given the very distinctive style of resorts such as Cap d'Agde, Gruissan and La Grange Motte, modern architecture is barely acknowledged. Also of interest is the low ranking of accommodation, especially as self-catering is an important feature of the resorts. Overall the ranking of texts and photographs is quite closely related.

One difficulty affecting the reliability of the analysis was the number and size of publications available at each resort. In some cases, particularly for resorts still being developed or which are smaller, the number of publications was five or less, whereas in the established and larger ones there were a dozen or more. It is also not at all certain whether a complete set of publications was obtained.

Some general observations

There is an interesting contrast between the

155

The Image of Destination Regions

Table 9.6: Content analysis of publications:text(%)

Category	A	B	C	D	E	F	G	H	I	T
Sport	8	52	27	30	30	20	16	15	27	25
Hist. Arch.	56	0	7	3	0	4	8	5	10	10
Beach	6	2	13	2	6	5	14	9	14	8
Nat. History	22	0	13	8	5	1	14	7	0	8
Art/Culture	3	4	0	5	16	9	4	25	1	7
Environment	3	4	20	2	1	20	0	10	5	7
Gastronomic	0	4	0	14	9	7	13	2	10	7
Accomm.	0	4	0	12	6	5	18	4	6	6
Communics.	0	4	7	2	5	6	0	12	21	6
Nightlife	0	4	13	11	10	3	0	0	0	4
Modern Arch.	0	0	0	2	1	2	0	2	2	1
Shopping	0	0	0	2	4	1	0	0	1	1
Other	3	26	0	7	9	17	13	11	5	10

Table 9.7: Content analysis of publications: photographs (%)

Category	A	B	C	D	E	F	G	H	I	T
Sport	20	49	31	41	24	22	9	20	36	28
Beach	4	4	26	3	7	15	25	4	10	11
Hist. Arch.	55	0	0	12	0	13	12	7	4	11
Accomm.	0	0	0	7	10	0	5	4	16	8
Nat. History	13	0	22	9	7	5	12	2	0	8
Art/Culture	0	3	0	10	6	16	9	20	2	7
Environment	9	2	13	2	8	19	0	11	13	7
Gastronomic	0	3	0	3	3	3	16	7	10	5
Modern Arch.	0	4	0	7	13	4	0	0	0	3
Communics.	0	0	4	3	3	0	0	11	0	2
Nightlife	0	2	4	2	5	0	0	0	1	2
Shopping	0	2	0	0	2	0	0	0	1	1
Other	0	33	0	2	12	3	12	13	7	9

Key:

A - Agde
B - Cap d'Agde
C - Carnon
D - Gruissan
E - La Grande Motte
F - Palavas des Flots
G - Port Camargue/Grau du Roi
H - Sete
I - Valras
T - All resorts

Note: Percentages may not add to 100 due to rounding

156

impression of the Languedoc-Roussillon resorts given by suppliers and the use made of them by visitors. It is evident that the promotional literature tends to 'play down' the traditional resort activities and attempts to promote diverse facilities. This may be part of marketing strategies to move away from reliance on sun and sea as attractions, perhaps to lengthen the season and make use of spare capacity in accommodation, entertainment and sports facilities. As the tables indicate, visitors' ranking of the beach, shops and restaurants is much higher than that given to them by suppliers.

Whether indeed, as a result of the study, the images of tourists and suppliers do not coincide has certainly not been fully demonstrated. The researchers involved in the project were painfully aware of shortcomings in the study which precluded the drawing of any firm conclusions. However, the value of the exercise lay in the exploration of likely methods of establishing image and that future research requirements and directions were revealed. Some indication of these is given below.

THEORY AND THE LANGUEDOC-ROUSSILLON STUDY

An attempt has been made to relate image to consumer and supply theory and to sketch the empirical requirements. It is clear from the preceding section that the study in Languedoc-Roussillon is very much a preliminary stage in the investigation of image and its role in tourism development. The survey of visitors did very little more than indicate their sources of information used and give the broad impressions they had of the eleven resorts in the survey. Certainly no claims would be made that tourists' images have been established to assist in the development of 'characteristics' - based consumer theory, or the evaluation of promotion by the resorts, as suggested by Nolan (1976), reflecting the objective of establishing the correspondence between tourists' and suppliers' perception of the resorts, i.e. what he terms the 'credibility' of information.

The supply side part of the project represents a first step in a more comprehensive evaluation of the promotion of image. The scope and relevance of what has been done can be ascertained by reference to the discussion of supply in the section on the

157

theoretical context. The study confined itself to printed material only in the destination region. Moreover, as indicated, some constraints were imposed on the classification of image in the interests of consistency, since one objective was to relate it to the land-use functions of the resorts. Extension of the study would necessitate looking at all forms of promotion with its simultaneous consideration in origin as well as destination regions.

What has been accomplished is the derivation and testing of a procedure for assessing published material which appears to be largely objective in identifying and ranking the resorts' attributes, as conceived by suppliers in relation to visitors.

Identifying image from the supply side is less difficult than from the demand side. Consequently, if it is assumed, based on whatever evidence is available of tourists' perceptions, that there is a reasonable correspondence between tourists' and suppliers' images of resorts, then exercises such as those conducted in Languedoc-Roussillon could contribute to the development of Lancaster/hedonic approaches to consumer behaviour.

FUTURE RESEARCH DEVELOPMENTS

The programme initiated in Languedoc-Roussillon could take two broad directions. It can be developed in order to contribute, first, to demand and supply modelling, and second, to practical marketing strategies.

Modelling

The study of tourists' motivations and perceptions has been pursued extensively, especially in the USA, but most of this research suffers from three main shortcomings because it:

(i) relates to the period before the 1970s fuel crisis and economic stagnation experienced by many industrial nations,
(ii) is largely in the context of the American social structure and mores,
(iii) tends to ignore economic factors.

Thus, there is a case for re-examining consumer behaviour with specific emphasis on the formation of images in a European context. In doing so research should be extended to cover both potential as well as actual tourists. With respect to supply, a similar extension, as already alluded to, needs to be considered again emphasizing promotion within the economic theory of the firm. The Languedoc-Roussillon region is a suitable study area because it not only appears to typify a major form of 'sunlust' tourism, but also is a good example of a specific attempt to generate and divert tourist activity.

Empirical considerations

There are a number of objectives, which might include the testing of hypotheses, of more empirically based research. Some reference to the nature of such studies has been made throughout the chapter, but it is worth summarising, and suggesting other lines of enquiry here, with particular regard to the Languedoc-Roussillon region:

(i) The analysis of the images held by consumers of the region, particularly the images:
    (a) held by different people depending on their region/country of origin and socio-economic group;
    (b) of different resorts of a given group of people.
(ii) The rationale for differences in the images promoted by the region which might relate to:
    (a) the attributes or facilities of specific resorts;
    (b) the target group or origin country or region;
    (c) seasonal variations.
(iii) Analysis of the correspondence of (i) and (ii) and the reasons why some resorts have favourable and others unfavourable images;
(iv) The nature of promotional material in both origin and destination regions;
(v) The use made of promotional material by both potential and actual tourists and their evaluation and ranking of it;
(vi) The effectiveness of promotional material in forming/changing tourists' destinations and activities.

The results of such research can hold implications for the future promotion of the Languedoc-Roussillon region, particularly if it indicates wide variations in the images held of it by different categories of potential tourists and actual visitors. In conclusion it ought to be emphasized that image, although it is a significant variable, is only one of many factors in determining the success of tourism development. It must be set alongside other variables such as natural and manufactured resources, access, infrastructure, accommodation and indigenous population attitudes.

REFERENCES

Brown, G.M., Charbonneau, J.J. & Hay, M.J. (1978) The value of Wildlife Estimated by the Hedonic Approach, US Department of the Interior, Fish and Wildlife Service Working Paper No. 6

Ehemann, (1977) What kind of place is Ireland?, J. of Travel Research, 16,-28-30

Freeman, M.R. (1979) The hedonic price approach to measuring demand for neighbourhood characteristics in D. Segal, (ed.) The Economics of Neighbourhood, Academic Press, New York

Hunt, J.D. (1975) Image as factor in tourism development. J. of Travel Research, 13 (3), 1-7

Lancaster, K.J. (1966) A new approach to consumer theory, J. of Political Economy, 84, 132-57

Lawson, F. & Baud-Bovy, M. (1977) Tourism and Recreational Development, Architectural Press, London

Maclennan, D. (1982) Housing Economics: an applied approach, Longman, London

Mathieson, A. & Wall, G. (1982) Tourism: Economic, Physical and Social Impacts, Longman, London

Mayo, E.J. (1973) Regional Images and Regional Travel Behaviour, Proceedings of the Travel Research Association, Fourth Annual Conference, Sun Valley, Idaho, USA, 211-17

McIntosh, R.W. (1972) Tourism, Principles, Practices, Philosophies, Grid, Columbus, Ohio

Murphy, P.E. (1983) Perceptions and attitudes of decision-making groups in tourist centres, J. of Travel Research, 21 (3), 8-12

Murphy, P.E. (1985) Tourism: A Community Approach, Methuen, London

Nolan, S.D. (1976) Tourists' use and evaluation of travel information sources; Summary and conclusions, J. of Travel Research, 14 (3), 6-8

Pearce, D.W. (1981) Macmillan Dictionary of Modern Economics, Macmillan, London

Quandt, R.E. & Baumol, W.J. (1966) The Demand for abstract travel modes, J. of Regional Science, 6 (2), 13-26

Rosen, S. (1974) Hedonic prices and implicit markets: product differentiation in pure competition, J. of Political Economy, 82, 34-55

Rugg, D.D. (1971) 'The Demand for Foreign Travel', PhD thesis, University of California, Los Angeles

Chapter 10

MARKETING THE HISTORIC CITY FOR TOURISM

Gregory Ashworth

'Celebrating the past was implicit to a sense of nationhood, statehood and locality. It was educational as a means of orientation to one's cultural heritage, but above all visiting historical attractions could be entertaining and relaxing. Historical sites offered a sense of permanence in an ever changing world of new, highly standardized landscapes. Historical flavours served as a counterpart to modernity' (Jakle, 1985).

INTRODUCTION

Historical artefacts and associations have long been one of the tourism industry's most marketable commodities. It can be argued that the 'grand tour' around sites of historical significance in search of educational or cultural profit, along with the pilgrimage in search of spiritual profit, is one of the oldest motives for travel (Burkart & Medlik, 1974).

The importance of history as a primary or supplementary motive for recreational travel can be demonstrated at a number of spatial scales. It is the principal motive for intercontinental tourism generating in particular what might be termed the 'colonial' tourist flows from the United States, Canada, Australia and Latin America to the European 'motherlands' such as Britain, France, Italy and Spain. It is this form of long-distance 'wanderlust' that accounts for the dominance of cities such as London, Paris or Rome as tourist resorts. It is a major motive for intracontinental and domestic tourism, in most countries being the second most important after beach tourism (Kosters, 1981). In addition it can provide useful 'back-up' facilities for holidays whose primary motive is quite different, by, for example, providing excursion possibilities in the course of beach holidays. It is an important objective for day recreation trips. A recent French study revealed that 60 per cent of the entire adult population had made at least one such trip in the year surveyed (Garay, 1980) while more than 20 million trips are made to the English medieval cathedrals each year.

Although not all sites and objects of historical interest are to be found in urban areas, cities play a disproportionately important role as the collection and display centres for the artistic productivity and historical associations of a nation or region. The importance of the ensemble of historical relics and buildings in creating an overall atmosphere of antiquity, that can rarely be achieved by an individual site, allows cities (or parts of cities) as a whole to become tourist attractions. This discussion will therefore be confined to cities as both containers of objects of interest as well as such objects in themselves.

Given the importance of marketable history to the tourism industry, it is necessary to be more precise about its definition and to introduce two related concepts to aid this analysis.

The historic city as a conceptualisation of a particular sort of urban phenomenon is derived from far more than just the antiquity of the buildings gathered together in particular towns. It is composed of three elements, viz. the characteristics of the urban form; the valuation placed on aspects of that form expressed through the preservation of a selection of the morphological elements and more broadly through a conservational philosophy of urban management; and the functioning of the city for both residents and non residents in such a way that the historical attributes are consciously exploited.

Such a concept with its accent on planning intervention and use can be directly related to particular consumer markets through the concept of heritage. This is the notion that there exists a demand for the preserved or reconstructed urban historical artefacts. This heritage demand, which may be 'actual' or 'optional' may be justified by educational, national-cultural, aesthetic or commercial motives, or more usually an inseparable mixture of many of these. Although the question 'whose heritage?' may rarely be posed, there is an inviolable link between the concepts of the historical city and of heritage - between the conservation of the urban fabric and a consumer.

163

The logical step is to regard heritage as a specific aspect of tourism supply to be marketed to an identified tourist demand. We arrive at what to many is the more or less self-evident proposition that antiquity converted into heritage provides a resource for a commercial activity, which in turn through its land demands and economic product, provides a justification, land use and financial contribution to the conserved urban form. It is at this point however that a number of inherent contradictions and potential conflicts arise to mar a happy symbiosis that has been more often assumed than demonstrated.

Although there are few tourism industries in the world that do not attempt some marketing of heritage, it has been most successfully achieved in Europe, and this paper will draw prinicipally upon the research experience of the Geographical Institute of the University of Groningen in Britain, The Netherlands and France. The research effort has been concentrated on the development of the concept of the historic city, its spatial delimitation, and its development modelling in the wider functional context of the city as a whole, as well as upon the problem of the development of appropriate planning and management strategies for urban tourism in the medium-sized cities. This research will be drawn upon in order to raise a series of questions about the problem of marketing the historic city for tourism.

CONFLICTS AND CONTRADICTIONS

Institutional

Historic cities, as was emphasized in the definition above, are created by the active intervention of institutions whether in the public or private sectors, which make a conscious selection from the available stock of antiquities, and using the available legal instruments and planning practices, attempt to conserve a particular interpretation of the past. The development of the urban conservation movement in Western Europe has been described elsewhere (Dobby, 1978; Burtenshaw, et.al., 1981) and it only needs to be stressed here that the evolution of the conservation ethic in local planning and its expression in national legislation (such as the French Loi Malraux 1961, Dutch Monumentenwet 1960 or British <u>Civic Amenities Act</u> 1967) gave rise to a particular set of institutions, principally but not exclusively at the local authority level, staffed by conservation specialists whose expertise was focused primarily on building preservation.

Urban tourism, far from being a creation of active public intervention, has long been regarded as mainly the concern of the private commercial sector. Policy was therefore a matter of the business decisions of firms and public intervention at the national level was late (beginning perhaps in Britain with the <u>Development of Tourism Act</u> 1969 which led to the creation of a network of national and regional tourist boards) and was generally confined to publicity exercises and the distribution of some national subsidies.

Policy-making bodies for tourism at the urban scale are rare and most local authorities have been content to react to the results of the influx of visitors, seeing tourism as a planning or traffic problem, rather than a real or potential major urban function in need of policy guidance and positive management. Some local authorities, especially those with a major tourism industry, have publicity or information departments and a few have attempted to co-ordinate departmental policies towards tourism through interdepartmental committees (Berkers, et.al., 1986). Very few cities however have a tourism department charged with shaping policy for the attraction of visitors, their management in the city and the development of an appropriate supply infrastructure.

The end result, for whatever reason, is that in most Western European cities the institutions concerned with the creation and maintenance of the historic city, and those concerned with the marketing of heritage to tourists, are not the same. They were established at different times, for different purposes under different legislative frameworks, operate at different spatial scales, have a different mix of public and private interests and are staffed by quite different groups of specialists with differing expertise. One set of institutions is attempting to market a product created and maintained by another with whom it has generally weak formal links.

Goals

It is self-evident that the ostensible goals

of tourism as a commercial activity and urban
conservation as a public service are different.
This need not in itself lead to conflict. There
are however a number of reasons why this is likely
to be the case.

The effective spatial scale of operation of
urban conservation varies in different parts of
Europe. Countries such as Britain and to a lesser
extent The Netherlands have tended towards a high
degree of local responsibility for the selection
and maintenance of historic buildings, while France
and the countries of Eastern Europe have tended
towards a more centralised system with national
governments playing a more active role (Dobby,
1978). This has significant implications for the
criteria used and thus for the choice of what is to
be conserved, or which historic city is created
from the alternatives available. The use of
national criteria implies a concentration on
artefacts of national or international
significance, as well as the projection of the
chosen national image, while regional and local
criteria can select a different, or more usually
supplementary, set of artefacts in accordance with
a local or regional self-image that may be quite
different. For example the stress on nineteenth-
century social and labour history in a number of
British cities is in contrast to the grander
imperial themes projected at a national level.

It has been argued that there is a tendency to
move from the national towards the local scale over
time, both because local offical involvement in
some countries, such as Belgium and France, lagged
behind national legislation, and also because
success in urban conservation inevitably leads to
an extension of the effort from the spectacular
monuments of national importance, which are
protected in the 'first wave' towards more modest
domestic buildings whose significance is inevitably
local (Ashworth, 1984).

Tourists have, in general, a more restricted
knowledge of, and interest in, the art and history
of a region than local inhabitants. The tendency
is for tourists to associate places with a few
easily recognised characteristics or landmarks of
international significance (Amsterdam is the
canals, Pisa a leaning tower, Edinburgh a castle,
etc.) and confine their visits to a pre-selected
handful of such attractions, largely ignoring those
of slightly lesser renown or merit. This aspect of
the spatial behaviour of visitors has been

adequately examined elsewhere and related to various visitor characteristics, such as distance travelled, motive, educational level, age and the like (Ashworth & de Haan, 1985 & 1986b). The result can be not only a conflict between national and regional goals, but between the local objectives of conservation and the needs of tourism. In the city of Norwich, for example, tourists concentrate their attention upon three small areas - the cathedral, the castle and Elm Hill, (which taken together account for 46 per cent of all tourist visits to objects of historical interest). Of these the castle is largely a nineteenth-century reconstruction of the contemporary idea of a medieval keep, and Elm Hill is an early conservation project that has effectively rebuilt a late medieval street facade. The efforts of the council's conservation programme over the last few years by contrast have been concerned with the more peripheral, and less spectacular domestic architecture, of the inner city ('Norwich-over-the-Wensum', King Street, St Benedict's) which attract very few tourists. Similarly on a regional scale the regional self-image of the French province of Languedoc has increasingly been bolstered by a stress upon the region's independence of spirit and resistance to Capetian imperialism and national centralisation from the thirteenth century. Local conservation policy therefore emphasizes the 'Cathar' castles and the 'hotels' of the local Montpellier gentry rather than the grandiose monuments of the seventeenth century that symbolise the conquest of the region and which have been the focus of central government conservation efforts over the last twenty years.

Whereas tourism may be an obvious use, in whole or in part, of the larger monuments located in the areas of tourist concentration, the smaller domestic monuments and those further from the narrow 'beaten track' of the visitors are far more likely to be in use by residents, especially for housing. Indeed, it can be argued, and has been demonstrated for the city of Groningen (Ashworth, 1984), that as conservation policy becomes more successful and extends its sphere of operation in the city beyond the nationally recognised monuments, so the relative importance of tourism as a use of the conserved city declines.

There is conflict between the goals of tourism and conservation planning in what can be termed the 'bowdlerisation' of the historic city as a consequence of its attempts to meet the expectations of visitors. Visitors require a simple, easily and quickly communicated historical experience that confirms their expectations, and they have neither the time nor inclination to accept the complications and subtleties of the city's historical development, and the generally confused mix of time periods and architectural styles that typify most city-scapes. A city such as Bath which comprises a single time period, and indeed a single facet of that period, viz. the eighteenth-century aristocratic health spa, is more readily appreciated than the more variegated morphological and functional patterning of most cities. It is therefore a short and logical step from Elm Hill, the preserved and reconstructed medieval facade of Norwich with its 'appropriate' cobblestones and street furniture, to the creation of an historical theme park in which the visitor is placed in what is effectively a stage set. The result can be either Jamestown, Virginia, where an existing site has been embellished and decorated with the contemporary American image of 'colonial' life, or Den Gamleby in Aarhus where a medieval town has been built in this century by assembling fragments from elsewhere. In both cases there comes a point where the goals of urban conservation have been not merely stretched but effectively abandoned. It is not that urban conservation policy is free from the necessity of choice, the exercise of value judgements and the necessity for much reconstruction of preconceived notions of antiquity. The historic city of the conservation planner is no more an accurate reflection of the city in past periods of time than is the tourists' open-air museum, but it is likely to be different. The pursuit of history as saleable heritage can result in the selling of York through Dick Turpin, of a region such as the Yorkshire Dales as the 'Bronte country' (or more recently the 'Herriot country'), and even of a whole country such as Romania, as the home of Count Dracula.

Locations

A fundamental and practical objection to the automatic association of the conserved urban fabric and tourism is that the two aspects of the city may not occur in the same place. The research undertaken for some years in a number of European cities, by the Geographical Institute of the University of Groningen, into the location, delimitation and evolution of the historic and touristic cities has revealed distinct differences in location. The historic city, in the sense of that part of the city that is valued as historic and designated as such under various planning instruments, is generally much more extensive than that part of the city either sold to visitors through the publicity of the local tourism agencies, or actually experienced by them. In addition the tourist city, in the sense of that part of the city that contains the facilities actually used by tourists, includes many areas outside the historic city, especially those providing accommodation, shopping, catering and entertainment services. Although the two cities generally overlap there are large areas that are exclusive to one or other function. With the exception of the small mono-functional 'gem' cities such as Elburg, Mont St Michel, Willemstad, Bergamo or Aigues Mortes, the historic city provides only one facet of the total tourism facility supply, while tourism impinges into only a relatively small part of the historic city.

Physical and environmental damage

Although frequently cited as a source of conflict between tourism and urban conservation, the physical and environmental impacts of visitors are in many ways of peripheral importance compared with the more fundamental issues raised above, although it frequently happens that the differences of institution and philosophy become focused on relatively trivial controversies about the physical damage caused by visitors.

Certainly the very presence of tourists en masse has an impact on the historic city and its monuments. The Tower of London in the summer has more the atmosphere of a fair ground than a prison, and a visit to Westminster Abbey is hardly a spiritual experience. But equally of course these buildings were not intended by their builders to be monuments of beauty or antiquity, but were in their time modern functional structures erected for specific uses that largely no longer apply.

There are well publicised cases of the supposed incompatability of tourism and

169

conservation as a result of the direct physical damage, whether wilful or not, caused by visitors such as the long standing controversy over access to Stonehenge. Such cases however are rarer than might be imagined, if only as was argued earlier that only a portion of the historic city is of interest to visitors, and are often the result of inadequate management, or at least can be ameliorated by effective management. Frequently it is the indirect environmental damage or inconvenience that is of more lasting importance and more intractable solution. Tourists, even those whose journey is motivated by historical attractions, have twentieth-century needs, and the provision of modern hotel accommodation and transport facilities are difficult to reconcile with the historic city (for some examples of controversial planning decisions resulting from tourism provision in historic cities (see Burtenshaw et.al., 1981).

CONFLICT RESOLUTION THROUGH THE INTERVENTION OF INTERMEDIARIES

The marketing of heritage is in essence much the same as the marketing of any other product (see Ashworth & Voogd, 1986a,b). At its simplest the process can be reduced to three tasks:

(i) the identification of the product,
(ii) the identification of the potential market,
(iii) the direction of a flow of relevant information about the former to the latter.

It is the intermediaries, i.e. those agencies, whether serving public institutions or private commerce, that are concerned with bringing together supply and demand, who undertake all three tasks. The complications arise from the inherent characteristics of historic city tourism, some of which have been outlined above, that renders the tasks of the intermediaries particularly difficult.

As far as the product itself is concerned, a major difficulty is that the marketing agencies can only select from an historic heritage that was not created by, or for, the tourism industry. The initiative in the definition of the product is therefore in practice largely in the hands of the local authorities and of the public sector. The

marketing agencies can only attempt to achieve a
degree of sensitive liaison with those designating
and managing the conservation of the built
environment, which in most cases must occur at the
local rather than the national scale. This in turn
involves a close permanent working relationship not
only between tourism agencies and local
authorities, but also within the local authorities
themselves. In very few cities does this in fact
occur although many local authorities have
developed the required expertise in similar liaison
with the private sector in industrial development
policies.

The second task falls squarely into the field
of responsibility of the tourism marketing agencies
who have the task of identifying the
characteristics of the existing market, and
recognising the potential of new markets. In
practice, however, very little systematic work has
been done, within the tourism industry or
elsewhere, on the relationship between the tourist
and the historic city. The characteristics of such
visitors, in terms of their age, family
circumstances, group composition, income, class,
educational background and the like in relation to
other sorts of tourists and of the population as a
whole, have been sketched in general terms in many
national and local studies (see Garay, 1980 and
Scheppers, 1986 for a French and Belgian example
respectively). But it is equally clear that
insufficient detail exists upon which to base
particular marketing strategies or to predict
future markets through projecting trends in those
characteristics. The behaviour of the consumer of
heritage in the historic city is similarly known
only in outline. Some comparative information has
been assembled on the length of stay, accommodation
choice, and crude estimates of expenditure, but how
the customer actually uses the historic city and
its facilities, in terms of the spread and
intensity of use, remains largely unknown, and yet
it is precisely these aspects of tourist behaviour
that are central to resolving a number of the
potential conflicts mentioned earlier. Finally the
question of visitor motivation has rarely ever been
posed and yet if the market for heritage is to be
accurately identified, the whole socio-
psychological field of the interaction of tourists
and historic monuments must be approached. It is
not enough to make broad unsupported assumptions
about nostalgia, escapism or romanticism, if the

heterogeneous market for an extremely heterogeneous product is to be understood.

A reaction to this plea for more information that has been frequently heard, especially from the tourism industry itself, is that the means of assembling such information do not exist in practice, and in any event such a research effort is unnecessary. Both points are not easily dismissed. The facilities for fundamental research of this nature largely do not exist within the tourism industry and it is beyond the scope and competence of most governmental tourism organisations. The rapid growth in the tourism market through much of the 1960s and early 1970s imposed a reactive role upon the tourism supply industry. A steadily increasing demand had to be met, and the industry developed the habit of response to a demand that they had little part in creating and had little time or incentive to examine too closely.

In undertaking the third task of bringing together the product and the market, the principal instrument available is the stimulation of a flow of information directed at the potential consumer. Some of this publicity originates from tourism marketing agencies, but much also orginates from quite different sources beyond the influence of tourism planners. On the basis of this information, however gleaned, the visitor makes not only the decision to holiday in a particular place but also the details of the length and type of visit and the activities to be undertaken. Historic cities in particular tend to have long established reputations which publicity can merely amplify and accent. Published information under the direct control of local tourism marketing agencies can be used to further such goals as a more satisfactory distribution of visitors in time or space. Such evidence as has been obtained from research suggests, however, that it is an inefficient medium for these purposes. A high proportion of such information is received by customers who have already made most of the critical decisions about their holiday, under the influence of first-hand experience and that of acquaintances rather than published literature, and research in Norwich (Ashworth & de Haan, 1986a) has indicated that only 32 per cent of visitors used a guide-book and only 16 per cent visited the local tourist information centre.

Even if such publicity material is less

effective than might be assumed, some studies of its content have revealed that it is rarely used to further existing policies for urban tourism. In a number of historic cities, for example, there are policies for the wider spatial spread of visitors through the inner city in order to diminish congestion and over use in a few limited areas, and yet the marketing information for such cities is in fact more heavily concentrated than the actual behaviour of visitors. The market is being followed rather than led. Exceptions can be found such as the City of Norwich Tourist Information Centre which has produced a series of tourist trails designed to broaden the sphere of interest of the visitor to include new aspects and areas of the historic city, but even here the attempt to draw visitors into the area of 'Norwich-over-the-Wensum' has been unsuccessful.

THE BROADER CONTEXT

In order to define and delimit the tourist-historic city it is necessary to isolate it, and this isolation is especially unreal and misleading in the development of marketing strategies. Hardly any historic cities, however extensive or imposing their heritage, can engage the attention of visitors for more than a few days, and in the case of most medium-sized cities a few hours. As any individual city can only provide a part of the total holiday experience, a collection of such cities may be packaged together by the consumer. The position of any one city within such a network in terms of accessibilty and complementarity is therefore critical and has obvious implications for marketing. There are notable examples of the appreciation and exploitation of precisely this point, such as the joint publicity of the 'East of England Cathedrals Route' or, on an international scale, the joint promotion of Maastricht, Liege and Aachen, but the institutional structure mentioned earlier inhibits such initiatives.

Second, historic city tourism is only one type of holiday which may be located within reach of quite different tourist regions possessing different holiday supply packages. This could present problems of competition for resources, or equally opportunities for complementary promotion. There are many examples of the tourist-historic city offering its historic attractions or its urban entertainment, catering and shopping facilities, as day excursion objectives for holiday-makers staying in neighbouring beach or inland rural holiday regions. In the case of Norwich, the city is within easy reach of both the Broads water-based tourist region and the Norfolk coast beach tourism, and offers some facilities for both, although the complementarity is not fully reciprocated (Ashworth & Bergsma, 1982) at least in part because the three distinct holiday regions are managed and promoted by quite distinct intermediary organisations.

The tourist-historic function is one of many urban functions, which compete or co-operate within the city, and planning for tourism without a consideration of the broader goals and problems of the city is futile. It cannot always be assumed that the marketing of the tourist-historic function will accord with the other legitimate objectives of the urban managers. Indeed the promotion of the conserved historic city may not present an image that is attractive to venture capital in new enterprises, and can thus be detrimental to economic development goals, while naive claims that the impact of tourism on the local economy is unqualified gain is quickly disproved by experience. Similarly urban conservation policy may have impacts upon the social structures of conserved areas that are contrary to the social policies of the local authority. Although such arguments can be found in the literature (e.g. Burtenshaw et.al., 1981; Mathieson & Wall, 1982) and more significantly can frequently be heard in the council chamber, they are more often a reflection of a failure of those responsible for the tourist-historic city to appreciate the broader context in which they must operate, rather than demonstrating irreconcilable differences of principle.

The marketing to visitors of the heritage of the tourist-historic city offers real economic possibilities to a wide range of cities. The successful exploitation of these opportunities depends to a large extent on the skill and sensitivity of the intermediaries, who must, as their name implies, come between and thereby bring together not merely the different institutions involved but also the range of interests and goals that comprise that city.

REFERENCES

Ashworth, G.J. & Bergsma, J. (1982) Impacts of the Boat Hire Industry in the Norfolk Broads: problems and policies, GIRUG, Groningen

Ashworth, G.J. (1984) The Management of change. Conservation policy in Groningen, The Netherlands, Cities, 605-16

Ashworth, G.J. & de Haan, T.Z. (1985) The Tourist-Historic City: a model and initial application in Norwich, UK, Field Studies Series, No. 8, GIRUG, Groningen

Ashworth, G.J. & de Haan, T.Z. (1986a) Uses and users of the tourist-historic city, Field Studies Series, No. 10, GIRUG, Groningen

Ashworth, G.J. & de Haan, T.Z. (1986b) De stad als vrijetijdscentrum - het vrijetijdcentrum als stad, Vrijetijd en Samenleving

Ashworth, G.J. & Voogd, H. (1986a) De Europees Erfgoed: een stimulus voor stedelijk economisch ontwikkeling, Plan

Ashworth, G.J. & Voogd, H. (1986b) City-Marketing: a new paradigm for urban planning and research. Paper to Symposium on Planning Studies and Practice, London School of Economics, Sept 1986

Berkers, M., et. al. (1986) The Planning and Management of the British Historic City, Field Studies series, No. 9, GIRUG, Groningen

Burkart, A.S. & S. Medlik (1974) Tourism: past, present and future, Heinemann, London

Burtenshaw, D., Bateman, M. & Ashworth, G.J. (1981) The City in West Europe, Wiley, Chichester

Dobby, A. (1978) Conservation and Planning, Hutchinson, London

Garay, M. (1980) Le Tourisme culturel en France, Notes et Etudes documentaires, Direction de documentation Francaise, Paris

Haan, T.Z. de & Ashworth, G.J. (1986) Funktie en gebruik: De bezoeker in de multifunctionele binnenstad, Onderzoekverslagen, No.14, GIRUG, Groningen

Jakle, J.A. (1985) The Tourist, University of Nebraska Press, Lincoln/London

Kosters, M.J. (1981) Focus op Toerisme, VUGA, Amsterdam

Mathieson, A. & G. Wall (1982) Tourism: Economic, Social and Physical Impacts, Longman, London

Scheppers, E. (1986) Het vakantie en recreatiegedrag der Belgen in het binnenland, Geotoer 3, Leuven

Chapter 11

DEVELOPMENTS IN THE PROMOTION OF MAJOR SEASIDE
RESORTS: HOW TO EFFECT A TRANSITION BY REALLY
MAKING AN EFFORT

Bryan J.H. Brown

PROMOTION AND THE BEGINNING

The historical development of the English
seaside resorts, and their close and early
relatives the inland spas, has been the subject of
considerable research (see for example Walton,
1983, who provides an extensive bibliography).
Much of this research has concentrated upon the
social history of the resorts, or upon the
development of their urban geography, and there has
been relatively little detailed investigation of
the topics such as promotion and marketing in an
historical context. However, both the large number
of general historical works and the more limited
range of detailed local investigations (for example
Brown, 1985) reveals quite clearly that almost
since the beginning of the modern seaside resort in
Britain deliberate promotion and marketing has been
undertaken, and that many resorts owe both their
initial foundation and subsequent growth entirely
to such activities.

Early methods were of course relatively crude
by modern standards, but made use of the available
contemporary media. Scarborough's early promotion
in the late seventeenth century for example
included the publication of a medical text
extolling the value of its spring and sea waters,
while the famous publication by Russell in 1751
which set Brighton on the road to rapid growth was
soon followed by many other works in similar vein,
culminating with Granville's famous two-volume epic
on the Spas of England in 1841. The power of this
type of medical text and the influence of the
medical profession in general on influencing the
decisions of the upper classes to visit particular
spas and seaside resorts, especially during the
eighteenth century, must not be underestimated.
Indeed, by the latter decades of that century the
use of the more popular media was developing, and

the purely medical influences upon resort growth
were in decline. In addition, there were growing
influences at work in society altering attitudes to
leisure, from philosophy and literature (in
particular the romantic poets), to the rapid spread
of non-conformism and its impacts upon personal
behaviour and lifestyle.

The situation is particularly well illustrated
by the early development of the seaside resorts of
the west of England. The present author has
recently documented the situation of Weston-super-
Mare in some detail (Brown, 1985), and at this very
unpromising site on the shores of the upper Bristol
Channel it was newspaper advertising which was used
in the initial promotion of the resort as early as
1779. A combination of advertisements for
accommodation, the publication and circulation of a
descriptive guide-book in the regional booksellers,
a number of editorial articles in the regional
newspapers and even a romantic article in a popular
national journal of the early nineteenth-century,
(Gentlemans' Magazine) undoubtedly helped to
develop in the minds of Weston's early potential
visitors a very positive view of the site. This
perception was at considerable variance with the
actual conditions at Weston in this period, where
the village actually offered very few facilities
for visitors and the muddy waters and high tidal
range of the Bristol Channel provided far less
favourable conditions than could be found at many
other sites in southern England.

Much later in the nineteenth century a similar
situation prevailed in respect of the development
of tourism in Cornwall. This relatively remote
part of the country had been almost untouched by
the tourism boom as a consequence of the lack of a
railway link to other parts of England until the
completion of the Royal Albert Bridge at Saltash in
1859. Although there was some early tourism, for
example to Penzance in the first two decades of the
century (where much store was placed upon the
exceptionally mild winter climate), the rapid
development of Cornwall as a major domestic tourist
destination owed a great deal to the deliberate
creation of a romantic image by the Great Western
Railway (GWR). The GWR's later nineteenth- and
early twentieth-century publicity campaigns for the
Cornish Riviera reached a large part of the
population through poster advertising, newspaper
articles, and even the publication of very high
quality guide-books and history books, many of

which are now valued collector's items. Walton
(1983) notes, for example, how after 1904 the GWR
achieved considerable success with this effort in
the Birmingham area, and by 1913 even such a
provincial paper as the Walsall Observer was
running a regular paragraph of 'Holiday Views from
Devon and Cornwall'. Careful use was made of
literary images of place, of Celtic legend, and of
high quality photographs to produce a sub-regional
image which persists very strongly in the mind of
the British population to the present day, to the
clear positive advantage of the county's
contemporary tourism industry.

These brief examples serve to illustrate that
there is a long and frequently successful history
of deliberate image-building on various spatial
scales within the domestic tourism industry in
Britain. In the early phase such efforts were made
either by the promoters of a resort, usually large
landowners, or at a later date by the main railway
companies. Walton (1983) points out, however, that
as the nineteenth century progressed the
increasingly democratic local government
institutions began to undertake a much wider range
of activities, and in the growing resorts the
emergent councils inevitably became concerned with
the welfare of the industry which supported so many
of the members of the councils. Thus we find
resort propaganda by the mid-nineteenth century
stressing essentially municipal issues such as the
levels of public health and the state of the
sewers.

Not surprisingly, in an increasingly
competitive world, the power to levy an advertising
rate was eagerly sought by many coastal local
authorities towards the end of the century.
Blackpool was in a leading position in this
respect, and for many years an unusual one, as in
1879 an oversight on the part of the Local
Government Board allowed the corporation the power
to levy a two pence rate to devote 'to the cost of
maintaining at railway stations and in other public
places advertisements stating the attractions and
amusements of the town' (Walton, 1983). This rate
initially provided £500 per annum, rising to well
over £4,000 in 1914, amounts well in excess of any
of the other major resorts of the period.

It is of considerable historical significance
that from the earliest years of being able to levy
such a rate, the Blackpool Corporation Advertising
Committee, which allocated the income, appears to

have been dominated by shareholders and directors of the town's entertainment companies. This resulted in strategic decisions to concentrate the resources into the extension of the town's catchment area through the classless, and for the 1890s novel medium of the coloured picture poster. As Walton pointed out, it was only when Blackpool's working-class catchment area had been firmly extended over a wide area of the Midlands and industrial Yorkshire that the Advertising Committee turned its attention to season extension at the turn of the century, after a building boom had greatly inflated its income and the entertainment company presence had been diluted by an admixture of high-class shopkeepers and estate agents from the Tradesman's Association.

However, Blackpool had a rather unique position among the British resorts for many years, for before 1914 the Local Government Board were most unwilling to grant similar rating powers to other towns - there is a long list of rejections in the records of the Board for the 1880s and 1890s! As late as 1912 Brighton was refused a half-penny rate for posters and placards for example, being confined to leaflet and newspaper advertising financed from deck-chair and bandstand profits. Indeed, local councils were forced to use rather underhand methods to provide at least some co-ordinated local publicity, a favourite method being to vote a 'mayoral salary' for advertising. Nevertheless, the seeds of corporate municipal promotion were sown very early in the development of resorts, and much experience was gained from related fields of destination promotion. Of these the most important from our contemporary viewpoint was undoubtedly the highly professional development of international destinations by the Thomas Cook organisation from the later nineteenth century onwards, but the details of this particular story are beyond the scope of the present chapter and are related in detail by Edmund Swinglehurst (1982).

NEW IMAGES FOR OLD: WHY THE NEED FOR CHANGE?

Within Britain there are many historical examples of seaside resorts which following a period of successful growth and development entered phases of stability or even decline. Changes in fashion, advances in transportation, and the influence of competition were for example to be found as much in the nineteenth as the twentieth century. A classic example has been discussed by the present author (Brown & Loosley, 1979) in respect of Weston-super-Mare in the early 1880s. Here, a severe loss of trade was apparently due to the competition being offered for the traditional middle-class clientele of the resort by Torquay. The reaction was heavy investment by the local authority to change the whole image of the resort, creating a vast new seafront promenade which radically changed the appearance and facilities of the town. It took Weston down-market, to a new and prosperous era catering for the needs of a growing working-class demand for seaside amusement, and greatly changed the whole pattern of building and development for the rest of the century.

The need for a new image is thus not new, but the problems which have had to be faced by Britain's traditional seaside resorts in the past few decades have been far greater than in the past, and to be overcome have required altogether more sophisticated solutions. The most favoured approach has been that of destination marketing, especially as applied by local authorities, and the general background and approach of this has been well described by Alan Clark (1985). The concept of a tourist destination area is one of some debate, since the drawing of boundaries is always a difficult task when dealing with socio-economic and behavioural as well as purely physical resources. However the set of criteria devised by Balmer and Crapo (Province of Ontario, 1980), including the natural resource base, population, transport, attractions and events, image and cohesiveness plus services and facilities, appears acceptable as a marker of their content in the present context. Administrative divisions, which are frequently highly arbitrary, are naturally less satisfactory as a tool on which to base marketing policy, but certainly within the United Kingdom context where tourism is frequently perceived as a vital part of local economic regenerative policy, such divisions frequently delimit many important destination regions in marketing terms.

This is most clearly seen in relation to the many very instructive examples of recent attempts to create new destinations for United Kingdom tourism. The majority of these are linked to the needs for inner city regeneration, and form part of major initiatives developed by successive governments following the 'discovery' of the inner

city as a political issue during the 1970s. Given
the often large scale of public investment in the
creation of facilities for recreation and tourism
it is not surprising that considerable attention
has been focused upon these both in the media and
the academic arena. Peter Buckley and Stephen Witt
(1985) provide an analysis of some important
examples of such developments in what they
described as 'difficult' areas, including Bradford,
Bristol, Glasgow, and the London Docklands; the
Merseyside area and Tyneside are additional
examples where publicly and privately funded
developments are currently taking place. They
conclude that the development of tourism in such
areas is a feasible strategy to increase employment
and prosperity, but that it is not a panacea and
can only be one part of an economic and social
programme. They also point out the necessity of a
concerted, targeted marketing effort, the need for
public-private sector co-operation and that the
investment of considerable resources is essential.
This high level of interest in new destinations in
the domestic market has however tended to
overshadow the problems being faced by the old
established coastal resorts, and we must now turn
to a detailed examination of two important case
studies in which considerable effort is being made
to revive the fortunes of older holiday
destinations.

The Torbay example

Torbay is an administrative area which
includes three major towns (Torquay, Paignton and
Brixham) and several smaller population centres,
grouped around the shore of Torbay in South Devon.
The current (1985) resident population is nearly
110,000, and this has in fact increased by some
4.2 per cent since 1981. Population increase is
largely the result of the in-migration of a retired
population, however, and does not offer a true
reflection of Torbay's economic position over the
recent past. From a peak in the middle 1970s there
has been a 22 per cent drop in tourist nights spent
in the resort and a significant reduction in the
length of the tourist season, hotels being 70 per
cent full for 14 weeks in 1977 but only four weeks
in 1982. Although this subsequently increased to
seven weeks in 1984 this is still a significant
decline.

Torbay grew rapidly during the nineteenth and early twentieth centuries primarily as a resort area, and there is relatively little local employment which is not connected with the tourism industry. In consequence there has been a major increase in the local rate of unemployment, which has in any case been consistently above both the national and regional levels. Industrial diversification is not easy as a response to this growing problem. The area has little land available which may be considered for industrial uses and the surrounding countryside is mostly classified as of very high landscape value (and itself is a major tourism resource). The local authority has therefore developed during the 1980s a comprehensive marketing and development strategy, beginning with the creation of a Torbay Tourist Board in 1982 in order to spearhead a co-ordinated approach.

The current strategy (Torbay Borough Council, 1985) builds upon the recommendations of a research study conducted by the English Tourist Board in 1982. It involves considerably increased investment by the public sector in new facilities (some of which are listed in Table 11.1), and the vigorous promotion of a new image for the three resorts is centred under the collective umbrella of the English Riviera. The latter has seen the development of a unified logo and a range of co-ordinated advertising materials and promotional activities, conspicuously avoiding use of the relatively new (1969) local authority name of Torbay, which had appeared to cause some degree of confusion among potential domestic customers. The new overall title makes it quite clear that three separate centres are involved.

It is too early in the campaign to expect concrete results from such a broad range of development activity, but the effort involved has been considerable and there can be little doubt that a much changed product image has been created - certainly among the trade itself - and that the Torbay approach demonstrates the potential for linking public and private investment to achieve sector growth. The degree of involvement is amply demonstrated by the extent of investment being generated (currently around £55 million), and it is forecast that this will bring about the creation of over 1,000 jobs and some 373,000 additional visitor nights in the resort area by the end of the century.

Table 11.1:   Examples of new facilities and
investment in Torbay

(a)   Development of new facilities:

English Riviera Conference Centre (for up to
1,500 delegates plus leisure pool, etc. (£3.1
million European Regional Development Fund
grant approved) for completion Spring 1987.
460 berth marina, completion 1987.
All-weather beach resort, themed leisure
complex and apartments, Goodrington,
commenced 1986.
New championship golf course, in planning
application phase.

(b)   Environmental improvements:

Enhancement of Torquay Harbour Conservation
Area, completion 1988.
Improvement scheme in Old Paignton
Conservation Area.
Babbacombe Downs Conservation Area improvement
scheme.

(c)   New countryside schemes:

Cockington Country Park, completion 1988.
Cockington Court, development of rural museum
and crafts/horticulture centre.
Improved visitor interpretation centres and
facilities including signposting.

Defence of the Realm project

A second major example of the use of
destination marketing to create new tourist
business is provided by the Hampshire and Isle of
Wight Defence Heritage Project. This major
project, which began in its present form during
1984, aims to provide co-ordinated marketing for a
wide range of military heritage sites, some of
major international significance such as HMS
Victory, the Mary Rose project and the Royal Navy
Submarine Museum. The castles, ships and museums
linked by this project at present receive over two
million visitors per year.

Previously the various heritage sites in this region had been developed and marketed with little regard for their historical relatedness, and indeed in a relatively prosperous part of the United Kingdom little consideration had been given to the potential of tourism. This situation changed during the later 1970s, however, especially in the City of Portsmouth, where the combination of a major closure programme for the Royal Naval Dockyard and the decline of the resort trade of Southsea (an integral part of the City) led to a rapid reassessment of the local economic scene. The City has been a particularly vigorous convert to the use of tourism as a tool for economic regeneration, and with a focus on the island city the Hampshire and Isle of Wight project is currently aiming to create a new awareness of the military heritage as a tourism resource.

As in Torbay, a relatively low-cost marketing and promotion unit has been established, in this case as a co-operative effort between a number of local authorities, providing a linkage between the largely independent attractions and a wide variety of funding and investment bodies. It is rather like taking the view that the whole area is a gigantic military theme park, and ensuring that visitors and potential visitors make the link as well. The project is now further supported by the designation of the Portsmouth area as an English Tourist Board Tourism Development Action Area. Again, this project is in too early a stage for conclusions on its success, but for Portsmouth alone it is estimated that the present phase of development will produce a one-third increase in tourism-related activity over the period 1986/9.

LARGE INDUSTRY - SMALL BUSINESSES

It is quite feasible to create new impressions of traditional resorts by a concerted marketing effort, arranging suitable publicity, putting together attractive new packages of accommodation and services for selected markets and co-ordinating the patterns of public and private investment on a large scale - Torbay, Portsmouth and many other examples are available to show what is possible, even on quite limited budgets. However, for many of our major seaside resorts the problems are more than just that of image or the lack of certain major public facilities. A recent study of the Bournemouth area (Brown & Hankinson, 1986) illustrates this very clearly.

Bournemouth, in common with the other major resorts, has a majority of its available accommodation in the smaller hotels and guest houses. Each of these is an independent small business unit with its own operating aims and structure which for the long-term planning of structural change in resorts must be taken into account. There are considerable problems in encouraging such businesses to invest in a higher standard of facilities (and for many this may actually be uneconomic), while substantial numbers do not wish to extend their operations above the level at which they would begin to pay Value Added Tax. Many are in any case run for family rather than strictly business reasons. Changing the mix of accommodation, widening the availability of central computerized booking, (in which Bournemouth is probably further advanced than any other UK resort) and encouraging the participation of these smaller businesses in larger marketing exercises is very difficult indeed.

In fact the main conclusions of the recent Bournemouth and SE Dorset Tourism Study (BTA/ETB, 1986) pay little attention to this problem, preferring instead to concentrate on the more traditional marketing and promotion areas. It may well be that in order to ensure the effective survival of our resorts into the next century far more effort is going to be required than has already been expended, for it is in the accommodation sector that the battle for survival is likely to be won or lost in the long term. The smaller hotels and guest houses appear at present to have low levels of marketing ability, a lack of strategic planning, poor pricing structures and low profitability. Such a situation perpetuates an excess of accommodation types relatively unsuited to the long-term development needs of the British resorts, and far more consideration needs to be given in future to the ways in which the legitimate needs and aspirations of the owners and managers of this sector can be matched with the requirement to provide our resorts with the accommodation they require. In this respect, the task facing the resorts has only just begun, and there can be little doubt that new techniques need to be developed by the public sector management bodies for the encouragement of change in the small business sector of tourism.

185

REFERENCES

BTA/ETB (1986) Bournemouth and South East Dorset Tourism Study, BTA/ETB Research Services, London

Brown, B.J.H. (1985) Personal perception and community speculation, a British resort in the 19th Century, Annals of Tourism Research, 12, 355-69

Brown, B.J.H. & Hankinson, A. (1986) Final Report of the National Small Hotel Study, Phase I, Economic & Social Research Council, September

Brown, B.J.H. & Loosley, J. (1979) The Book of Weston-super-Mare, Barracuda Books, Buckingham

Buckley, P.J. & Witt, S.F. (1985), Tourism in difficult areas, case studies in Bradford, Bristol, Glasgow and Hamm, Tourism Management, 6 (3), 205-13

Clark, A. (1985) Destination marketing - Gwent county approach, Tourism Management, 6 (4), 297-300

Province of Ontario (1980), Tourism Development in Ontario: A Framework for Opportunity, Provincial Government of Ontario, Toronto, Canada

Swinglehurst, E. (1982) Cook's Tours, The Story of Popular Travel, Blandford Press, Poole, Dorset

Torbay Borough Council (1985), The English Riviera 2000. An Integrated Tourism Strategy for Torquay, Paignton, Brixham, The Council, Torquay

Walton, J.K. (1983) The English Seaside Resort, A Social History 1750-1914, Leicester University Press, Leicester

Chapter 12

TOURISM DEVELOPMENT PLANNING IN LANGUEDOC: LE MISSION IMPOSSIBLE?

Gregory Ashworth and Michael J. Stabler

INTRODUCTION

This chapter investigates the role of a particular tourism agency in stimulating development in a specific region, and is thus intended to act as a case study illustrating some of the more general themes discussed earlier. It examines the objectives and methods of the official tourist organisation in the region and attempts an assessment of its effectiveness in terms of both the development of the region as a whole and the evolution of individual resort complexes. The ultimate aim is not to arrive at specific criticisms or suggestions relevant to the case under consideration but to use the specific regional experience to develop a comparative methodology for the study of tourism development in such regions.

The joint Groningen-Reading research programme has concentrated upon the general topic of the impacts of tourism development in disadvantaged regions. The choice of the coast of Languedoc-Roussillon as one of the regional illustrations of this theme was made despite the existence of a considerable body of official and unofficial literature from both French and foreign sources, which has monitored progress in the region over the last 20 years. In particular the University of Montpellier Department of Economics and the Centre Régionale de Productivité et Etudes Economiques conducted a large-scale monitoring study in the late 1970s (CRPEE 1976), and among foreign observers notably both Pearce (1981) and Murphy (1985) have reported on developments in the region.

The 1986 Groningen-Reading field programme consisted of three main data collection projects undertaken by students, who were located for the whole of the study period in eleven resorts between Port Camargue and Gruissan including the town of

Sete. These projects consisted of:

(i) The mapping of relevant land-use functions, especially visitor accommodation and tourism services.
(ii) A questionnaire study of visitor characteristics and behaviour combined with an observational exercise of the origins of motor cars. The survey of visitors concentrated mainly on the place of origin, group size, length of stay, trip patterns, accommodation choice, travel mode and expenditure patterns. Other questions on the interview schedule covered the use of publications and opinions of the specific resort and the Languedoc-Roussillon coast in general. This aspect is dealt with more fully elsewhere in this volume (see Chp. 9).
(iii) A study of the image of the resorts as presented in official and commercial promotional material.
(iv) An analysis of the addresses of all second-home owners with accommodation in the resorts.

The methods of data collection had been developed over a number of years in other coastal resorts (Haan & Ashworth, 1985). The substantive information gained from these field projects is currently being processed and will be published later.

The Regional Context

The Languedoc-Roussillon region of South West France has a Mediterranean coastline stretching 200 km from the Rhone to the Pyrenees. It consists of the five departments of Aude, Gard, Herault, Lozere and Pyrenees-Orientales and covers 27,500 km^2 (about 5 per cent of the area of France), with a population of nearly two million (4 per cent of the national total). The terrain consists of sandy beaches, backed by étangs and a hinterland rising to nearly 2,000 m (Ferras, Picheral & Vielzeuf, 1979).
The economy of the region prior to the initiation of the development programme was predominantly agricultural (especially wine production), with some mineral extraction (iron ore) and localised industries (textiles). Depopulation was occurring at an accelerating rate as the labour demands of these activities declined.

Although the Mediterranean coast of France was one
of the first regions to exploit the climatic and
scenic advantages for tourism, such development was
concentrated on the more accessible coast of
Provence, which was not only more scenically
attractive but also did not suffer from the
disadvantages of malarial marshes. Tourism in
Languedoc-Roussillon was weakly developed, and
largely local, attracting about 300,000 visitors
per annum during the 1950s, of which fewer than
half came from outside the region (Pearce, 1981).

THE MISSION

In the immediate post-war period French
planning was characterised by the initiation of
imaginative grandiose projects designed to
modernise the French economy (Ardagh, 1982).
Centralised state direction and large public
investments in infrastructure typified such
schemes. The lagging economy of Languedoc-
Roussillon was an obvious target for such planning,
and given the natural features of the area, the
development of tourism appeared to be the most
feasible instrument for stimulating growth. The
main specified objectives of the project were:

(i)   to diversify the economy, thus providing
new employment especially for young people and
thereby reverse the depopulation trend,
(ii) to raise the level of regional incomes,
(iii) to meet the rising demands for tourism
facilities from both French and foreign
visitors. This would relieve pressure on the
Cote D'Azur, which itself was reluctant to
adapt to the new mass tourism demands, and
help to correct France's growing adverse
international balance of tourism payments.
Although the domestic demand for tourism was
rising, the receipts from tourism in France
had been declining in real terms since 1960.

In addition there was originally an element of
social justice alongside this economic nationalism,
as much of the new tourism provision was to be
designed for visitors on average incomes.
An inter-ministerial commission (Le Mission)
was established in 1963. This central government
body had two roles: the co-ordination of the five
concerned government departments and the

maintenance of the unity of the project and its implementation. It had its own budget to facilitate development and promote the region. The state took responsibility for the infrastructure including roads, harbours, water supply, drainage, and environmental aspects such as afforestation, as well as financial planning and technical surveys and studies. Mixed development boards, comprising bodies at provincial and local level, were formed and were responsible for preparing the land and erecting administrative buildings within the framework of the development plan. In effect the boards constituted the link between the state and the communes. The boards sold the prepared land to the private sector developers and social groups, such as trade unions, sporting organisations, pension funds and the like.

Five resort units, i.e. clusters of new and existing resorts separated by open conserved landscapes, were proposed stretching from Port Camargue in the north-east to Perpignan in the south-west (see Fig. 9.4). The plan for development was to maintain harmony of urbanisation and the natural environment. Each of the five units was to have a similar tourist capacity, including 9,000 boat moorings in ports less than a day's sailing apart, a space standard of not more than 800 people to the hectare, 45,000-50,000 new tourist beds and at least 25 per cent low cost accommodation in each resort.

The five units are:

(i)   Le Grau du Roi/Port Camargue/La Grande Motte/Carnon/Palavas des Flots,
(ii) Sete/Cap d'Agde/Grau d'Agde,
(iii) Valras/Narbonne Plage/Gruissan,
(iv) Port Leucate/Port Barcares,
(v)   Canet/St Cyprien/Argeles.

Of these, the resorts in the first three units were included in the fieldwork undertaken in the late spring of 1986.

Construction of hotels, apartments, campsites, sports and entertainment facilities was assigned to the private sector under the urbanisation plan supervised by the architects and engineers employed by the commission.

Progress in the implementation of this grand design is described by the commission's chairman in a book with the grandiloquent title of Le Mission Impossible (Racine, 1980). The principal elements

in the plan had been created by the mid 1970s
although not all the individual resorts have yet
reached their capacity targets.

ASSESSMENT OF REGIONAL DEVELOPMENT

Given the objectives of the project, its
success should be measured from two main
standpoints, namely, regional economic development
in general and the development of tourism in
particular. The secondary goals, such as nature
conservation and the various social aims, can be
set aside because of difficulties in establishing
objective measures. The study of the Languedoc-
Roussillon development has tended to be piecemeal
and descriptive and there is some discrepancy in
the statistics collected. Consequently it is very
difficult to give a detailed evaluation and the
estimates of increased employment given below
certainly cannot be confirmed.

Some indication of changes in the region can
be obtained from official statistics, such as Les
Collections de L'INSEE (Statistiques et Indicateurs
des Régions Françaises) and Eurostat. With respect
to tourism, evidence can be gained from research on
individual aspects of the resorts, for example as
published in the <u>Bulletin de la Société Géographie
Languedocienne</u> (1983) and the <u>Revue de Geographie
de Lyon</u> (1984).

Regional development in general

In regional analysis the most common
indicators used to ascertain the effectiveness of
policy measures are population (structure and
migration), unemployment (level and by sector),
income (in total and per head), investment (total
level and by sector), and output (volume and
value). Clearly a more useful approach would be
to consider the rate of change in these indicators
and to compare this with other regions. Moreover
as shown earlier in stating the specific objectives
in Languedoc-Roussillon, policy may be selective,
such as concern for the employment of those under
25 years of age.

Tourism development

Following what has now become a well established technique, tourist multiplier analysis would embrace the indirect and induced effects of tourism development as well as the direct impact, in an economic approach. (See Escudier and Miossec, 1983, for an application of this approach in the study region.) This would necessitate, as a basis for estimating revenue, costs, etc. the straight counting undertaken by tourism agencies and others in terms of bed-nights. In a full impact analysis, which might embody environmental and ecological factors, social costs and benefits would be included. Such an approach is inhibited by the absence of adequate regional accounting, as well as by the difficulty of drawing areal boundaries around the areas to be considered.

The kinds of tourism statistics normally to be found are, both purely physical counts, such as number of visitors, number of bed-nights, occupancy rates of accommodation units, numbers employed in tourism and tourism-related activities, and also financial estimates, of for example, the expenditure of visitors, foreign currency earnings from tourism, incomes from tourism, property values/rent levels, and investment in tourism facilities and services.

As with the more general regional indicators, rates of change in the variables and comparative analysis are essential, perhaps internationally in addition to consideration at a national level. While reasonably accurate estimates of the first three can be obtained, as can some indication of employment and expenditure, the last two are in practice very different to determine.

Results

Some of these indicators have been used in the appraisal of regional development in Languedoc-Roussillon (see the special edition of the Bulletin Société Géographique Languedocienne, 1983), together with more qualitative indicators such as raising the standards of wine produced, greater diversification of agricultural and manufacturing output and infrastructural improvements, perhaps most notably in transport.

With regard to tourism the development can be counted a success in terms of the sheer size of the building programme implemented and from what Pearce (1981) describes as a 'technical point of view'. However, growth has not been as rapid as anticipated and the nature of the accommodation provided, with the accent on privately-owned apartments of a great variety of types, and the lack of facilities for more active pursuits has tended to narrow the market. Also the intermediaries involved in promoting the region have been rather slow in exploiting certain segments in the market, especially the off-season use of the resorts.

The statistics that are available show a growth in bed-nights, number of visitors (especially visitors from outside the region and from outside France), and a lengthening of the season. The programme has not appreciably reduced unemployment in the region as a whole, which continues to have one of the highest unemployment rates in France, in the face of higher than average increases in population. Regional incomes also remain substantially below the national average (L'INSEE, annually).

Most of the data collected is still concerned with 'head counting' so that there is a need for further and more detailed research in order to relate supply more closely to tourists' requirements and preferences. By 1980 it was estimated that investment by the commission, the mixed development boards, local authorities and the private sector was in excess of 6,100 million francs. The estimated employment generated by the development in 1980 was 30,000 permanent and 20,000 seasonal jobs in the sectors of direct tourism services, tertiary/quaternary services linked to tourism and construction/public works. Future development is likely to be at a slower pace as demand levels off and based mostly on the development of the existing resorts in the units south-west of Gruissan.

ASSESSMENT OF RESORT DEVELOPMENT

A review of the research literature on the region suggests, as indicated earlier in this chapter, that there are gaps in the analysis of the tourism development. In particular no attempt has been made to consider the individual stations or the five units of the coastal development within resort structure and evolution models as derived at

Groningen (Haan & Ashworth, 1985). Also more sophisticated approaches to the investigation of the patterns of tourist demand have not been applied. Yet these kinds of study may be more appropriate than 'blanket' methods to assess the success of the regional policy for tourism because they allow for much more heterogeneity on both the supply and demand sides.

The comparison of the existing resorts with the developmental models derived from experience from other coastal tourism regions was a major objective of the field programme. The data collected will allow potential surfaces to be constructed from elements of tourism supply, and this together with the behavioural information and the image analysis will permit such a comparison to be made.

Two main questions are raised:

(i) Does resort development sponsored by centralised intervention differ in essentials from that resulting from the spatial economic processes of the free market that have been used to power development models? A positive answer would necessitate modifying such models when they are applied to the many cases where intervention is an important element in development, while a negative answer casts doubt on the efficacy of such schemes in regulating the pre-existing processes. In either event the result is an assessment of an important aspect of the Mission.

(ii) To what extent does differentiation exist both between and within the tourist units at the level of the individual resort? Variations in the type of tourism infrastructure, the image appeal and thus characteristics of visitors and of their holiday behaviour would be revealed by such modelling techniques.

Although much of the definitive analysis is not yet completed, it is becoming clear that not only is there considerable variation between the resorts, but that the influence of the Mission has been substantially overestimated. Given the extensive and powerful propagandising resources of the central government agency, and the inevitably somewhat superficial reporting of many outsiders, this is in itself not surprising. An examination of development at the resort level reveals four important aspects that have been either ignored or underplayed in most of the literature.

First, considerable tourism development had already occurred on the coast of Languedoc-Roussillon before it captured the attention of the Mission. Considerable that is by the standards of the early 1960s, before the subsequent boom in mass tourism to the Mediterranean, and by comparison with stretches of coast other than the Cote D'Azur which can be regarded as exceptional. A number of the more accessible points between the étangs have a history of serving the holiday demands of the inland urban regions which stretches back into the nineteenth century, and which was reinforced by railway connections as at Grau du Roi, Palavas, and Narbonne Plage. The Mission was thus not operating upon a tabula rasa but was including in the schema resorts whose character and clientele were already clearly established.

Second, the Mission had no monopoly of commercial initiative nor was it able to regulate comprehensively the initiatives that originated from the lower local authorities. Narbonne Plage, being administratively a part of the commune of Narbonne, is an obvious example where development was initiated, planned and implemented at this scale. Equally there exists a long tradition of local investment and local development initiatives that have been important in shaping Palavas, Valras, Sete, Grau d'Agde and Grau du Roi both before and during the operation of the Mission.

Third, an investigation of the tempo of growth in the individual resorts reveals the existence of a momentum of development before 1963. Although considerable growth occurred after 1963, this was not at a noticeably faster tempo than in other western Mediterranean coastal regions where tourism was developing, which in turn poses the question of whether spontaneous growth would have occurred in any event, leaving the Mission with the function of channelling development between resorts, conserving green space between the units and in particular sponsoring the new developments at previously neglected sites, such as Port Camargue, Grande Motte, Cap d'Agde and to a large extent Gruissan.

Fourth, all three of the aspects raised above will tend to increase the degree of differentiation between resorts, as will accessibility both at the scale of distance from the main French market, determined in practice by spacing along the 'Languedocienne'/'Catalane' motorways, and more locally accessibility from the coast to the main road system which runs well inland and not between the resorts along the coast. Such differentiation will be both reflected and furthered by the projection of distinctive images.

CONCLUSIONS

Despite the more than 20 years' experience of operating the Languedoc coast tourism development programme, and the copious literature that has been produced during that period, it is clear that a number of important questions remain unanswered. In particular the question of central importance to the Groningen-Reading programme, concerning the efficacy of such large-scale, centrally conceived development plans, is difficult to answer definitively. The plan, even after such a time has elapsed, is not complete; the target capacities of a number of the stations have not yet been achieved, let alone the necessary maturity of the resorts.

The statistics referred to earlier give some indication of the regional economic consequences of the developments and thus its success in achieving its primary goal. The extent to which such changes would have occurred without the stimulation of the plan is impossible to estimate, as is the influence of external economic circumstances beyond the control of the regional planners, not least changes in tourism demand. In addition the extent to which tourists have been diverted from other destinations rather than 'new' tourists generated is unknown. Although diversion was one of the goals of the Mission, it is likely, given the rapid growth in holiday-making during the period of the project, that most of the demand is 'new'.

An assessment of the consequences at the resort level cannot fail to take note of the distinctive design and stylistic features of the 'green field' resorts. The effects upon land-use patterning, however, are expected to be much less radical. In particular the stress in the plan on the idea of 'tourist units', that is clusters of resorts separated by conserved landscapes, has little relevance to the resorts in terms of functional links, as they have evolved. There are however a number of functional relationships between resorts and the existing inland settlements which provide historical attractions, such as Aigues Mortes, and shopping and other services such as Montpellier, Narbonne, Bezier and Perpignan.

It is hoped that the results of the 1986 fieldwork will allow further investigation of both topics and thus permit the Languedoc-Roussillon experience of centralised planning for tourism to be effectively evaluated and its practical value as an example to other areas appreciated.

REFERENCES

Ardagh, J. (1982) France in the 1980's, Penguin, Harmondsworth, Middx
Bulletin de la Société Géographie Languedocienne (1983) Vol. 106 No.3/4, Montpellier
Centre Regionale Productivite et Etudes Economiques (1976) Tourisme et croissance Urbaine, 5 vols., Montpellier
Escudier, J.L. & Miossec, J.M. (1983) Aspects methodologique de l'économie spatiale touristique Bull. Soc. Lang. Geog., 106 (3/4), 539-69
Eurostat (annual) Yearbook of Regional Statistics
Ferras, R., Picheral, H. & Vielzeuf, B. (1979) Languedoc et Roussillon, Atlas et géographie de la France moderne, Flammarion, Paris
Haan, de T.Z. & Ashworth, G.J. (1985) Modelling the Seaside resort: Great Yarmouth UK, Field Studies series No. 9, Geographical Institute, University of Groningen
Les Collections de L'INSEE (1985) Statistiques et Indicateurs des Regions Francaises, Annex au projet de loi de France, Institut National de la Statistique et des études économiques, Paris
Murphy, P.E. (1985) Tourism: a community approach, Methuen, London
Pearce, D. (1981) Tourist Development, Longman, London
Racine, P. (1980) Le Mission Impossible, Midi Libre, Montpellier
Revue de Geographie de Lyon (1984) Panorama du Tourisme en France Vol. 59 (1/2)

Chapter 13

CHANGING TOURISM REQUIRES A DIFFERENT MANAGEMENT APPROACH

Martinus J. Kosters

The modern tourist has rejected organised temptations in a large way. Notwithstanding professional research and marketing studies, which suggested the opposite, the holiday-maker has gone his own way. The majority of the travel trade has resigned itself to this situation and tries to supply more or less partial tourism products instead of complete (or final) products.

National, regional and local governments are also involved in tourism, even more heavily than they may realise. Usually, they consider it is sufficient to subsidise the promotional activities of the respective tourism organisations. Yet there are so many changes currently taking place in tourism that such a passive attitude is inadequate. This causes problems for those governments that have to deal with tourism, without having a basic knowledge of the management of this increasing, economic activity.

No government can ignore its innovative role, and thus the management role, it has to play in tourism. When a customer is tired of a product, he looks for a new one. So, when a tourist is no longer satisfied with a given destination, he will look elsewhere and the original'destination has lost a client. The suppliers of tourism products are not always capable of adapting to a new market situation and need a strong, guiding hand to respond. Will the government respond and provide the guidance needed?

The changing economic tide makes it more difficult to intervene because of a general lack of investment capital in both public and private sectors. As a result plans for tourism projects and facilities are shelved or cancelled. It is difficult to predict to what extent this policy will 'queer its own pitch'. Even so, many governments continue to do no more than contribute to the promotion for tourism. They overlook the fact that promotion in tourism is a part of the marketing mix: product, price, promotion and distribution. In this chapter this situation of increasing tension is monitored and new directions suggested to alleviate it.

STATUS QUO

Although tourism in the world is increasing slowly, tourism of the traditional, Western industrial countries, like Great Britain, West Germany, Belgium, The Netherlands, and France is not growing significantly any longer. Here a situation exists which is characteristic of a saturation level. The holiday participation level seems to have stabilised at 65 per cent, the average holiday duration remains at two weeks and there are hardly any new big tourism projects being developed or under construction. The only encouraging fact in these countries is an upward trend in the number of holidays a year per holiday-maker.

What has not changed during the years after the Second World War is the self-made character of a tourism product. The majority of the tourists compose their holidays themselves, instead of buying a complete package. In the 1950s and 1960s the travel trade, however, expected a trend to more ready-made tourism products.

So, many new firms entered the tourism industry expecting to earn abnormal profits in a growth market. They expected a substantial and rapid increase in holiday participation based on a considerable increase in personal income and, therefore, a huge increase in the demand for tourism arrangements, especially complete tourism products, particularly to foreign destinations. In this growing market there was room for many newcomers as suppliers, but now that the market has stabilised, it cannot support all these firms. Only the stronger ones and the organisations with a strong management will be able to survive.

'DO-IT-YOURSELF'

Although tourism in the world is seen as a mass movement, the holiday is - and remains - a very individual product. The main objective of each holiday-maker is to do something - or not do something - in a completely different environment to their normal home and work environment and that implies - many people, many different minds. Therefore, it is very difficult to standardize a holiday as a total product. It is of course possible to provide some standards in travel to and accommodation in the popular destinations. But even then there are considerable financial benefits that attract consumers, rather than the qualitative aspects and the attraction of the product as such. The supply of ready-made holidays, when the consumer is 24 hours a day in the care of the producer, as for example during a sea cruise, is and will remain a very small share of the total tourism supply.

The majority of consumers prefer an individual programme, but people do accept recommendations of professional (tourism) organisations. These consumers travel en masse and often prefer to see many fellow tourists en route and in the destination. In a way, many tourists need each other to feel comfortable and gain added enjoyment.

There is an increasing demand for activity holidays: windsurfing, walking, sailing, cycling, watching animal life, fishing and so on. Again these are holidays which are frequently arranged by the individual participants. Compared to other countries Dutch holiday-makers prefer self-catering holidays. In the domestic tourism situation they use camping-sites, bungalow parks, apartments and marinas, but rarely hotels or pensions. People often want to behave like what the Dutch call, 'God in France': they do not like to accept rules, they prefer to do whatever they wish. Thus they like to break the daily rules they will accept when at home: during their holidays people go nude, men go unshaven, people frequently have sexual contacts with different partners, consume much more alcoholic drink than they would normally do, and so on. Therefore the question in more and more destinations is: how can we control the unco-ordinated mass of tourists who invade a village, a town, a region, a province, a country and who behave as they like, causing many problems besides providing income and work? A further question then arises: how to balance these aspects? What is acceptable and what is not and how far should we go in promoting tourism?

UNITY IN DIVERSITY

Tourism is not only a complexity of millions of people on their way to, returning from or staying in places away from their normal place of residence, who as a group form the demand side of the many suppliers of all kinds of services tourists need. No, tourism is something more. Let us compare it to the car industry. At the global scale there are only a few dozen car producers who make some hundreds of models of cars. Together they control the supply side. The thousands of sub-contractors are all dependent on the instructions of the few car producers. The final product is a ready-made car in a showroom. The government has hardly anything to do with such a production system: it only has to produce a good infrastructure of roads and public utilities. When a government wishes to get in contact with the car industry an invitation to a few producers is enough to reach them.

In tourism the situation is completely different: there are, depending on the size of the country, thousands, tens of thousands or even hundreds of thousands of suppliers of tourism services. Moreover, there are hardly any suppliers of final products as in the car industry. There are all kinds of interests: the various modes of transport, the travel trade, the accommodation and lodgings industry, the sector providing all kinds of attractions (e.g. from swimming pools to safari parks), the tourist destinations, the various groups of shopkeepers, banks, insurance companies, and the food and beverages sector. This is a complexity of suppliers who together form the tourism industry or the tourism sector. Even then the group of tourism promotional organisations, the architecture in a region or country, landscape and nature and even the language or climate have to be added.

These latter aspects belong to the heritage of a nation and normally the 'consumption' of these aspects is free of any charge, although they are in fact the core of the final tourism product. Thus, it may be claimed that the local, regional, provincial and national governments are fellow-producers of services in tourism: the government is the manager of the common property supplied to tourists. But the government is also the supplier of the various public utilities and the infrastructure in tourism. So, in tourism the

201

situation is very different from the car industry. Tourism is in fact a disorderly field of many firms and organisations, and also of the government who do not feel a strong, mutual dependency. There is a unity in diversity. In the best case there is some collaboration, but mostly there is no collaboration at all.

So, the government is involved in tourism. It is the manager of the various types of infrastructure, the landscape, nature, the villages and the towns, the waterways, the beaches, the forests, the mountains and many attractions like museums. Therefore we might expect a very close contact between the government and the private sector of the tourism industry, but that is not the case. Perhaps the main reason is that the authorities are very seldom suppliers of a part of the traded tourism products. The policy-makers do not have the feeling that they are actively involved in tourism as a commercial activity. They do not realise enough the essence of the tourism product and consider the private diverse industry responsible. In fact, this is a ridiculous situation: governments should be involved and interested, not only for political reasons, but also because of the particular character of tourism. It is hard to believe that many governments do not have any experts in tourism on their pay-roll! Perhaps the exceptions are to be found at the local level, because of the shorter lines of communication between government and the tourism industry at that spatial scale.

Missing policies

It is deplorable that governments of many European countries, and also of many municipalities, ignore their involvement in tourism. This is particularly so now that there is considerable unemployment in all European countries: there is hardly any government attempting to use tourism as a means to generate employment. Governments still act in the traditional way and try to attract new industries, the bigger the better.

But in tourism the majority of the suppliers are small-scale firms. It is a service industry spread throughout the various sectors of economic life. Where governments are involved in tourism they mostly confine their actions to giving financial help for the promotional activities of the tourism organisations and towards providing some facilities.

The question is whether promotion is still the right answer now that tourism is changing so rapidly in character, destinations and customers. In every economic sector the suppliers have to deal with the marketing variables mentioned before: product, price, promotion and the places of distribution of the products. This marketing principle also holds good for tourism. Why then should a government restrict itself to supporting promotion? Tourism needs a higher priority considering its economic impact and, therefore, governments or special councils should concentrate efforts on tourism in all its aspects. But as long as political parties neglect tourism as a relevant aspect of society, I doubt if we will make progress. As a result, many things in tourism will neither be improved nor optimalised. As scientists we therefore have a duty to act in this respect, namely to persuade the government that things have to be improved.

MANAGEMENT

Every company of any importance has a management structure with a related organisation scheme. There is an executive team which is responsible to the board of directors. The executive team is responsible for daily management, assisted by specialists and heads of departments. As a rule, there is a technical department and a commercial department. This model should serve as an example to be used in tourism.

In every country there is a cabinet and occasionally there is a special minister or under-secretary for tourism. Normally, tourism is only one of the many responsibilities a minister has: but that minister does then have some experts in tourism at his disposal.

The Netherlands has been fortunate in having two active under-secretaries for tourism for the last ten years. Tourism in The Netherlands is a responsibility of the Ministry of Economic Affairs. Until the end of the 1970s recreation was under the control of the Ministry of Culture, but today it is a part of the Ministry of Agriculture, Fisheries and Nature Conservation. At the Ministry of Economic Affairs there is a main section for tourism with a full-time staff of just six employees. Such a small staff is not a reflection of the economic importance of tourism in The Netherlands: if that were the case there would be an independent Ministry of Tourism, because tourism, recreation and leisure activities account for nearly 10 per cent of the national income. But the National Tourist Organisation (NTO) which acts as the national council for the promotion of tourism to The Netherlands and has 125 employees, is subsidised by this Ministry to the extent of over 70 per cent.

This main section for tourism of the Ministry of Economic Affairs has been very successful in developing policies for tourism in The Netherlands, compared with many other governments in Western European countries and their involvement in tourism. In the past this section invited the many representatives of the various sectors in tourism to feed them ideas for those tourism policies they wished to see implemented. The result was that two reports of the Ministry of Economic Affairs were issued which outlined the official views on tourism and the priorities for tourism at the national level (Ministerie van Economische Zaken, 1979 & 1984). Many ideas of the private sector were incorporated, but others were left out.

As a reaction to the first national note the twelve provinces started to produce official reports for tourism and recreation. The notes demonstrate the main views of the provincial governments concerning the further development of tourism and recreation: where there should be redevelopment, where improvements in infrastructure are necessary and where there is scope for new projects and developments. Although new projects have to be initiated by private industry, provincial governments are prepared to support special projects with subsidies to overcome the unprofitable slice of the operation when necessary.

Finally, the municipalities have now started, at their level, to produce official notes for tourism. In so far as tourism and recreation are important or needed at the local level, priorities for tourism are now being established. The result of this process is that in The Netherlands the knowledge of tourism in government bodies has increased and more experts in tourism are participating in the work of the governments at the respective levels. The approach to tourism has therefore improved considerably in the last ten years. The organisational structure of tourism in The Netherlands is summarised in Fig. 13.1. And yet we are not satisfied, because tourism requires even more professionalisation. So far the result has been that the involvement of the official bodies in tourism has moved from the 'obligatory' subsidy for promotional activities to a more fundamental approach in co-operation with the various commercial tourism sectors. Governments must acknowledge more responsibility for tourism products and be more critical of the benefits of promotional activities in tourism.

Creative management

Developments in every market are dynamic. The demand is continually changing and requires creative action on the part of the many suppliers. If a given destination wants to stay in the market, then at least it is necessary that the local industry and local government enlist assistance from experts in tourism and marketing research. Then they will be able to learn how to reshape their products or how to react to new market opportunities. For example: in a given resort there may be excellent accommodation but in the long run there is a fair chance that this destination will not survive in the tourism market if there is no organisation providing entertainment for holiday-makers.

This is now acknowledged by tourism agencies who have learned from research that a tourist considers his holiday or his trip as a complete product and, therefore, that the many suppliers should co-operate in their production of services. Destination agencies will then be able to monitor the many changes in the market and the changes in consumer tastes. As a result it will then become clear that two resorts need not compete so severely if they specialise in different market segments, which means different social groups. To achieve such a course of action, professional expertise and management is needed.

The traditional tourism organisations, specialising in tourist information and promotion, should be converted into professional market organisations with a flexible and creative management. Governments should encourage this, because official bodies and governmental organisations are not the best possible form of

Figure 13.1: Organisational structure of the tourism industry in The Netherlands

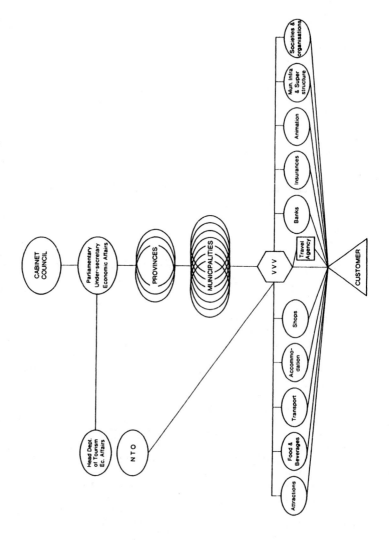

206

central tourism management. A private tourism organisation is better equipped and can take on such a new role in addition to the old one, although 'fresh' and skilled managers in tourism would need to be employed by even these organisations.

MARKETING

It is encouraging that marketing techniques are increasingly common in parts of the tourism industry, particularly in the transport and hotel sectors. In resorts there is now much more attention paid to factors like product and price, besides promotion. The distribution of information is also being considered more carefully than ever before. Yet, the real key to success is professional management that uses the right marketing techniques and stipulates the policies to be adhered to. Unfortunately, too few suppliers of tourism services are aware of their place within the total product and this mitigates against effective marketing on their part.

A client does not come to Bournemouth, Scheveningen, or any similar resort just because of the excellent hotel room, he comes for the nice atmosphere in the town, the clean beaches, the competitive prices as well as for the good bed. Permanent marketing activities on a professional scale will teach the many suppliers how important it is to collaborate with each other. It will then be possible to finance adequately management and marketing activities. It is important that the respective governments join these activities, but on the understanding that the private trade does not expect the government to pay the bill.

All resorts should develop strategies for the special target groups they want to reach. The clearer each tourist destination is, in this respect, the better the consumers will understand the promotion messages. To obtain such results is a matter of professional management. When the management knows which goals have to be attained, it can work well towards them and it is also much easier to keep in close contact with the market. In fact, promotion for tourism will then become a different and more effective way of marketing than it is today in the majority of cases. Currently promotion is often too general and destinations do not promote themselves in distinctive ways. There is too little differentiation because there is a lack of market information. This implies, in fact, that today much promotion is a waste of both money and effort: a professional approach would achieve better results, and cost, most likely, less money.

In order to improve the tourism performance in many places the remedy is therefore very simple: co-operation between the many suppliers, the adoption of professional management in a re-organised tourism organisation with the backing of the respective governments and the use of the right marketing techniques. It sounds very easy, but it is very difficult in practice. Yet, there are excellent examples: for instance, the rural village of Norddeich in northern Germany. This village has a small harbour from which the ferries sail to the German Kurort and island of Noderney. In Norddeich the residents saw the many holiday-makers passing through, but they did not make money out of these tourists. Then a manager was appointed to develop the ideas described above. With the help of the local government he saw to it that everybody who could make some money out of a tourist would pay a small percentage of his turnover to the tourism organisation, whether he was a grocer, a hotelier or a doctor. A sound financial basis for tourism marketing was therefore established. Within ten years the whole economy of Norddeich changed. The manager stimulated farmers to provide camping facilities for tourists and encouraged other inhabitants to start bed and breakfast ventures. With the backing of the municipality he laid out a sandy beach on the sea side of the dike and added some catering facilities: later on he built a complete swimming pool there and another indoor, heated, ultra-modern swimming pool in the village, along with bungalow parks, camping sites, a leisure centre where children and adults can meet each other and where they can do something creative, and, finally, he introduced sports facilities for guests. People now come from all over Germany, because he has created facilities for an existing (latent) market. As a result of marketing research it was found that the German North Sea islands were rather exclusive and expensive, so, there was a lack of facilities in Germany for the less prosperous Germans who wanted to go to the coast! Further examples can be found in the Austrian Tirol.

Strength-weakness analysis

In the future, more than in the past, the quality of tourism products should be better related to prices. Every supplier should be better informed of the strengths and weaknesses of his part in the chain of tourism products. With a bird's eye view every supplier is able to attune better to the total product. A strength-weakness analysis is possible when the suppliers of tourism services and the government are co-operating well and join forces in a professional tourism organisation. After such an analysis the conclusion may be that certain sub-products in a destination should be improved in quality in order to maintain their attraction to their target groups; or that marketing activities should be aimed at other groups of tourists, because a place is losing its attraction to the traditional clients and it should be rebuilt in order to reach new target groups with better prospects.

An example of such an approach is the seaside resort of Scheveningen in The Netherlands. It is one of the very first examples of a resort where obsolescent accommodation was pulled down and renewed on a large scale as a result of marketing studies and a sound belief in the product life cycle of a destination. It should be clear that this was a very radical process and could only be done by the very enthusiastic involvement of the municipality in co-operation with the various local suppliers. The result is a 'reborn' seaside resort with a fresh character and new spirit that attracts new groups of tourists. And what a success!

But before that stage is reached, much work has to be done, of which the strength-weakness analysis is the basis, and a professional management team, with a skilled and modern organisation, has to be established.

The tourism organisation as a wholesaler?

The process of professionalisation of the Dutch local tourism organisations was accomplished differently from that described above. There was a belief that to improve market results, local and regional tourism organisations should offer facilities for central bookings and for complete holiday arrangements. Some tourism organisations obtained excellent results with central booking systems for accommodation. In that way they competed with travel agencies, who traditionally were very passive in the domestic market.

When destination area tourism organisations also started to organise the arrangements for trips and holidays to their destinations and to sell these products directly to the consumers, the travel agents were furious. They forced the tourism organisations to deal with them, accusing them of unfair competition. The tourism organisations are subsidised by their respective municipal/provincial governments and, in fact, act as private companies. Although this is true, it was surprising that the travel trade - both agencies and tour operators - who hardly produce any services for domestic tourism, complained when the tourism organisations filled a gap in the market.

The question remains: is it correct for a tourism organisation to produce tourism products? Traditionally, the tourism organisations are places for information for tourists and they are the producers of tourism promotion. Because many tourism organisations were too weak to be reorganised in the way outlined in this chapter, they took their chance at an easier level in the hope of increasing their grip on the tourism industry. Although it was a success in a more practical sense in the short run, in the long run it may not be so certain, because the reaction to the developments was not fundamental enough.

With some new facilities for bookings and offers of organised holidays different groups will be attracted to the destination. The question is whether these new groups of clients are accepted by the host population, or not. It cannot be denied that for some tourism organisations these new services helped them raise funds in order to survive. To that limited extent they were, and are, successful. But to be successful in the long run the experts believe that tourism organisations should be further reorganised into central marketing organisations with a strong professional management and expertise. This is a process of blood, sweat and tears and will take years and years. However, it is recognised as the only, modern way to approach tourism promotion. Success will depend on the local situation. Where successful, it is also possible that tourism organisations will offer services for central bookings and will also sell holiday packages. But then it is a result of a marketing-research process and a conscious choice and not a form of defence to survive.

CHANGING ORGANISATIONS

It has been stressed in this chapter that success in tourism is associated with professionalism in tourism management and expertise. These two functions can be self-financing only when the organisation has been improved. In The Netherlands this process has begun because the national government has laid down in two reports (Ministerie van Economische Zaken, 1979 & 1984) what the national policies are. Then followed the provincial government and after them the municipalities with their respective views. These views provided a much-needed clarification. To date the result has been an increase in employment in tourism. Moreover, government investment in tourism is a relatively cheap investment to decrease unemployment, because of the big share of labour, compared with capital, in a tourism product. So, to decrease unemployment in a country, tourism is a good investment (depending on country, region, or place) and when tourism is improved, the economic structure of the country is also improved. Of course, there are limits, you cannot continue investing in tourism indefinitely. But for the 1980s, and perhaps for the 1990s, it appears a good policy.

It is also important to ask in what ways will tourism organisations in other Western European countries reorganise themselves. They are able to do so only, when and if their respective governments give support and even then they are still dependent on the co-operation of the many suppliers in the private sector. But there is a tendency elsewhere to adopt the directions described here and similar schemes to those presented here. The tourism organisation in a destination remains the central institution for priming the market and monitoring both the quality of the product and the competitiveness of prices in relation to the products in its own destination and in relation to developments elsewhere. The tourism organisation is also responsible for the joint promotion of the destination, but only after a very intensive process of marketing development. This process indicates which type of promotion for which

Tourism requires different Management

groups, to what extent and in which places is needed for a resort, a region or a country.

REFERENCES

Ministerie van Economische Zaken (Ministry of Economic Affairs) (1979) <u>Nota Toeristisch Beleid</u>, Staatsuitgeverij, Den Haag
Ministerie van Economische Zaken (Ministry of Economic Affairs) (1984) <u>Nota Toeristisch Beleid</u>, Staatsuitgeverij, Den Haag

Chapter 14

TOURIST IMAGES: MARKETING CONSIDERATIONS

Gregory Ashworth and Brian Goodall

COMPETITION IN THE TOURISM INDUSTRY

Tourism is a growth industry, and holiday-taking is an established habit. The long-term trend is for the number of domestic and international tourists to increase and the prospect for tourist destination areas, whether countries, regions or resorts, seems set fair. However, the competition to entice potential tourists to take a particular type of holiday or visit a particular destination is intense.

The capacity to produce tourism products and services, that is the holiday package, must be established ahead of the time the holiday-maker arrives at the destination. Having invested in the necessary infrastructure and facilities it is essential from the viewpoint of the tourism organisations in the destination region, both public and private sector, that a steady flow of tourists is received. However, the marketing of tourist destinations differs in some important respects from the marketing of other goods and services, and an awareness of these differences is important in a successful promotion of the images of tourist places. It can be argued that the impossibility of storing, transporting and transferring the tourism product, which must be consumed at the moment and point of production or be wasted, and consequently the short-term inflexibility of tourism production in terms of the nature, quantity, and place of production, renders a matching of supply and demand more critical, and thus marketing to achieve such a match more important. Although this simple point is well taken and justifies relatively high promotional expenditure by tourism producers, the tourism industry shares these characteristics with many other place-bound services in the public and private sectors.

213

Tourism products, especially within a given holiday type such as 'sun, sea and sand' or winter skiing, are relatively substitutable. Destination areas must therefore compete in the market place for customers: broadcasting their ability to satisfy the holiday requirements of potential tourists. This is done by generating and transmitting a 'favourable' image to which the potential tourist is exposed in his or her home region. However, in terms of image promotion the most troublesome characteristic of tourism is the difficulty of defining both product and customer, and clearly the successful promotion of destination images presupposes a knowledge of what precisely is to be promoted and to whom. The fact that many promotion campaigns in this field have neglected these questions, perhaps because they are difficult to answer, explains the abundance of vague, generalised, and thus ineffective geographical marketing of which there are too many examples, e.g. the northern Netherlands (Veen & Voogd, 1987). This search for definition on both the supply and demand sides should not be dismissed as an obsessive academic pursuit of unnecessary abstractions, even though too much research effort in tourism has sought taxonomic classifications for their own sake rather than for their explanatory value. Ashworth and de Haan (1986a) have argued explicitly against these approaches, and more broadly the theme of this book is an implicit criticism of attempts to isolate and define either the tourism facility or the tourist except in relation to each other.

The destination images may be conveyed directly to the potential tourists' home regions by advertising and by establishing tourism information offices. This often occurs where a government organisation represents the tourism interests of the destination area; for example, the work of the British Tourist Authority abroad which is essentially a 'come to Britain' campaign extolling the virtues of a wide range of places and of holiday activities throughout the country. Whilst such activity contributes to the information available to potential tourists it is not usually presented in the form of a purchasable holiday package. The destination area's viewpoint therefore does not hold centre stage in the tourist-generating region and the image it projects is not the critical one in the tourist's holiday choice. It is the holiday that is marketed, not

the image of the destination area.
The significant element underpinning effective marketing of holidays is the structure of the commercial tourism industry. Marketing is via a distribution system whose functions are (i) to make information available to the right people at the right time and in the right place to allow a holiday purchase decision to be made, and (ii) to provide a means whereby the consumer can book and pay for the holiday (Mill & Morrison, 1985). Thus it is distribution, primarily a private sector activity in the case of tourism, which bridges the gap between the supply of and demand for holidays. To do this the tourism industry depends, much more than in other industries, on sales intermediaries, tour operators in particular, who package complementary tourism services (travel, accommodation, excursions, etc.) into inclusive tours designed to satisfy the tourist's need for a holiday experience. These holidays are promoted in a brochure and sold through retail travel agents. Competition between tour operators, not between destination areas, is the most significant aspect of the market in tourist-generating regions. Any competition between destination areas is subsumed into the competition between tour operators.

Tour operators are the front-line organisations, the risk-takers, but competition between them is not just on the basis of what destination areas have to offer. Since many tour operators offer holidays to the same destination areas, competition reflects other aspects of their service as well, such as price. Moreover, whilst tour operators do compete in respect of the range of holiday destinations they each offer, a tour operator's allegiance to any particular destination is tenuous - it holds only so long as it is sufficiently profitable!

Thus there exists a dichotomy in tourism marketing. On the one hand there is the promotion of destination areas by indigenous tourism organisations, emphasizing the attractions of the destination area rather than particular holiday packages per se. On the other hand there is the promotion of holiday opportunities by tour operators who advertise widely the holiday packages they offer. The latter have a clearly defined market - the final consumers - but questions must be raised as to the appropriate market towards which the promotional activites of destination area tourism organisations should be directed in the

Tourist Images: Marketing Considerations

tourist-generating regions. Is it the general public in such regions at whom the promotion should be targeted? Or is it more important to convince the tour operators and other tourism sales intermediaries that a given destination area is a desirable location for a holiday package to be sold by the tour operator?

IMAGES AND MARKETING

The central importance of images in the bringing together of the tourist destination and the potential tourist has been mentioned a number of times in the preceding chapters. Stabler (Chp. 9) has tried to introduce hedonic pricing into economic demand models, both Ashworth (Chp. 10) and Brown (Chp. 11) are concerned with the translation of the facilities of the tourist resort, of one sort or another, into a marketable product, while Buck (Chp. 4), Bowes (Chp. 5) and Kosters (Chp. 13) investigate details of the operation of such markets. All these are partial analyses in that aspects of a much more comprehensive model are being applied to part of the tourism system.

The theme of this book as a whole is anchored firmly in the idea of the promotion of destination regions, and thus the three related, but not synonymous, processes of place image creation, place promotion and place marketing are seen as the essential links matching the tourism product and the tourist experience - the holiday and the individual. The importance of this synthesis in providing coherence in an otherwise highly disparate topic deserves closer attention. Previous attempts to find a workable integrative structure for the understanding of tourism have borrowed explanatory frameworks from economic analysis (Lundberg, 1976), the psychology of needs (Smith, 1977) and even the sociology of group behaviour (Cohen, 1979). The integrative structure of this book is similarly borrowed, in this case from marketing science, in which a set of concepts are combined in a philosophy that includes, but is more than, a procedural technique of organisation and planning. In the same way that the success, or otherwise, of previous approaches has depended to a large extent upon an understanding of their basic concepts as a necessary preliminary to an application of the procedures they generate to a new situation, so also does a successful use of

216

marketing techniques in tourism presuppose a
redefinition of some of its basic elements in the
light of this new approach.

If marketing is the 'continuous and permanent
orientation of the production process to the needs
of consumers as expressed through market
transactions' (Kotler, 1986), then tourism supply,
broadly interpreted to include the entire packet of
facilities, whether ostensibly produced for tourism
or not, becomes the product, and the tourist, the
customer. The translation of such ideas from the
selling of physical products by commercial firms
for short-term profit, to the tourism market where
the product is frequently a service, or even less
tangibly an experience, and the firm often a public
enterprise with long-term and welfare objectives,
was made possible by the development of four
concepts in the course of the 1970s, viz. 'social
marketing', where the objective is to influence
behaviour other than purely consumer behaviour;
'socially responsible marketing', where the longer
term interests of the customers, or society as a
whole, are built into the notion of profit; 'non-
business marketing', for organisations with public
responsibilities; and 'image marketing', where
images are sold without direct reference to
particular physical products. The four concepts
combined make possible the idea of 'place' or
'geographical marketing' (Ashworth & Voogd, 1986)
and thus underpin the concept of tourist
destination images and the process of tourism
destination promotion.

The content of the tourist destination image
is necessarily diffuse but need be neither vague
nor contradictory. In Chapter 10 the historic city
was considered as a marketable product where
buildings, solid physical objects created for many
different purposes, were transformed into
'heritage' an idea compounded of many different
emotions, including nostalgia, romanticism,
aesthetic pleasure, and a sense of belonging in
time and space. There is no contradiction here
implicit in the promotion of ideas through physical
objects (any motor car salesman does the same) but
unlike many products the city is multi-sold. The
same city is sold to many different customers for
different uses, by means of different images. Nor
is the problem solvable, as has been pointed out in
Norwich, by market segmentation in a physical
sense, as the historic city is principally a way of
viewing the urban experience as a whole, not a

physically delimited district that can be
separately packaged. The same difficulties apply
in all tourist destinations that are not mono-
functional, including seaside resorts, rural
tourist areas, and large metropolitan cities.

The multi-functional nature of the tourist
destination is paralleled on the demand side by the
multi-motivated consumer. It just is not possible
to segment potential customers into large
homogeneous groups to which labels such as
'tourist', 'resident', 'business visitor',
'excursionist' and the like can be attached. The
pursuit of this chimera, which has occupied the
attentions of many researchers, contributes no
useful definition of target groups to marketing.
The users of the destination facilities are varied
and recreation or tourism are motives of the
moment, defining the potential customer at that
point in time alone. This phenomenon of the multi-
motivated user may be more or less self-evident in
the multi-functional city, but even in a set of
tourist destinations specifically developed for
recreation such as the Languedoc coast resorts, it
is clear that the user is far more heterogeneous
than the simple designation 'tourist' implies
(Ashworth & de Haan, 1987). To whom then should
the image be promoted, or, using marketing
terminology: can target groups of potential
customers be identified and which image should be
promoted to which segment of the market?

THE MARKETING DIMENSION

Tourists need information about destinations
so they can make a choice. Herein lie the
opportunities for promotion by the tourism
industry. Marketing seeks to identify potential
customers' desires; to meet those desires from
existing or newly-developed resources; to
communicate to the customers, directly or
indirectly, the attraction of the product; to
facilitate purchase; and to secure satisfaction for
the consumer (O'Driscoll, 1985). Successful
marketing requires that the product is tailored to
accurately identified patterns of demand.
Marketing is therefore a process of communication
between buyer and seller: its goal in the case of
tourism promotion being the modification of
tourists' behaviour - namely, to persuade the
potential tourist to make a holiday purchase where

none was made before; to induce a change in holiday behaviour by getting the tourist to purchase a different destination or type of holiday; or to reinforce the tourist's existing behaviour by maintaining the purchase of a given holiday 'brand' (Mill & Morrison, 1985). How does the tourism industry set about changing the images potential tourists hold of a destination in order to increase the likelihood of those persons visiting that destination?

Marketing activity in the tourism industry

The tourism product - the holiday - is an amalgam of several products and services, the individual components of which are usually supplied by different firms. Potential tourists may be vague about the destination for their coming year's holiday and from the marketing viewpoint the problem is one of establishing a particular destination as a unique place offering particular benefits to satisfy the tourist's needs. Various organisations within the tourism industry will be involved in that part of the marketing process which is designed to make available information on destinations and holidays, that is, to create the producer or 'supply image'. Indeed the organisational structure of the tourism industry introduces certain peculiarities in the promotion of tourist destination images as compared to the usual marketing model that was developed for the selling of goods and services by profit-making private companies in which the entire marketing procedure was under the organisational control of the firm. The marketing of tourist destination images involves not only the promoters of the products of a large number of quite different producers, whose individual share in the total package may be small (as Brown has stressed in Chp. 11) but frequently also an institutional hiatus between those responsible for production and for promotion.

Most production of tourist accommodation and catering is performed by private companies, or in the case of much tourist travel, especially inclusive tours, by publicly-owned companies or their subsidiaries that act in much the same way as private concerns. Promotion, especially generalised place promotion, however, is usually the responsibility of local authorities, or public and semi-public bodies such as regional or national tourist boards. In this respect tourism is almost unique. Those promoting tourist destinations are not responsible for the management of the services they are marketing, and only indirectly profit from the success of the promotion. Conversely those engaged in the commercial provision of the tourism product in the destination area are generally too small and too distant to appreciably influence the nature of the promotion of that product, which is likely to be highly generalised.

Tourist boards and similar destination organisations aim their promotional activities at both the potential tourist and the travel trade. In the tourist's home country their media advertising highlights attractions of the destination area and indicates the existence of a national tourist office or agency. Such offices provide information and advice to personal callers and in answer to postal enquiries, as well as offering illustrated talks to voluntary societies and clubs. Most important, however, is the approach tourist boards make to the private sector travel trade. This involves various promotional activities, for example, tourism workshops and familiarisation visits designed to acquaint tour operators and travel agents with the destination's tourism products. If successful the outcome is the inclusion of holidays to that destination in a tour operator's brochure. Destination area tourism organisations also play an 'at-home' promotional role once tourists have arrived by providing information on forthcoming events and persuading visitors to participate in additional activities.

However, few destination area tourism organisations directly market holidays in tourist-generating countries. The latter is normally undertaken by tour operators whose base, more often than not, is in the generating country and who use a variety of advertising media. Their advertising message concentrates on the availability of the tour operators' brochures and may indicate any 'special offers' available but (other than for direct-sell tour operators) travel agents are involved in the distribution of the brochures. The travel agent frequently provides the initial point of contact between the trade and the potential tourist and where the latter is unsure of the possibilities (i.e. the opportunity set) the agent may be instrumental in conditioning the tourist's images of destination areas.

The contrast has been drawn between market-orientated management philosophies and practices, and those which are best described in a Weberian sense as bureaucratic, i.e. governed by norms intrinsic to the organisation itself, by Ashworth (Chp. 10) from empirical studies of the operation of public sector tourism management, and is implicit in the contrasting approaches of Buck (Chp. 4) and Bowes (Chp. 5). The point being stressed here is not that one or other of these two approaches is more suitable for tourism management but that the marketing of tourist destinations has the intrinsic difficulty of accommodating both.

In marketing as a planning procedure, promotion is of course only a single stage, dependent upon the adequate completion of preceding stages, including the identification of the product and its 'positioning' in relation to competing products (Dietvorst, 1981 writes of 'geographical positioning'), the identification of the target consumer groups and the resulting 'segmentation' of the market, and the 'auditing' that relates the market situation as revealed to the producing organisation (Ashworth & Voogd, 1987). Promotion can then be seen as one aspect of the 'marketing mix', instigated at this point in the 'marketing plan'. If promotion is defined as the presentation of information about the product to potential consumers, in such a way that actual consumption is achieved, then the image of the product, in this case the tourist destination, or more precisely the destination as a location of the particular tourist experience desired by customers, is obviously important.

It is useful therefore to distinguish between the three different aspects of the use of such images in promotion, viz. their creation or projection, their transmission and their reception, each of which, despite their obvious functional links, is controlled by a separate set of variables and thus needs a separate analysis.

IMAGE PROJECTION

Tourist destination images created and projected by tourism agencies, at various spatial scales, have been investigated by a number of researchers (such as Dann 1976; Crompton 1979) and form a part of a line of geographical investigation into place perception which has a 20-year pedigree.

221

Three main problem areas emerge from such research. The most important is that the images projected by the destination agencies, what can be termed the 'official' image, are not the most important source of ideas about the tourist destinations held by the potential visitor, indeed in quantitative terms it may be relatively insignificant. The images shaped by the news media, by the personal experience of the visitor on previous holidays and by the second-hand experiences of personal contacts of the potential visitors, have emerged in many studies as far more important than the publicity emanating from the tourist destination itself. This need be no disadvantage as long as there is no serious conflict between sources, but in practice much official (destination-area) tourism promotion is 'defensive', that is endeavouring to correct or counterbalance images obtained elsewhere.

A second difficulty concerns the selection of elements in the image and its relationship to the more fundamental goals of the marketing exercise. The effectiveness of a destination image is dependent upon the ease of its recognition and its conformity to the predisposition of the recipient. Clarity, simplicity and a minimum of dissonance with pre-existing prejudices are the essence of success. The objectives of the marketing exercise, however, may determine that image promotion be used as an instrument for encouraging the tourism industry in new directions, rather than merely reinforcing existing patterns. The place images needed for 'selective demarketing', 'remarketing', 'stimulational marketing' and many other forms of marketing will be far less immediately acceptable. The Norwich dilemma, to refer to one example of many (Berkers, et.al., 1986), is whether to project the simple recognisable and expected image based on the three most well-known symbols of the historic city, or to project the less acceptable and more complex image of a spatially and functionally more varied tourist destination and thus further the deconcentration and diversification aims of the city's planning policies.

A third general problem is that of conflict, or at best a lack of complementarity, between images projected by different destinations in the same region, and even on occasion between images for the same destinations projected by different agencies. One variant of this problem is that of spatial scale, when, as is usual in tourism

marketing, different authorities are responsible for the tourist images at national, regional and local levels.
Finally those creating all product marketing images must make a choice between the specific and the general. The former runs the risk of creating a gap between the promise and the reality, quickly discovered when the tourists' expectations are not met. Although it has never been quantified, the idea that tourism services generate a higher than average level of complaint and thus customer dissatisfaction can be attributed in part to this. The alternative, and safer option is to project an image so generalised as to fail to differentiate the destination being promoted from many others offering the same broad package of experiences.

IMAGE TRANSMISSION

Once an image of the destination region has been created by the relevant tourism authorities it must be successfully transmitted to potential tourists through whatever media are appropriate. It is curious that far less attention is generally paid to this stage in the process compared with image creation, and the monitoring of the effectiveness of transmission is frequently neglected. Yet it is precisely during this stage that the 'official' desired images have to compete for the attention of recipients with the so-called 'noise' or message interference from the other sources of information and ideas.
Obviously tourists need information before they can choose a holiday and they obtain information, by external search, from both formal and informal sources, i.e. commercial and social environments, and which go beyond the marketing information provided by the tourism industry itself. The industry will always have to contend with the fact that tourists' images, particularly naive images of destinations, are also conditioned by other information and experiences. Even for information directly associated with holiday opportunities, the industry's marketing message will be in competition with information tourists receive from their social environment, e.g. opinions and actions of friends, relatives and peer reference groups. Tourism organisations therefore need to ensure that their marketing message, targeted at potential tourists, contains the type

and quality of information the tourist can readily absorb (Mill & Morrison, 1985).

The promotional message must be distinctive, yet easily understood and believable, whether conveyed to the target audience by advertising, publicity, sales promotion or personal selling. To reach the travel trade destination-based tourism organisations use advertising in the trade press, distribute publicity materials (newsletters, information manuals), promote sales via participation in trade shows and personal selling via familiarisation visits. To reach the potential tourists both destination area organisations and tour operators use general media advertising (newspapers, television, etc.) as well as travel posters, distribute publicity material largely in the form of brochures, promote sales by contributing to travel exhibitions open to the public, and emphasize personal selling via enquiry and information services, including travel agencies. Advertising, especially in newspapers and magazines, accounts for over half of the industry's promotional expenditure and most of the 'consumer literature' (i.e. the brochures) which provide the basis of sales support is published by tour operators (Schmoll, 1977).

The marketing message seeks to convince potential tourists of the desirability of a particular tourism product or destination by creating a supply image which is positive in terms of quality, price, distinctiveness and availability. These elements are building blocks or inputs, termed significative stimuli (Mill & Morrison, 1985), of the marketing message. Various 'technical' ploys are used to communicate the message effectively. For example, in advertising holidays large advertisements give an impression of quality (because size is often equated with quality and the larger the tour operator, hotel or cruise liner the better the service is perceived to be). Similarly the use of colour in advertisements attracts more attention than black and white. Intensity, movement, position, contrast and isolation are further factors contributing to effective advertising (Mill & Morrison, 1985).

The image transmitted for any destination area also relates to the distance(s) separating it from tourist-generating areas. The domestic tourist living in south-east England may perceive clearly the difference between London's West End and the City but not so the potential visitor from, say,

Australia. Wherever the tourism industry is able to recognise similarities and differences between tourist-generating areas the opportunity exists for collaborative marketing by destinations in some markets whilst maintaining individual promotion in others (Hunt, 1975). Thus tourist resorts and regions in Great Britain may combine to promote 'Britain' in the North American market but within the country individual seaside resorts market themselves independently. Furthermore the image projected of a given destination could vary between tourist-generating areas in which it is marketed, as with the marketing of Britain in Australia on the basis of kinship and historical ties but in The Netherlands on the basis of its physical and scenic diversity. Therefore different markets may be allocated different proportions of the destination area's promotional budget.

Research into the transmission of tourist destination images has stressed two particular difficulties. First, a very large proportion of the publicity effort is only accessible to tourists after most of the fundamental choices about holiday destinations have been made. It is much easier to transmit information within the originating town or region than in the place of residence of the potential visitor. Potential visitors to any one holiday destination are widely spread through their home regions which renders it all but impossible to convey more than a highly generalised national or regional image to the undifferentiated general public or even to selected target groups within that potential market. Most official publicity is only in practice available after the important decisions, such as the taking of a holiday, the choice of timing, length, accommodation type, country and probably region, have already been made. It is available on request directly or through distributing agents and thus serves principally to confirm existing expectations and influences only details of holiday behaviour within the chosen destination.

Secondly the effectiveness of the transmission even to actual visitors is low. For example research in the important tourist-historic city of Norwich on the role of the Tourist Information Centre (TIC) as a means of transmitting information to existing visitors revealed that only 16 per cent of all visitors made any use of its services during their visit, despite the fact that it was located close to the main tourist attractions, and offered a wide range of information services, largely free of charge (Ashworth & de Haan, 1986b). The effectiveness of TICs varies according to a range of visitor variables with use being positively influenced by length of stay, lack of previous visits to the city and distance travelled, but it is equally clear that only a minority of all types of visitors are being successfully reached by this medium. Similar work on the use of printed publicity information has revealed its low level of effectiveness in tourist destinations as far apart as East Anglia (Ashworth & de Haan, 1986b) and Languedoc (Chp. 9; Ashworth & de Haan, 1987). In both these cases only a minority, and generally a very small minority, of visitors of all types makes any use of printed publicity information distributed through the local tourist authorities (8 per cent in Norwich and 2 per cent in Languedoc). Non-official guide book information, such as that published by motoring organisations or commercial publishers, is used by a similarly small minority of visitors, either before or during the visit (9 per cent in East Anglia and 15 per cent in Languedoc). Such use as is made of the printed information sources declines rapidly with familiarity with the place, region and country.

Thus the official tourism authorities and also independent commentators on the tourist destination are in practice rated well below the experience of the visitor himself, although the experiences of acquaintances, which as Buck (Chp. 4) has pointed out could include commercial travel specialists in the region of residence, can be influential. This in turn has implications for the use of promotion as a means of managing the market and influencing tourist behaviour within the destination region itself. The low effectiveness of transmission determines that tourist images projected by the tourism authorities can frequently do little more than confirm and reinforce the existing expectations of the existing market, and attempts to use such images as a planning instrument for managing future tourist behaviour in destination regions or develop new market segments is likely to be extremely difficult.

Marketing strategies

Since the product sought by the potential tourist can be satisfied by any number of destinations, the marketing effort of the tourism industry requires a guiding philosophy or orientation (Mill & Morrison, 1985). Several orientations are possible but not all are equally effective. Destination areas are often guided by product orientation which highlights the products and services available, such as the areas' physical, historical and cultural resources. However, where many destinations compete for the same tourists the emphasis is on a selling orientation: what is available for sale in the area. Both product and selling orientations are firmly rooted in supply side considerations. A further development adopts a demand orientation where the requirements of the tourists are given highest priority and the destination area seeks to provide services to meet those requirements. But to aim solely at satisfying the needs of tourists implies certain risks for the host community.

Since tourism demand is heterogeneous market segmentation, the process by which groups with similar requirements are targeted is an accepted strategy. Segmentation is possible because:

(i)   Each group has distinctive needs and preferences;
(ii)   Each group's members have similar socio-demographic characteristics;
(iii)   Certain products will appeal to some segments of the market more than to other segments;
(iv)   Tourism firms can improve the effectiveness of their marketing by developing specific products to cater for specific market segments.

Market segmentation can be based on socio-economic variables, e.g. age or life-style segmentation as with the 'Golden Oldies' (over-50s), the 18-30 years age group, and school parties; on product-related variables, e.g. cruising, adventure holidays, and self-catering accommodation; and on geographic variables, e.g. concentration on a given set of destinations such as long-haul or a specific country.

The product life cyle - a concept based on the development of total demand for a product over the lifetime of that product - can be applied to destination marketing and will serve as an additional guide to targeting markets. The early stages of the product life cycle correspond to the introduction and adoption of a new product, in this case a new destination when the potential tourists know little or nothing about the opportunity. Marketing's primary role at this stage is to inform tourists of the existence of the opportunity. With the growth phase of the product life cycle marketing's role is to persuade more tourists to purchase a holiday in a given destination rather than in one of an increasing number of destinations offering similar holidays. During the maturity stage of the cycle, when demand has reached its saturation level, marketing needs to remind tourists to continue to purchase a holiday in a particular destination (rather than turn to alternative destinations and alternative types of holidays). The responses of potential tourists to marketing messages will depend upon whether the supply side tourist image of the destination and the holiday match up to the demand side tourist image(s).

IMAGE RECEPTION

The final stage in the promotion of the destination images is their reception by the intended target groups. Research into the place images actually held by holiday-makers can in the first instance focus upon the nature and consistency of these images themselves and relate variations to particular characteristics of visitors. The central importance of such image formation in the whole process of geographical marketing necessitates subsequently that such images be compared with both those projected by the tourism agencies, thus monitoring the effectiveness of transmission, and with the existing supply packet on offer in the places concerned, as well as the use made of these facilities in the actual activities of visitors.

Marketing seeks to ensure potential tourists are exposed to information on destinations and holiday opportunities. But exposure to and use of does not imply effectiveness of information. The tourist's image of a destination is not simply a function of the promotional image conveyed but an amalgam of images that have evolved on two levels:

an organic image, derived from non-tourist information, and an induced image, the result of holiday experiences and conscious promotion by the tourism industry (Gunn, 1972). Tourism marketing may well have to counteract an unfavourable organic image.

Although there is some published comparative research on the images of tourist places held by visitors, e.g. the study of a range of national destinations by Dilley (1986), or of The Netherlands by the National Bureau voor Toerisme (1986) and rather more on inventories of tourism supply and tourist behaviour, only very rarely is the whole interrelated process examined for any one tourist destination. A problem in comparing the projected with the received images is that the methods of measurement and description are likely to be quite different. Projected images are nearly always investigated through some form of content analysis of publicity material, while received images are obtained through attitude questionnaires or tests of the visitors themselves. In addition it is easier to investigate the images held by actual visitors, than to obtain similar information on the images held by those not consuming the tourism product. A notable although small-scale exception is Dietvorst's (1987) investigation into the image held of the city of Nijmegen by a random sample of respondents drawn from The Netherlands as a whole. More usually only success is being monitored and not failure, while the latter is of equal importance in assessing the efficacy of the transmission and the original projected image.

The tourist's image of a destination is very much influenced by how that individual perceives the message being conveyed. Tourists vary in their sensitivity to information exposure. Much depends on how inclined tourists are to use the information received, i.e. their information-receiving processes control the quality of the information taken in and the promotional message, however clear its original formulation, is likely to be distorted by perception. Thus if potential tourists have already decided not to holiday in Ireland because of the political situation, their preference to go to Ireland will be low, and hence their sensitivity to information about Ireland. The chances of information being taken in are greatest if the potential tourist already has a preference for the holiday package or destination being marketed.

Tourists view the various information sources

229

differently. Destination-specific literature, which is non-personal, is generally regarded as serving an informing function whereas opinions of friends and relatives and the advice of travel consultants assumes an evaluating or legitimizing function (Gitelson & Crompton, 1983). However, where potential tourists are vague about possible destinations and holidays there is a marketing problem to establish a particular destination as the unique place offering various unique benefits to satisfy the tourists' needs. The fact that there is normally a considerable time-lag between the decision to book a holiday and its actual consumption generates further opportunities for misunderstanding, if not misrepresentation.

From the tourist's viewpoint, the credibility of the information contained in the marketing message is open to question. Nolan (1976), using a semantic differential approach across four dimensions of authenticity (accurate-inaccurate), evaluative (informative-uninformative), personalism (exciting-unexciting), and objectivity (biased-unbiased), demonstrates that guide books and official tourist board information services are seen as the most credible sources, with travel advertisements in newspapers and magazines the least credible. The World Tourism Organisation (1985) confirms that national tourist administrations are viewed as authoritative sources of information. Nolan concludes that tourists do recognise bias and promotional distortions in tourism information sources yet still find the information offered by those sources useful.

Aspects of the official locally projected images of seaside resorts on the Languedoc coast have been investigated together with attitudes of actual visitors to the same destinations. Some of the problems of comparison are evident. The official projected images have been measured by a quantitative content analysis of text and photographs in freely distributed general publicity information, while the attitudes of visitors was measured by their reactions on a three-point scale to a series of adjectival constructs. Useful general conclusions can be drawn about each set of images, including variations among the resorts, and among visitors of different nationality, length of stay, familiarity with the coast and the like (Ashworth & de Haan, 1987). Comparison between the two sets, except in the most general terms, is however clearly difficult.

Comparison between various aspects of the images held by visitors is much easier. Differences between the individual resorts, and between the resorts and the region as a whole, revealed some interesting discrepancies, in particular that such images varied more strongly with the characteristics of the visitor than with the characteristics of the place, and that a strong similarity between resort and regional images existed for each group of visitors.

Similarly comparison between tourist attitudes and both the tourism facilities available and the actual use made of such facilities, revealed many discrepancies, which in turn could, and in market planning exercises should, form the basis of a marketing exercise. The relationship of destination images to tourism policy, and specifically the use of the former as an instrument for executing the latter, which was referred to earlier, again becomes evident at this stage. Resorts that were consciously attempting to influence behaviour through their image promotion were likely to experience the largest discrepancy between projected and received images, while those content to project images conforming to the existing predispositions of the visitors suffered fewer discontinuities.

Thus the analysis of the reception of images, illustrated here by only one briefly described example, provides not only a means of monitoring the effectiveness of place promotion, essential though that is, but also invites an approach into facility supply and demand behaviour and ultimately policy analysis.

CONSEQUENCES OF DEMAND-SUPPLY IMAGE MISMATCH

It can be argued, from the discussion above, that promotional or supply images and tourists' naive (or demand) images of destination areas may not coincide. This is the crux. A distorted image - whether the result of supply projection or demand perception - detracts from a destination area's ability to realise its tourism development potential. Where fact and perceived image differ there will be a gap between the holiday expectations and the holiday experiences of the tourist: the larger the difference between image and reality, i.e. between expectations and experiences, the more dissatisfied the tourist will be and the more likely he or she will seek alternative holidays and destinations on future occasions. The consequences of mismatch between demand and supply images is critical at two stages in the tourist's holiday cycle - the decision stage of holiday choice and the reflective stage on return from holiday. Naive (demand) images represent tourists' perceptions of whether destinations contain the holiday attributes that they consider necessary for a successful holiday and when these images are compared with whether or not the destination actually contains those attributes (which a factually accurate supply image would reveal), four situations can be hypothesized:

(i)   Positive demand and supply images, in which case the marketing message is on target and the destination(s) will be considered amongst the final group from which a holiday is chosen. A holiday booking is therefore highly probable.

(ii)   Positive supply image but a negative demand image, leading potential tourists to reject such destination(s) as falling below their evaluative images. The destination area therefore needs to improve both the targeting and the nature of its promotional image.

(iii)   Positive demand image but a negative supply one, implying any marketing message(s) have been misunderstood and the attributes perceived by the tourist are imaginary. Because the naive image of the destination may exceed the tourist's evaluative image a holiday booking is possible. The destination area needs, most of all, to improve the product(s) it offers, as well as polishing the supply image presented.

(iv)   Negative demand and supply images meaning destinations are perceived as unsuitable and do not possess the attributes tourists require. Such destinations will not be considered as holiday locations. Major improvements are needed to the product(s) available in such destinations and to the way those products are marketed.

Tourists select their holiday destination on the basis that its naive image exceeded their evaluative image or aspiration level by the greatest amount. Choice is based on expectations of holiday pleasures but experiences may or may not measure up to expectations so two further situations may be hypothesized at the reflection stage:

(a) Positive demand image at booking stage and also on return from holiday. Since expectations were realised, or even exceeded, the tourist will consider a repeat booking for that type of holiday or that destination in a subsequent year.

(b) Positive demand image at booking stage but negative image on return. The holiday was a disappointment for the tourist who is, therefore, likely to seek at least an alternative destination, if not a different type of holiday, for the following year. This situation is most likely to occur in the case of situation (iii) above but could also occur in (i) if the tourist suffered some unfortunate experience (such as losing money, being involved in a car accident or taken ill) whilst on holiday.

Thus not only must destination areas get their marketing message right and target the appropriate market segment(s) but they must also provide tourists with quality experiences within a range of affordable prices if their long-run success in tourism is to be sustained.

THE WAY FORWARD

For the tourism industry, especially destination area-based organisations, marketing of holidays is beset by uncertainties. Even in those cases where the destination image is accurately and successfully marketed and the tourists who visit a particular resort in the area have an enjoyable holiday (which exceeds their expectations), those same tourists are highly likely to go elsewhere for their next holiday! Tourists demonstrate a high propensity to visit new destinations on each holiday and even where a repeat visit is made to a general destination region (country) new resorts will be selected. This reflects the ease of substitution of tourism products between destinations. In a growing market resorts attract new or generated business (e.g. persons taking a first holiday abroad, etc.) but in a static market resorts are very much more dependent upon diverted business, i.e. holiday-makers attracted from other resorts. The importance of professional marketing is clear. Tour operators, based in tourist-generating regions, are better placed because they can pick and choose which destinations to include in their programmes.

It is clear from many of the chapters in this book that there is a large and growing volume of work accumulating on many of the aspects of tourism investigated here, and large quantities of factual information on the characteristics of tourism as an industry, as an activity and as a legitimate field of policy have been gathered in the twenty years since it captured the attention of analysts and policy makers. It is however equally clear that yawning gaps in understanding remain. In particular there is an absence of an explanatory framework that incorporates the diverse separate elements discussed. The central suggestion of this book is that marketing as an approach, and specifically the promotion of destination images, can provide such a coherent framework. As early as 1973, Medlik and Middleton applied some of the conceptual ideas drawn from marketing to the tourism product, and tourism promotion in both private and public sectors has been dominantly staffed by executives with a marketing background. However, to be successful as an analytical structure such marketing should offer a means of relating supply and demand, facility and use, the tourism place and the tourist. It should provide a basis for conscious management intervention, and avoiding the clear cut and in practice rather sterile distinction between the theoretical study of tourism as a social phenomenon and the tourism industry, or between the commercial goals of the private sector and the wider responsibilities of public organisations. A future research agenda therefore must concentrate on the causal relationships between the elements.

Image promotion can only be understood as a continuous process from projection to reception, and must in turn be related on the one side to the existing goals of public and commercial policy and on the other to the actual behaviour of visitors. It is easy to state in marketing terminology that promotion is part of the marketing mix that brings together product and customer, but it is far more difficult to actually trace the relationship between promotional activity and either the tourism

234

product being presented or the characteristics and
behaviour of the consumer being targeted. Neither
product nor consumer can be isolated from the place
and the society in which each is set and within
which each interacts.
A better understanding is required of how the
naive images of potential tourists can be changed
to increase the likelihood of those persons
visiting particular destinations. Producers
examine the reactions of consumers: namely which
holiday packages and destinations are selling well,
which holiday types and destinations generated most
complaints. Attitudes of potential tourists are
not considered by the producers but from a
marketing standpoint the successful stimulation of
additional business could hinge on understanding
the reasons why tourists did not choose a holiday
in a particular destination (and book through a
particular tour operator). As long as the market
is buoyant the incentive for such commercially-
sponsored research is limited.
Segmentation has been an important and
increasingly commonplace ploy in effective tourism
marketing, encouraged in Europe by new travel forms
and policies, e.g. time-share accommodation and
flight-only arrangements. There still exists,
however, a need to obtain more systematic
information on potential markets for tourism if
segmentation is to realise its full economic
potential. In that context tourist images need to
be investigated not only in a spatial context but
also in a temporal dimension. To promote
effectively second or off-peak holidays it is
necessary to know whether the tourist's image of a
destination in the off-season differs significantly
from that in the main holiday season.
At least one tour operator admits to a lack of
knowledge about how and why people choose holidays
(Travel Trade Gazette, 1987) but in commissioning
research the objective is as much reduction in use
of their viewdata system to search for holiday
options for clients as to understand the holiday
selection process. On average seven different
options are currently looked at before one of them
is taken up and it is the tour operator's view that
this range of options could be reduced if the
holiday selection process were better understood.
Matching of demand and supply in the light of such
a development can be interpreted as satisficing
behaviour when viewed by the client. If holidays
and clients are matched more readily the tour

operator benefits from cost savings whilst the potential tourist enjoys time savings. The latter, however, is achieved by the sacrifice of choice (unless the tourist has done a lot more 'homework' before approaching a travel agent or tour operator). In any event a reorientation of marketing messages is likely to be required.

For destination areas the problem of matching demand and supply is more difficult. A prerequisite remains the identification of the area's comparative advantage in one or more tourism products and the marshalling of factors of production to exploit that advantage (Goodall & Ashworth, 1985). The marketing approach adopted should be a community or societal one (Mill & Morrison, 1985; Murphy, 1985) which focuses on the satisfaction of tourist needs while respecting the long-term interests of the destination community. In this way the destination safeguards the resources, natural and cultural, which gave it a comparative advantage in the first place: it does not attempt to adapt its resources totally to the needs of tourists and therefore avoids joining the increasing number of 'identikit' destinations which take on an increasingly similar and familiar appearance. The destination will then retain a distinctive marketing image with which to entice a continuing stream of tourists.

For the researcher the importance of image vis-à-vis other factors, such as accessibility, intervening opportunity, economic and family circumstances, in the potential tourist's choice of holiday has yet to be clearly established. There are also other avenues to explore. How do tourists' preferential, evaluative and naive images change as they receive more information? Are there important differences in this context between the different types of tourist that have been recognised? How does information made available to potential tourists in their origin regions differ in content (and effectiveness) from that available to them on arrival in destination areas? It is to these, and associated marketing questions, that future emphasis will be given in the Groningen-Reading tourism research programme. In part the difficulties are technical, involving details of research design, and in part they are more deeply embedded in the diverse nature of tourism as a social activity, as an income-generating industry and as a function of places. The answers to at least some of these questions is the task that the

Tourist Images: Marketing Considerations

Groningen-Reading research team has set itself in the belief that through the application of such an integrated framework this important phenomenon can be given the prominence it deserves.

REFERENCES

Gunn, C.A. (1972) Vacationscape: Designing Tourist Regions, Bureau of Business Research, University of Texas, Austin

Hunt, J.D. (1975) Image as a factor in tourism development, J. of Travel Research, 13 (3), 1-7

Kotler (1986) Principles of Marketing, Prentice Hall, Englewood Cliffs, New Jersey

Lundberg, D.E. (1976) The Tourist Business, CBI Publications, Van Nostrand Reinhold, New York

Medlik S. & Middleton, V.T.C. (1973) The Tourist product and its marketing implications, International Tourism Quarterly, 9

Mill, R.C. & Morrison, A.M. (1985) The Tourism System: An Introductory Text, Prentice-Hall International, Englewood Cliffs, New Jersey

Murphy, P.E. (1985) Tourism: A Community Approach, Methuen, London

Nationaal Bureau voor Toerisme (NBT)(1986) Imago studie Nederland: Wat de nederlanders van nederland als vakantieland vinden, Leidschendam

Nolan, D.S. (1976) Tourists' use and evaluation of travel information sources, J. of Travel Research, 14, 6-8

O'Driscoll, T.J. (1985) European Travel Commission, Tourism Management, 6 (1), 66-70

Schmoll, G.A. (1977) Tourism Promotion, Tourism International Press, London

Smith, V.L. (1977) The Hosts: The Anthropology of Tourism, University of Pennsylvania Press, Philadelphia

Travel Trade Gazette (1987) Horizon commissions holiday research study, 2 April

Veen, W. van der & Voogd, H. (1987) Gemeentepromotie en bedrijfsacquisitie, Geopers, Groningen

World Tourism Organisation (1985) Identification and Evaluation of those Components of Tourism Services which have a bearing on Tourist Satisfaction and which can be regulated, and State Measures to ensure Adequate Quality of Tourism Services, WTO, Madrid

Index